VOLUME 30   NUMBER 4   2024

Queering the Domestic

HOW TO QUEER THE DOMESTIC

Lauren Jae Gutterman, Martin F. Manalansan IV,
and Stephen Vider

*I*n the widely admired third episode of the HBO series *The Last of Us*, two men, Bill and Frank, find love in a hopeless place. While the world falls victim to a zombie-borne virus, Bill's beautifully preserved Colonial home (and survivalist bunker) becomes the setting for a new queer domesticity. But that queer domesticity is shadowed by another queer pair at the heart of the series: the orphaned and miraculously immune youth Ellie and a before-times contractor named Joel. Both have lost their biological ties, and the show's emotional center is watching the two essentially adopt each other. Their queer kinship is rooted not in a defined home space but in dislocation, as they strike out on the road to bring Ellie to doctors who hope to derive a cure for the zombie virus from her blood. Each episode follows Ellie and Joel to a new city or community, where survivors struggle to build a new sense of social order and safety. Bill and Frank's home is the most idyllic of the options (albeit with an electric fence), but it too cannot last. Between Bill and Frank and Ellie and Joel, *The Last of Us* effectively weds home stories and road stories—both a domestic tale and a picaresque. In doing so, the show suggests how queer kinship has variously troubled conventional ideas of what constitutes the home in the first place: Who gets to belong at home? Where might home be found? What does home provide? And how does it fail us?

This interplay between the lure of the home as a bounded and protected space and the need to make home where you are is a key tension of this journal issue. The essays here address both the potentialities and the impossibilities of queer domestic space, dwelling in both utopian and itinerant imaginaries. Home is idealized as stable and safe, yet as Craig Willse (2015: 2) writes, "housing"—the biopolitical systems that make house and home available to some and not to others—is a monster, "a technology for the organization and distribution of life, health, illness, and death." To have a home or to be "homeless" is simply to find oneself on

GLQ 30:4
DOI 10.1215/10642684-11331066
© 2024 by Duke University Press

different sides of the beast, to be sheltered or made vulnerable. Still, the underlying secret is that no home or house is ever perfectly secure, as a single conversation with an insurance agent will lay bare. To live in a home is to live in a state of denial about the potential disasters looming outside and the mess hidden within. The discursive divide between "shelter" and "home" enacts this denial, with some spaces of rest, kinship, and care imagined as more real and more lasting than others.

That fantasy—idealizing, valuing, and enabling some forms of home and family over others—rests at the core of Western conceptions of "domesticity": the historically generated ideology that roots family and privacy to the material borders of the home. Domesticity (at once marshaling and exceeding domestic spaces and practices) is a product of Western modernity and a tool of European and American imperialism. Isabella Beeton, the English Martha Stewart of the nineteenth century, for example, wrote in her *Book of Household Management* ([1861] 2006: 1) that the "mistress of the house" is a prudent and chaste "commander of an army" waging a "campaign" for happiness in the home as a refuge of comfort and security for husband and children. Such a domestic space is imagined as a shelter, far from the wild hordes of presumably immoral, uncivilized, sex-crazed people in the public realm. Scholars Amy Kaplan (1998) and Rosemary George (1998), too, note how the split between the private domestic sphere and the public mirrors imperial geographies of what constitutes the "domestic" and the outside world ready to be colonized. Domesticity is not a placid location or condition. Rather, it is the result of unequal socialities and political structures and an ongoing process of struggle, wars, and messy encounters. Domesticity is a fictional product of the modern West's understanding of itself enforcing violent regimes of hygienic social order in the world.

To queer the domestic, then, is to attempt to dislodge and disrupt these Western binaries and hierarchies to expose the entangled mess inherent in power relations. Queer studies since the 1990s has often positioned itself against traditional models of domesticity, espousing the potential of public space over the confinements of privacy, most directly in critiques of same-sex marriage.[1] At the same time, Black feminist studies, queer ethnography, queer diasporic studies, queer area studies, and queer of color critique all have troubled the modern bifurcation of the domestic and the public, revealing the home to be a site of labor, irregular shelter and care, leisure, consumption, and carceral surveillance.[2] To queer the home is not necessarily to purposefully or self-consciously reinvent the home in practice but to make legible the already queer practices of homemaking that are often and otherwise disregarded—to recognize the home for its own queerness, revealing, in Sedgwick's (1993: 8) words, "the open mesh of possibilities, gaps, overlaps, dissonances and resonances, lapses and excesses of meaning" the home materializes.[3] The essays in this collection attempt to map out these entanglements to find alternative forms of togetherness, spatiality, and temporality that might enable minoritized subjects to live, survive, and flourish.

Today, record numbers of individuals and families across the globe confront new forms of displacement and forced migration as a result of genocide, persecution, climate change, and the ongoing impacts of US imperialism. Neoliberal economic and social policies have reprivatized forms of caregiving once managed by the state. At the same time care work has emerged as a global industry, with service-industry migrants and guest workers moving from one nation to another. Gentrification in major cities has widened the disparity between those with stable housing and those without, while global inflation and rising rental and mortgage costs have put housing stability even further out of reach for people around the world. Amid these shifts, home is still promised as a space of sanctuary, even as neoliberal privatization hollows it out from within and makes it more difficult to achieve in the first place.

The issue begins with Rasel Ahmed and Efadul Huq's essay demonstrating both the possibilities of queer domesticity and its limits. Drawing on ethnographic research and their own personal experiences, Ahmed and Huq analyze an apartment known as Nanur Basha ("Grandmother's House"), the home of a Bangladeshi queer activist and community leader, in the 2010s. Looking closely at Nanur Basha, they argue, reveals "quotidian practices of queer worlding" in the postcolonial global South. The apartment housed queer dance parties and performances, hookups, and community organizing events. The site also provided a foundation for the launch of *Roopbaan*, a groundbreaking LGBTQ+ magazine. But as much as the space served as a sanctuary for queer Bangladeshis, it also enabled surveillance by neighbors and attacks by queerphobic nationalists.

Ariel M. Dela Cruz also finds political potential in queer remakings of home in Hong Kong. Dela Cruz explores the carework performed by Filipino tomboy Leo Selomenio, a domestic worker and organizer of migrant laborers' beauty pageants as shown in the 2016 documentary *Sunday Beauty Queen*. Selomenio—exceptional among Filipino domestic workers in his ability to live on his own, outside of his employer's residence—carves out what Dela Cruz terms a "tomboy domesticity." By turning his apartment into a community gathering space and site of unremunerated caretaking for other migrant laborers, Selomenio resists the structures of race, class, and gender inequality that define transnational domestic care work and affirms the value of Filipino domestic workers' lives on their own terms.

Holly Jackson suggests that queer kinship formations can only transform the home so far. Focusing on "the archive of polyamory's emergence" in the late nineteenth century, Jackson argues that political radicals conceived of sexual "varietism" or "free love" as a means of building a more just and egalitarian society, rather than as an end in and of itself. These early theorists of polyamory insisted that without a broader social revolution overturning capitalism, women's subordination, and the privatization of domestic work, polyamory would—for all but the wealthy—merely increase the financial stresses and labor demands of married life. This warning, which Jackson finds in Edith Wharton's 1911 novel *Ethan Frome*, among other sources, carries particular salience given polyamory's recent rise, and many polyamorists' demands for access to rather than disruption of legal marriage.

Several of the writers here draw our attention to the queerness of housing precarity and homelessness. They do so both in terms of how gender- and sexual-nonconforming people are at greater risk of losing housing and how being deprived of or unable to access a home, in the conventional sense, is in itself a queer experience. Maggie Schreiner focuses on the former. Schreiner's essay examines the 1985 case of Michael Brown, a gay New Yorker who was evicted from his apartment in Chelsea after his lover died of complications from AIDS. Tenants' rights advocates and gay and lesbian activists in Chelsea rallied behind Brown and fought for him to be able to remain in his home. They were ultimately unsuccessful, but Schreiner argues that their campaign shows how queer activists in the early AIDS era contributed to and were deeply influenced by New York City's long-standing housing movement.

While many authors included in this special issue examine how queer people make or find home beyond the nuclear family and the private dwelling place, Miguel A. Avalos considers the meaning of "queer domesticity" in a theoretical sense, distinct from gender and sexual nonconformity. In particular, Avalos analyzes the daily routines of transborder commuters, that is, people who cross the US-Mexico border in the San Diego-Tijuana region on a daily or near-daily basis for work or education. Avalos argues that due to the time-intensive nature of going through border security (an undertaking of several hours), transborder commuters "queer" the domestic by creating ephemeral, transnational homes where and when they can: they eat, dress, and study in their cars; they crash on friends' couches and shower in public places. In doing so, Avalos's subjects carve out a new form of domesticity defined by physical movement rather than structural stasis and stability.

If most of the queer figures discussed thus far find or create homes of some sort, Cody C. St. Clair focuses on those defined by their houselessess: homeless people during the Great Depression. St. Clair's essay highlights Depression-era poetry, music, and fiction that depicts homelessness as a profoundly "disgendering" experience, one defined by exclusion from both the heteropatriarchal family and the gender binary. This disgendering, St. Clair contends, works to justify the violent, dehumanizing treatment homeless people have faced under racial capitalism, both in the 1930s and today. At the same time, St. Clair finds hope in homeless individuals' queer kinship bonds as depicted in other writing of this period. For St. Clair, networks of care and support among chosen kin as depicted in Depression-era literature function as a counterpoint to experiences of disgendering and provide models of kinship beyond the nuclear family.

Many other queer figures discussed in this issue find ways to claim "home" in public or semipublic spaces, challenging white, middle-class, Eurocentric notions of the domestic sphere as confined to a single structure or private space. René Esparza, for example, looks to the fictional characters of John Leguizamo's *Mambo Mouth* (1991) and the more recent *Tangerine* (2015) for representations of how queer and trans people of color have responded to gentrification by using urban, public spaces for resistant acts of caretaking typically thought of as "private." In the hands of Leguizamo's character Manny the Fanny and *Tangerine*'s protagonist Sin-Dee Rella—both trans sex workers—the street, the laundromat, the coffee shop, and the bathroom become domestic; that is, they become places of collective sustenance and support, which Esparza terms "communal intimacy."

Similarly, the queer, trans, and nonbinary youth depicted in Laila Annmarie Stevens's evocative series of documentary photographs "A House Is Not a Home" feel more at home in New York City parks, streets, and shops, and in the arms of friends and lovers, than they do in the houses where they reside with parents or other family members. Having stable housing, Stevens's project demonstrates, is not the same as being *at* home, as feeling safe, loved, and accepted. As art historian Virginia Thomas writes, Stevens's photographs suggest "an intergenerational history of queer and trans home-building in the city that extends beyond private property." Yet Stevens's work does not portray New York City as a straightforward alternative to unwelcoming family homes; rather, Stevens's photographs capture the persistent tension between young people's identities, communities, and domestic spaces.

Finally, in the forum feature, scholars Shoniqua Roach, Jules Gill-Peterson, Jina B. Kim, Gayatri Gopinath, and Sara Matthiesen each touch briefly on the meaning of the domestic in their work on Black homemaking, trans history, disability justice, queer diasporic communities, and reproductive politics, respectively. Their short essays, and their scholarly work more broadly, open up even more avenues for thinking about what it means (or doesn't) to queer the domestic.

The essays here remind us that home is not inherently a space of violent normativity but also a space of racialized and gendered work and a capacious realm of contingent relations, scripts, structures, and aspirations. Home is not always a space of negation, death, and no future but rather a place of survival, longing, persistence, and even joy. It is not necessarily the mess we escape from; it can also be the mess we live with and through. LGBTQ+ people in particular have historically been excluded from state-sanctioned visions of home and family, yet they have also consistently adapted domestic spaces and practices to interrogate gender and sexual norms and to develop new models of kinship and connection. "Queering the Domestic" seeks to investigate these messy relations: the many ways in which the spaces and practices of home both structure and challenge norms of intimate and collective belonging as they play out in everyday life, historically and in the present.

Notes

We are grateful to the many people who worked with us to realize this special issue. Thank you to Lillian Nagengast, who served as editorial assistant on the issue; to managing editors Liz Beasley and Karen Dutoi for guiding us through the editorial process; to *GLQ* editors Chandan Reddy and C. Riley Snorton for their encouragement and feedback in conceptualizing the issue; to Greta LaFleur for sharing insights and advice; to Holly Jackson for many thoughtful suggestions and questions on the introduction; and to our own domestic entanglements for many other forms of care and support during the time we spent working on this issue. Thank you finally to the many scholars who reviewed article submissions and provided vital feedback on these essays.

1. See, for example, Berlant and Warner (1998) and Duggan (2002).
2. We build here on a growing body of scholarship in LGBTQ+ studies that rethinks and reevaluates domesticity, kinship, and care as sites of queer and trans potentiality, including work by David Eng (2010), Karen Tongson (2011), Heather Murray (2010), Daniel Winunwe Rivers (2013), Marlon Bailey (2013), Martin Manalansan (2003, 2014), Lauren Gutterman (2020), Ghassan Moussawi (2020), Marty Fink (2020), Sara Matthiesen (2021), Stephen Vider (2021), Jafari Allen (2022), and Allan Punzalan Isaac (2022), as well as edited collections by Scott Herring and Lee Wallace (2021) and Teagan Bradway and Elizabeth Freeman (2022).
3. On Sedgwick and home, see also Moon et al. (1994).

References

Allen, Jafari S. 2022. *There's a Disco Ball between Us: A Theory of Black Gay Life*. Durham, NC: Duke University Press.

Bailey, Marlon M. 2013. *Butch Queens Up in Pumps: Gender, Performance, and Ballroom Culture in Detroit*. Ann Arbor: University of Michigan Press.

Beeton, Isabella. (1861) 2006. *Mrs. Beeton's Household Management*. Hertfordshire, UK: Wordsworth Editions.

Berlant, Lauren, and Michael Warner. 1998. "Sex in Public." *Critical Inquiry* 24, no. 2: 547–66.

Bradway, Teagan, and Elizabeth Freeman, eds. 2022. *Queer Kinship: Race, Sex, Belonging, Form*. Durham, NC: Duke University Press.

Duggan, Lisa. 2002. "The New Homonormativity: The Sexual Politics of Neoliberalism." In *Materializing Democracy: Toward a Revitalized Cultural Politics*, edited by Russ Castronovo and Dana D. Nelson, 175–94. Durham, NC: Duke University Press.

Eng, David L. 2010. *The Feeling of Kinship: Queer Liberalism and the Racialization of Intimacy*. Durham, NC: Duke University Press.

Fink, Marty. 2020. *Forget Burial: HIV Kinship, Disability, and Queer/Trans Narratives of Care*. New Brunswick, NJ: Rutgers University Press.

George, Rosemary Marangoly. 1998. "Homes in the Empire, Empires in the Home." In *Burning down the House: Recycling Domesticity*, edited by Rosemary Marangoly George, 47–74. Boulder, CO: Westview Press.

Gutterman, Lauren Jae. 2020. *Her Neighbor's Wife: A History of Lesbian Desire within Marriage*. Philadelphia: University of Pennsylvania Press.

Herring, Scott, and Lee Wallace, eds. 2021. *Long Term: Essays on Queer Commitment*. Durham, NC: Duke University Press.

Isaac, Allan Punzalan. 2022. *Filipino Time: Affective Worlds and Contracted Labor*. New York: Fordham University Press.

Kaplan, Amy. 1998. "Manifest Domesticity." *American Literature* 70, no. 3: 581–606.

Manalansan, Martin F., IV. 2003. *Global Divas: Filipino Gay Men in the Diaspora*. Durham, NC: Duke University Press.

Manalansan, Martin F., IV. 2014. "The 'Stuff' of Archives: Mess, Migration, and Queer Lives." *Radical History Review*, no. 120: 94–107.

Matthiesen, Sara. 2021. *Reproduction Reconceived: Family Making and the Limits of Choice after Roe v. Wade*. Oakland: University of California Press.

Moon, Michael, Eve Kosofsky Sedgwick, Benjamin Gianni, and Scott Weir. 1994. "Queers in (Single-Family) Space." *Assemblage*, no. 24: 30–37.

Moussawi, Ghassan. 2020. *Disruptive Situations: Fractal Orientalism and Queer Strategies in Beirut*. Philadelphia: Temple University Press.

Murray, Heather A. A. 2010. *Not in This Family: Gays and the Meaning of Kinship in Postwar North America*. Philadelphia: University of Pennsylvania Press.

Rivers, Daniel Winunwe. 2013. *Radical Relations: Lesbian Mothers, Gay Fathers, and Their Children in the United States since World War II*. Chapel Hill: University of North Carolina Press.

Sedgwick, Eve Kosofsky. 1993. *Tendencies*. Durham, NC: Duke University Press.

Tongson, Karen. 2011. *Relocations: Queer Suburban Imaginaries*. New York: New York University Press.

Vider, Stephen. 2021. *The Queerness of Home: Gender, Sexuality, and the Politics of Domesticity after World War II*. Chicago: University of Chicago Press.

Willse, Craig. 2015. *The Value of Homelessness: Managing Surplus Life in the United States*. Minneapolis: University of Minnesota Press.

BETWEEN QUEER JOY AND INJURY

The Making and Unmaking of a Queer Sanctuary, Nanur Basha, in Bangladesh

Rasel Ahmed and Efadul Huq

*H*ow do global South queers make and expand domesticity under heterosexist nationalist surveillance and organized violence? We engage this question from the vantage point of Nanur Basha, which was a queer sanctuary in a postcolonial global South city. In 2012, a group of friends, predominantly gay men, created a queer refuge that evolved into a place of kinships, shelter, leisure, care, joy, eroticism, and political organizing in Dhaka, the capital of Bangladesh. From the social and political intimacies at Nanur Basha's homespace, an LGBTQ+ magazine named *Roopbaan* came into being in 2014. The magazine published two issues and provoked the ire of Bangladeshi society. Religious conservatives marched and called for the punishment of *Roopbaan*'s editor, Rasel Ahmed (this article's first author), who was eventually forced to go into exile. In 2016, a local chapter of Al-Qaeda murdered Xulhaz Mannan (*Roopbaan*'s publisher) and his fellow organizer Mahbub Rabbi Tonoy in Nanur Basha. Nanur Basha's short-lived everyday practices and organizing, from pamphleteering to parades to magazine publishing to its ultimate demise, heralded a new era of LGBTQ+ (in)visibility politics in Bangladesh.

The dominant archives related to the 2016 murders contain narratives to suit specific interests. Secular nationalists read the murders as evidence of uncontrolled Islamization (Hossain 2017). Islamist groups framed LGBTQ+ organizing as a front of US imperialism and the violence as a legitimate response to neocolonialism. Elite intellectuals critiqued the LGBTQ+ organizing behind *Roopbaan* as being rooted in class privilege and blamed the media for advancing Islamophobia by covering the murders. These dominant archives, by centering a singular

GLQ 30:4

DOI 10.1215/10642684-11331130

moment of violence and reducing the incident to a cautionary analysis of Islamo-phobic "imperialist tropes" in the era of global war on terror, erased the worldmak-ing agency of care, hope, and imagination nurtured within Nanur Basha's queer domesticity.

Taking inspiration from a rich body of scholarship (Ahmed 2006; Banerjea and Browne 2023; DasGupta 2014; Manalansan 2005; Manalansan 2004; Puar 2017; Shakhsari 2020), we bring a postcolonial queer-feminist lens to remembering the lived experiences of queer community members—gay, *koti*, lesbian, *hijra*, and trans-identifying people—who gathered for hangouts, parties, and political organiz-ing at Nanur Basha. We argue that global South queer domesticities, constituted through quotidian practices and expanding from apartments to rooftops to streets, aspire to greater political freedom by deploying imaginative, transgressive, and counterhegemonic agency. Such queer domesticities underpin an affective sanctu-ary, where the term *sanctuary* refers to a relational freedom ("You can be a bit more yourself here") in the threshold between the queerphobic world and queer domes-ticity. Sustained at the borderlands between queer joy and injury, queer sanctuary, unlike legal or political sanctuary, is not shielded from state or organized violence. As queer domesticities open up interstitial sanctuaries for queerness in nationalist discourses and within the urban fabric, queer domesticities are reshaped and queer sanctuaries unmade by interfacing with competing postcolonial nationalisms.

Queer domesticities like Nanur Basha are crucial sites for maneuvering through heteropatriarchal social barriers. Within them queer subjects can be their full "complicated" selves and dream up multiple possibilities for the world. Pay-ing attention to Nanur Basha takes us closer to engaging with "how non-normative lives are lived" within and beyond Bangladesh's heteropatriarchal nationalism and urbanization, without assuming that lack of legal and political rights make queer lives impossible (Banerjea and Browne 2023: 4).

Through autoethnographic recollections, journaling, personal archives of photographs and videos, and secondary sources (news reports), we explore the making and unmaking of Nanur Basha. We show how the making of Nanur Basha involved queers performing caring practices towards themselves and others, nego-tiating and appropriating heterodomestic space, and organizing politically in hope of gender and sexual freedom. While South Asian apartment living is predomi-nantly understood and regulated through heteronormative expectations that pri-oritize the reproduction of nuclear families, we present a queer archive of how apartments are remade by a "vernacular queer worlding" composed by everyday practices and affects that eventually extend beyond the physical confines of the apartment (Manalansan 2015). Understanding the relational nuances of space and queerness in Bangladesh enriches understandings of "home" regionally and globally.

South Asian queer studies have drawn attention to digital spaces (Dasgupta 2018; Malik 2018), but less documented are the range of subterranean spaces where sexually marginalized subjects practice alternative kinships and intimate relations and agitate for freedom. In the global North literature, the spatial focus of queerness has been on suburbia, urban neighborhoods, and public spaces (Tongson 2020; Rivers 2013). Documenting and interrogating the messy placemaking dynamics of Nanur Basha located in a global South megacity offers a southern vantage point to inquiries of queer urban worlding and depicts the ambivalence of queer sanctuaries as sites of both joy and injury. Fabulously interscalar, moving from homes to rooftops to streets to print media, Nanur Basha's practices in our theorization join hands and advance existing scholarship on queering domesticities by depicting counterhegemonic and insurgent placemaking practices (Huq 2020; Miraftab 2009) that pave the path toward queer urbanisms of "freeing queer futurity" (Vallerand 2013: 64).

The unmaking of Nanur Basha involves violences embedded in Bangladesh's unresolved political contestations over secular versus Islamist postcolonial national identity. Queer communities continue to face surveillance, violence, and discrimination across Bangladesh. Drawing from its inheritance of colonial laws, Bangladesh penalizes homosexuality, although prosecutions under section 377 have been rare. Several nongovernmental organizations (NGOs) and community-based organizations provide health care and other services to LGBTQ+ communities. In 2014, Bangladesh recognized *hijra* as a gender category, although misunderstandings about *hijra*, trans, and intersex people proliferate in media and society. In 2013, two lesbians who eloped were publicized in the media and forcefully separated. In 2017, the police raided a party and arrested twenty-seven men suspected of being gay. Since the pandemic, dating violence and blackmail of gay men have increased. LGBTQ+ organizations continue to receive threats, and an active anti-LGBTQ+ bloc has been organizing book publications, webinars, and other queerphobic activities. Queer underground publications, organizing, and parties continue while navigating these threats. Queer perspectives in Bangladeshi academia remain in the closet or are deemed irrelevant for analyzing the construction of Bangladeshi nationalism, authoritarianism, and communalist politics. This article challenges that stance by contributing to existing scholarship that weaves together nationalist conflicts, surveillance, and the global war on terror. We highlight how Nanur Basha enacted and spatialized a dissenting Bangladeshi identity that embraced social fluidity and political contradictions.

It is important to acknowledge that while both authors originate from Bangladesh, we are situated within global North academia and hold certain class and social privileges, both in Bangladesh and in the United States. While these privileges afford us certain resources and shape our perspectives, our positionalities remain complicated. Both authors, who are gender nonconforming and nonbinary, are actively engaged in organizing, archiving, and participating in the Bangladeshi queer community. One of the authors played a pivotal role in creating and shaping Nanur Basha and served as the editor of *Roopbaan* magazine. They were targeted for this involvement and were ultimately forced to leave Bangladesh, and they are currently a political refugee in the United States. Given the relational matrix of privilege and oppression that we both navigate in our lives, it is important to acknowledge that our analysis may not center class critiques of Nanur Basha. Instead, we bring our mourning and compassion with us and into our method in returning to Nanur Basha as a site of autoethnography. Traumatic events, like the 2016 incident at Nanur Basha, can often be scripted into geopolitical tensions, and they can also be rescripted into activist struggles to oppose "state violence and savior politics" (DasGupta 2019). But, following Alexander's (2005) provocations, although memories of violence can be powerful grounds for staging radical queer politics, we start from the premise that centering violence may be inadequate for the purposes of expressing the fuller, complicated, unromanticized portraits of queer worlding in the global South. Our method, therefore, involves remembering the quotidian happenings preceding the traumatic event. When woven together and theorized, these everyday practices and their messiness have the potential to speak more intimately to comparable queer urbanist experimentations occurring across urbanizing global Souths.

In what follows, we first situate ourselves within ongoing scholarly conversations on queer homemaking and queerness's relationship to nationalisms. We then unfold our investigation in two interrelated sections on queer appropriation of heteronormative apartments, rearranged intimacies, and political organizing. We end with implications for queer understanding of domesticity under authoritarian nationalist regimes.

Queer Homes and Nationalist Worlds

Queer homemaking practices disrupt and reimagine dominant notions of domestic life and relationships, and they challenge normative arrangements of family values, caregiving, and socialization. Homes have been seen as a site of familial violence for queer people, but queer subjects also establish reciprocal relations with their families and reclaim their Indigenous roots (Murray 2010; Morgensen 2009). Queer scholarship shows diverse manifestations of queer subjects making their own "homes" outside familial bonds and through queer kinships (Cook 2014; Gorman-Murray 2006). Quite critically, queering domesticity involves living "with, against, and despite the mess," which refuses legibility and hegemonic categorization (Manalansan 2014: 105). Queer homemaking disrupts and blurs spatial and symbolic binaries such as public versus private. In other words, queer domesticity is an expansive concept encompassing houses, apartments, neighborhoods, public spaces, and bars (Andrucki 2017). The microrelations within the home—communal dynamics, interpersonal relations, object relations—are critical for understanding the fluidity and antinormative dimensions of queer domiciles (Gorman-Murray 2008; Pilkey 2014; Vider 2015). Queer domesticity can include appropriation of suburbia, public space, and entire neighborhoods that support queer socializing and child-raising (Rivers 2013; Tongson 2020). Domesticities crafted outside familial bonds are not free from scrutiny. They may stand out in the neighborhood or the cityspace and may be surveilled with the potential for undermining safety and community as well as finding shared purpose (Gorman-Murray 2012). In Nanur Basha, the neighbors monitored queer people from adjacent windows and balconies, and they complained about regular parties and visitors who were *hijra*s and "effeminate" men. The widely circulated photograph of Mannan's lifeless body after his killing, taken discreetly from a neighboring window adjacent to his bedroom, serves as compelling evidence of heightened surveillance.

Queer of color critique highlights how queer domesticities can be part and parcel of "queer liberalism" by giving economic and political empowerment to certain gay communities as well as by incorporating queerness into neoliberal city making and surveillance (Eng 2010; Manalansan 2005). Queer appropriation of public spaces has been folded into a neoliberal rubric of multiculturalism where gayborhoods index the cultural capital and cosmopolitanism of cities, and work at times in collaboration with a classed and racialized urban development agenda of neighborhood safety (Hanhardt 2014; Rushbrook 2002). Yet, queer homemaking practices are undeniably tied to advancing social justice, innovating cultural practices, sustaining communities during public health crises, and organizing for queer liberation—practices that need further exploration, particularly beyond the global North's urban centers (Fink 2020; Bailey 2013; Shanker 2022; Vider 2021). Although attention has been given to the global South's digital queer culture, formal laws, and informal practices of marginalization, attention paid to the diversity of queer domesticities is lacking—a gap that our article addresses (Banerjie 2019; Dasgupta 2017).

Exploring queer domesticity in the global South reveals how subordinate queer communities, who are denied substantial citizenship, imagine and produce transgressive and counterhegemonic spaces. Queering strategies in "postcolonies" grapple with the intractable realities of coloniality's continuance, deeply entrenched inequities, and intensifying aggressions of nationalisms and global wars. In the postcolony where national identities are under contested construction, queer identities are often conflated with other marginalized identities and imperial hegemony (Caron 2016; Fernàndez 2000; Kawasaka 2018; Malik 2018; Mbembe 2001; Spurlin 2013). Queer narratives can be read as dissenting with nationalist aspirations. In Bangladesh, LGBTQ+ communities are anathema to the cultural and nationalist hegemony of Bangali patriarchy and are folded into contestations between divergent Islamist and secular nationalisms. The geopolitics of the global war on terror further complicates nationalisms' relation to queerness. Particularly, the global war on terror's recasting of "homonationalism" in the biopolitical mold marginalizes queer communities. On the one hand, the systematic oppression of queers in the global North is whitewashed by portraying Western intervention as the savior of queerness in "backward" countries (Puar 2017; Shakhsari 2012). On the other side of the coin, as we show in this article, local ruling regimes instrumentalize the agenda of the war on terror to the detriment of queer survival in the global South. Bringing queer domesticity scholarship into conversation with scholarship on queerness's relation to postcolonial heteropatriarchal nationalisms, as we do in this article, nuances theorization of global queer domesticities. It is impossible to understand the unmaking of Nanur Basha without contextualizing it within Bangladesh's participation in the global war on terror. Such theoretical gestures illuminate how southern queer communities make and expand situated "queer futurity" against the exclusions of dominant models of nation-state, citizenship, and cities (Muñoz 2019).

Remembering Everyday Intimacies

Nanur Basha was constructed in layers through everyday negotiations and spatial modifications reflecting a physical and affective "waywardness" (Manalansan 2014). The resulting spaces were temporary, time bound, provisional, always having to be renegotiated or rearranged over time. Nanur Basha formed through "dispersed, tactical, and make-shift creativity" in two important ways (Certeau 2013: xv). First, the spatial modifications were composed of Mannan and his visitors' wayward and messy relationships to domestic objects and the physical space of

Figure 1. Party at Nanur Basha, 2013. Image courtesy of Rasel Ahmed.

Nanur Basha. Second, the negotiations were composed of Mannan's arrangements with his mother and the building guards.

Mannan took Ahmed to visit the Kolabagan apartment in 2012. It was a spacious, modern unit with two bedrooms, a guest room, a dining room, a living room, a domestic worker's room, and a kitchen. The two primary bedrooms had balconies and walk-in closets. Nanur Basha, constrained by a predominantly heteronormative floor plan, proved inadequate to fully accommodate the unique needs, ephemeral practices, privacy, and intimacy of queer socialization. For example, Nanur Basha's design was not conducive to hosting large gatherings (fig. 1). When Mannan furnished the apartment, he used a minimalist arrangement for easy movability to support the group's changing needs.

The second bedroom, Mannan's personal space, was smaller and was used for intimate encounters. Gay men hung out, played board games, snuggled, and had sex in that area. Mannan refreshed the aesthetic and ambiance of the apartment every couple of months by rearranging the furniture layout and changing the color of the curtains, resulting in variations within the same space. Mannan created a balcony garden, the main attraction of which was a pink water lily inside a clay bowl containing water and fish. The garden's plantscape catalyzed community building as Mannan and his visitors chatted about plants for hours.

Mannan kept the apartment fragrant and curated a distinctive olfactory experience for community members. Mannan kept scented candles and dried flowers such as lavender inside the house, and he sprayed fragrant mist on the bed. The careful maintenance of Nanur Basha created sensory memories that expanded the apartment beyond its physical confines. Visitors could feel that they were "present" in Nanur Basha by encountering the apartment's distinctive smells elsewhere.

At Nanur Basha, queer community members established subversive relations with traditional domestic objects, transforming them into catalysts for collective pleasure and self-affirmation. For example, community members would arrive at Nanur Basha directly from their workplaces, dressed in full formal attire. Inside Nanur Basha, they would promptly discard their clothing and drape themselves with patterned bedsheets or curtains, embracing and expressing their queerness and longing to embody femininity. They would repurpose other ordinary domestic objects such as mirrors, candles, and electronic gadgets in their playfulness. These reimagined objects, displaced from their conventional domestic functions, allowed for temporary transitions and performing queer living within a more intimate terrain of kinship.

Mannan and his visitors negotiated the access, use, and privacy of Nanur Basha with Mannan's mother, the building's guards, and the neighbors. The placement of the apartment in a densely populated neighborhood necessitated constant awareness and tactical maneuvering of gender/class presentation to mitigate violent neighborhood surveillance and discrimination. In Dhaka, a regular flow of unmarried men into a residential building would be likely to prompt complaints to the landlord.

Sakhina, Mannan's ailing mother, was not fond of having visitors, especially bachelors. In order to host gay men in the house, Mannan had to negotiate with his mother. Ahmed recounts one such instance: "During one of our discussions on the role of religion in understanding sexuality, Sakhina barged into the room and started an argument about the number of men visiting the house. Xulhaz, at the end of his patience, told her, 'Don't you know it's not safe outside? Where should we go? The police are outside.'" At other times, Sakhina had dinners with Nanur Basha's visitors. Mannan would invite his closest friends, including Ahmed, to dine with her. Over time Sakhina became more comfortable with the gatherings. She joined queer community members in making props for rallies, and she attended fashion show events held in the apartment.

Mannan tipped the building's service workers to enroll them in the making of the queer sanctuary and so they would permit the frequent visitors wearing flamboyant or feminine clothing. The building gates would close at around eleven every night, but if community members lingered in the apartment later, the service workers had to wake up to open the gate. The service workers helped Mannan organize large parties, setting up chairs and stalls.

In Bangladesh, although urban queers commonly meet in outdoor settings, expressing queer sexuality and sociality within heterodomestic spaces like urban apartments is less common. Gay men often resort to introducing their friends or dates as colleagues or classmates. Lesbians face stricter scrutiny of their relationships. Intimacies within Nanur Basha dismantled internalized queerphobia within domestic spaces. For example, Ahmed consistently declined Mannan's invitations to participate in social gatherings for several years. As he recalls, "I was absolutely terrified at the thought of being surrounded by so many queer people at a traditional event like Iftar or Poila Boishakh. It was something I had never experienced before. I had no idea what to expect, so all I felt was overwhelming anxiety and fear about being with my own community."

Ahmed's hesitation and anxiety, like that felt by many others, foregrounds the epistemic wedge between domestic space and sexualized subjects in Bangladesh. Bangali domesticity holds profound connotations of blood kinship, communal sharing, and a sanctuary of "pure" emotions. So when visitors started meeting at Nanur Basha, queer sanctuary feeling involved overcoming two internalized queerphobic scripts. First, visitors had to normalize expressing queerness collectively within traditional domestic spaces. Second, visitors had to move beyond the reductive gaze of erotic desire that only saw other queer people as potential sex partners. While queer erotic practices were welcomed and supported within Nanur Basha, Mannan and others like Ahmed aspired to a new and more plural relational mode of queer living (fig. 2).

One strategy that was deployed to create a new plural sociality within Nanur Basha's domestic space was the recoding of conventional familial relationships to identify queer relations. Some regular visitors began referring to Mannan as Khala (Auntie) and his home as Nanur Basha (Grandmother's House). Community members used other familial designations for individuals, such as *ma* (mother), *bon* (sister), and *meye* (daughter), to invoke less sexually charged ways of relating.

Performing domestic practices like cooking and social events like birthdays and farewells was part of enacting a more expanded set of queer socialities within Nanur Basha. Cooking and eating were more than a means of sustenance and nourishment; they were also means of crafting and sharing intimate attachments through which visitors grounded themselves in each other's lives. People laughed, gossiped, and counseled each other during food preparation and after-

Figure 2. Leisuring at Nanur Basha, 2015. Image courtesy of Rasel Ahmed.

meal cleaning (fig. 3). The cooking sessions seeded what later emerged as political and cultural organizing out of Nanur Basha.

Nanur Basha's ambivalent sanctuary feeling offered a performative double-ness marked by class, regional, religious, color, and gender inequalities. Often the focus of any celebrations revolved around people who were close to Mannan, primarily gay men. Individuals from rural areas, particularly those with regional accents, darker complexions, or low-income backgrounds, faced insults and humil-iation. Queer caring, as enacted within Nanur Basha, emerged from urbanizing Bangladesh's social fabric with embedded hierarchies of internalized oppressions and exclusionary dynamics. For instance, the existing hierarchy of male domina-tion reemerged as queer male-centric cultural patterns in Nanur Basha. It was not warranted to be safe; the site of caring was also the site of injury for those receiving care. Nanur Basha was a refuge for criminalized subjects who are excluded from Bangladesh's heteronormative citizenship. When read through these structural exclusions, Nanur Basha was a place where queers could express their criminal-ized desires freely, but at the same time it was an enclosed space where they could hide together in an extended "closet" and find physical security. In that sense, the border between concealment and disclosure within Nanur Basha collapsed.

Eventually, Nanur Basha's queer domesticity expanded beyond its immedi-ate walls. Figure 4, showing a rooftop party, encapsulates the intricate interplay

Figure 3. Cooking preparation at Nanur Basha, 2014. Image courtesy
of Rasel Ahmed.

Figure 4. Performance at Nanur
Basha's rooftop, 2013. Image
courtesy of Rasel Ahmed.

among Nanur Basha's expanding aspirations, neighborhood surveillance, queer joy, and privilege. The photo captures a drag show on Nanur Basha's rooftop, a liminal space that blurs privacy and public visibility "in the open." The photo shows an individual (from the *hijra* community) performing at a New Year's celebration. Traditionally, neighbors within the same apartment complex gather and engage in shared hobbies like gardening, drying pickles, or flying kites on rooftops. Rooftops of middle-class apartments are also utilized for occasional family-oriented gatherings such as weddings or birthday parties. In Bangali cultural practices, rooftops have been associated with feminine kinship and relief from household pressures. For Bangladeshi queers, quasi-private rooftops can be refuges at night, where they can meet their dates and sexual partners.

In the photographed event, Nanur Basha's rooftop was utilized as an open space. Away from community surveillance, the elevated rooftop permitted a degree of openness, allowing queers to celebrate in public while breaking class and gender norms. The opportunity to host a queer gathering under the open sky, free from the constraints of enclosed spaces, was especially liberating for many. Mannan invited his heterosexual friends to these rooftop gatherings, disrupting the barrier between heterosexual and queer socializing. Ahmed recalls, "In many ways, Xulhaz's rooftop was the first place where we openly expressed ourselves to the public as a group." The transition to the rooftop represented a significant expansion of Nanur Basha's territorial boundaries and political ambitions, signifying that Nanur Basha was no longer a static physical entity, but rather, in Ahmed's words, "a transformative force for redefining our perception of queer time, space, and kinship."

Sanctuary Dreaming under Nationalist Violence

In the affective flows of Nanur Basha, a collective dream for queer recognition emerged. Among other initiatives, Nanur Basha members created *Roopbaan*, an ambitious political project in the form of an LGBTQ+ magazine. Within two years of *Roopbaan*'s publication, a local chapter of Al-Qaeda attacked Mannan's apartment, resulting in the tragic death of Mannan and fellow activist Mahbub Tonoy. We argue that this was not an isolated homophobic attack, but rather the outcome of multiple points of convergence among Bangladeshi nationalists, secularists, atheists, Islamists, and the nascent LGBTQ+ rights movement embedded within the politics of the global war on terror. Therefore, unpacking Bangladesh's political events between 2013 and 2016 is instructive.

In 2013, Bangladesh witnessed the coexistence of two opposing social movements (Zaman 2018). The Shahbag movement, organized by urban "proliberation" and secular activists, sought capital punishment for war criminals involved in the atrocities committed during the 1971 liberation war. In response, Hefazat-e-Islam, a newly formed far-right Islamic advocacy group, organized around a set of "ultraconservative" demands, which included advocating for harsh punishment against the self-declared atheist bloggers associated with the Shahbag movement (Zaman 2018). The ruling political party initially showed overwhelming support for the Shahbag movement and attacked Islamic counterprotests because, by riding the wave of the secular movement, they were able to ban Jamaat-e-Islami, then the third-largest political party in Bangladesh, right before the 2014 election (Gomes 2013). The tumultuous tenth parliamentary election, boycotted by the main opposition parties, was "marred by the lowest turnout and worst electoral violence in Bangladesh's 43-year history" (Riaz 2014: 119). This moment was widely interpreted as a significant turning point in Bangladesh's postcolonial democracy, marking the advent of a "one-party state" under the guise of secular politics in Bangladesh (Mahmud 2018).

Nanur Basha's political projects navigated Bangladesh's volatile 2013–2014 landscape and were reshaped by it. Mannan, who was frustrated by alienating Westernized cultures within dominant community groups and NGOs, firmly believed that queer recognition could be achieved through a culturally relevant queer movement. One of Mannan's earliest moves in this direction was a pamphlet-distribution campaign in 2012. At that time, Nobel laureate Muhammad Yunus had cosigned a statement in support of LGBTQ+ Ugandans (AFP 2013). Bangladeshi religious groups were outraged at this news, and they launched a public campaign against Yunus that involved disseminating around six hundred thousand leaflets all over the country. In a tactical move that mirrored this religious pamphleteering, Nanur Basha members organized a counter-pamphleteering campaign to spread pro-LGBTQ+ messages. Ahmed recollects, "We didn't have the money like the Islamic organizations to distribute in all different subdistricts. So Xulhaz came up with a clever solution. It was the time of Eid, when people who live in Dhaka leave town for their home districts. Xulhaz printed thousands of pamphlets and gave them to Nanur Basha visitors who were visiting their hometowns. The idea was that they would find busy places in their districts, throw the pamphlets in the air, and then disappear."

Nanur Basha's aspiration to achieve political visibility by tactically appropriating nationalist myths and motifs, as we will show next, emerged and solidified at a time when multiple actors were contesting the legal, social, and political boundaries of nationalism in the country. Nanur Basha was animated in many ways by the social movements' energies. Bangladeshi national identity had been thrown up in the air for redefining, and Nanur Basha members were determined to tactically claim Bangali nationalism to perform an extension of that nationalism to include queerness. For the ruling party, Nanur Basha's organizing was likely insignificant at the time. Following the pamphleteering effort and several other queer events, Nanur Basha ventured into a visible political project in the form of *Roopbaan*, the nation's first printed LGBTQ+ magazine. Ahmed, the cofounder and editor of the magazine, recalls that the publication prioritized Bangladeshi ethnic and linguistic identity and its cultural significance in queer lives. The magazine was released on January 14, 2014, a mere two weeks after the contentious tenth parliamentary election. The publication's sensitive nature, coupled with the politically charged timing and extensive coverage by international media, catapulted *Roopbaan* and all those publicly associated with it into a space of heightened surveillance and intensified fear for personal safety. Right after the magazine's launch, an Islamic advocacy group named the Bangladesh Tafsir Parishad held a press conference demanding Ahmed's immediate arrest. Ahmed received numerous hate messages and threats on his social media accounts. He was socially exposed, which particularly affected his university life. Subsequently, Ahmed went into hiding for several months before he started to work on the magazine's second issue.

Soon thereafter, with the Shahbagh movement's conflict with Islamist groups in the background, coupled with a violent electoral climate wherein the largest Islamic party was barred from participation, a spate of targeted killings occurred. From 2014 to 2016, these attacks took the lives of thirty individuals perceived as secularists and atheists (Graham-Harrison and Hammadi 2016). During this period, the ruling party adopted a twofold strategy to exploit the situation. On the one hand, they withheld support from the allegedly atheist victims, so that conservative voter groups would not turn against them. In some cases, the ruling regime even blamed those who had been threatened for writing atheist content and imprisoned them in order to "protect" them from violence. On the other hand, the ruling regime amplified the fear-mongering public discourse about an Islamist takeover and the alarming growth of terrorism in the absence of a secular party like themselves in power. Bangladesh had been drawing upon the technical and informational support of the United Kingdom, the United States, and Israel to be a regional player in the global war on terror. In line with those priorities, the ruling party made a compelling case for allocating a larger budget toward countering terrorism, coupled with the amendment of an existing antiterrorist law to include provisions for the death penalty (Rahman 2008). Doubling down on combating Islamist terrorism, the government established a separate agency called Counter Terrorism and Transnational Crime (CTTC). The FBI provided support to the CTTC in the form of forensic equipment, training in cyber investigations, and surveillance techniques (Roy 2017). Although the counterterrorism initiatives were presented as "protectors" of peaceful civil society, they were soon used to suppress Islamic political parties and other dissidents (Associated Press 2016). Numerous religious party leaders went into hiding to avoid arrest or extrajudicial killing. Heightened activity among several transnational terrorist networks in the South Asian region coincided with this period (Liow 2016). Many religious political leaders who went into hiding in Bangladesh became more likely to enroll in the local formations of transnational terrorist networks like ISIS and Al-Qaeda.

Nanur Basha members, particularly those associated with the magazine, were out in the public sphere. They were visible to Islamist and secular nationalist groups as well as the state. Amid the ruling regime's partisan instrumentalization of counterterrorism, the propensity for violence and counterviolence intensified. The cascading chain of events increasingly pulled Nanur Basha in from the periphery of the nationalist debate to its bloody center. Journalists reported that terrorist hit lists included the names of Nanur Basha members. Some Nanur Basha organizers were determined to pursue political organizing, although there were disagreements among them. Ahmed did not want to move forward with political organizing under such conditions of threat and surveillance. Mannan, a steadfast organizer, proposed that Nanur Basha undertake a new project for the Poila Boishakh (Bangali New Year): a rainbow parade that would blend seamlessly into the festivities and colors of the celebration. Poila Boishakh is a day of public processions and does not require special police permission for parades. Mannan and his co-organizers saw the day as a window of opportunity in an otherwise heavily policed public space, and they planned to create a human rainbow as part of the event. Instead of the banners and rainbow flags seen in pride rallies, participants would wear individual colors of the rainbow and walk in a line, forming an invisible rainbow when viewed from the ground. However, from a distance or from above, the rainbow would become visible. Nanur Basha was the focal point where the organizers prepared for the parade. By symbolically integrating the rainbow parade into the cultural practices of Poila Boishakh, Nanur Basha disrupted the prevailing exclusion of queers in Bangladeshi identity formation and reclaimed public space.

Mannan and his co-organizers organized two Poila Boishakh parades (2014 and 2015), but the third one (2016) was canceled due to increased death threats and police calls to organizers. Eventually Nanur Basha was attacked by the same transnational terrorist network that was targeting bloggers, writers, and activists. Mannan and Mahbub were brutally murdered. In Bangladesh's paradoxical scenario, imperially resourced counterterrrorism programs were weaponized to suppress and persecute political opponents. Counterterrorism, filtered through local interests, created the conditions for reinvigorated terror networks that orchestrated the violent attack on Nanur Basha.

Conclusion

Nanur Basha represents a subterranean modality of southern queer urbanism that is both a vector of queer freedom and the target of violent heterosexist attacks. Reflecting on Nanur Basha, we offer three critical implications for queer understanding of domesticity under authoritarian nationalist regimes in the global South. First, global South queer domesticities need to be understood as messy sites of everyday negotiation, resistance, and structural as well as internalized violence, where queer individuals navigate the shifting landscapes of personal, social, and nationalist tensions that shape and reshape the contours of such domesticities. These unruly queer domesticities blur the boundaries between heterosexist urban order and queer worlding practices. Queer worlding practices in turn extend, moving from apartments to rooftops to streets to print mediascapes, producing a relational and affective sanctuary landscape between joy and injury. Bangladeshi queer subjects, as we have shown, navigate such ambiguous borderlands through a contingent set of tactical practices that are dispersed, fragmented, and even contradictory. Everyday spatial negotiations, intimacies, and political organizing manipulate events to turn them into opportunities for individual and collective pleasure, leisure, kinship, eroticism, and political recognition. Queer domesticities mirror, subvert, transgress, and play with heteronormative expectations of domesticity and nationality. They involve opening up new relational modes to experience each other's complicated fuller selves beyond rigid forms of romantic and sexual relationships.

Second, global South queer domesticities cannot be isolated from local politics. In the case of Nanur Basha, the sanctuary feeling was unmade by its relation to competing postcolonial nationalisms, particularly as organizers tactically surfaced Bangladeshi queer identity and were caught in the heteropatriarchal complicities between authoritarian nationalism and Islamist nationalism embedded within an imperial war on terror. Translated more broadly, the potential of violence against southern queer domesticities is inevitable, and this violence against queer domesticities cannot be solely attributed to homophobia; instead, it must be understood as the function of competing heteropatriarchal nationalisms. In the case of Nanur Basha, we argue that the ruling regime's co-optation of the global war on terror's agenda to consolidate power produced the conditions under which Nanur Basha was targeted. Integrating such local political nuances of the imperial war on terror reveals the situated ironies of global homonationalist politics. In Bangladesh's case, while the United States supports LGBTQ+ activism in Bangladesh, it also supports Bangladesh's counterterrorism initiatives that target gay parties (Associated Press 2017). Drawing out such political nuances further in Bangladesh and across other global South contexts would create generative ground for building transnational coalitions and solidarities for queer liberation.

Third, global South queer domesticities cannot be romanticized as spaces of liberation, privacy, care, and safety. Instead, queer communities engaged in crafting sanctuaries need to seriously engage with national and global politics. Queer domesticities need to be seen as crucial sites for producing transient and affective sanctuaries that are borderlands between joy and injury, and where safety is not warranted. We suggest that this is far from a pessimistic insight; rather, engaging with the political contingencies that unmake sanctuaries is necessary for queer survival.

Queer domesticities like Nanur Basha persist in Bangladesh. They grapple with dilemmas around safety, surveillance, and the need to prevent further injury. These spaces are limited to trusted members. Some are more cognizant of the intersectionality of issues (e.g., the divides between rural and urban or working class and elites) and the effects of racism in our communities. What can be said from the experience of Nanur Basha is that tactical practices of interstitial queer urbanism have limits. However, we remain hopeful, seeing that many Bangladeshi queer domesticities maneuvered toward critical visibility after 2016 and even appropriated invisibility at times as a source of safety while continuing to organize for queer liberation and generating novel sanctuaries.

References

AFP. 2013. "Muhammad Yunus, Nobel Prize Laureate, Prompts Bangladesh Protest over Gay Rights Support." *Huffpost*, September 30. https://www.huffpost.com/entry/muhammad-yunus-gay-rights-bangladesh_n_4018184.

Ahmed, Sara. 2006. *Queer Phenomenology: Orientations, Objects, Others*. Durham, NC: Duke University Press. https://doi.org/10.1515/9780822388074.

Alexander, M. J. 2005. *Pedagogies of Crossing: Meditations on Feminism, Sexual Politics, Memory, and the Sacred*. Durham, NC: Duke University Press.

Andrucki, Max. 2017. "Queering Social Reproduction, or, How Queers Save the City." *Society and Space*, October 31. https://www.societyandspace.org/articles/queering -social-reproduction-or-how-queers-save-the-city.

Associated Press. 2016. "Massive Crackdown in Bangladesh Raises Questions about Government's Motive." *South China Morning Post*, June 18. https://www.scmp.com /news/asia/south-asia/article/1977087/massive-crackdown-bangladesh-raises -questions-about-governments.

Associated Press. 2017. "Bangladesh Arrests 27 Men on Suspicion of Being Gay." *Seattle Times*, May 19. https://www.seattletimes.com/nation-world/bangladesh -arrests-27-men-on-suspicion-of-being-gay/.

Bailey, Marlon M. 2013. *Butch Queens up in Pumps: Gender, Performance, and Ballroom Culture in Detroit*. Triangulations: Lesbian/Gay/Queer Theater/Drama/Performance. Ann Arbor: University of Michigan Press.

Banerjea, Niharika, and Kath Browne. 2023. *Liveable Lives: Living and Surviving LGBTQ Equalities in India and the UK*. London: Bloomsbury Academic.

Banerjie, Ajita. 2019. "Beyond Decriminalisation: Understanding Queer Citizenship through Access to Public Spaces in India." *NUJS Law Review* 12, nos. 3–4. https:// nujslawreview.org/wp-content/uploads/2020/03/12-3-4-Ajita-Banejie.pdf.

Caron, David. 2016. *My Father and I: The Marais and the Queerness of Community*. Ithaca, NY: Cornell University Press.

Certeau, Michel de. 2013. *The Practice of Everyday Life*. Berkeley: University of California Press.

Cook, Matt. 2014. *Queer Domesticities: Homosexuality and Home Life in Twentieth-Century London*. Basingstoke, UK: Palgrave Macmillan.

DasGupta, Debanuj. 2014. "Cartographies of Friendship, Desire, and Home: Notes on Surviving Neoliberal Security Regimes." *Disability Studies Quarterly* 34, no. 4. https://doi.org/10.18061/dsq.v34i4.3994.

DasGupta, Debanuj. 2019. "Rescripting Trauma: Trans/gender Detention Politics and Desire in the United States." *Women's Studies in Communication* 41, no. 4: 324–28.

Dasgupta, Rohit K. 2017. *Digital Queer Cultures in India: Politics, Intimacies, and Belonging*. London: Routledge.

Dasgupta, Rohit K. 2018. "Online Romeos and Gay-dia: Exploring Queer Spaces in Digital India." In *Mapping Queer Space(s) of Praxis and Pedagogy*, edited by Elizabeth McNeil, James E. Wermers, and Joshua O. Lunn. Queer Studies and Eduction, 183–200. Cham: Palgrave Macmillan.

Eng, David L. 2010. *The Feeling of Kinship: Queer Liberalism and the Racialization of Intimacy*. Durham, NC: Duke University Press.

Fernàndez, Josep-Anton. 2000. *Another Country: Sexuality and National Identity in Catalan Gay Fiction*. MHRA Texts and Dissertations. Leeds, UK: Maney for the Modern Humanities Research Association.

Fink, Marty. 2020. *Forget Burial: HIV Kinship, Disability, and Queer/Trans Narratives of Care*. New Brunswick, NJ: Rutgers University Press.

Gomes, William. 2013. "Shahbagh: What Revolution, Whose Revolution?" openDemocracy, February 26. https://www.opendemocracy.net/en/opensecurity/shahbagh -what-revolution-whose-revolution/.

Gorman-Murray, Andrew. 2006. "Homeboys: Uses of Home by Gay Australian Men." *Social & Cultural Geography* 7, no. 1: 53–69. https://doi.org/10.1080/146493 60500452988.

Gorman-Murray, Andrew. 2008. "Reconciling Self: Gay Men and Lesbians Using Domestic Materiality for Identity Management." *Social & Cultural Geography* 9, no. 3: 283–301. https://doi.org/10.1080/14649360801990504.

Gorman-Murray, Andrew. 2012. "Queer Politics at Home: Gay Men's Management of the Public/Private Boundary." *New Zealand Geographer* 68, no. 2: 111–20. https://doi .org/10.1111/j.1745-939.2012.01225.x.

Graham-Harrison, Emma, and Saad Hammadi. 2016. "Inside Bangladesh's Killing Fields: Bloggers and Outsiders Targeted by Fanatics." *The Guardian*, June 11. https://www.theguardian.com/world/2016/jun/11/bangladesh-murders-bloggers -foreigners-religion.

Hanhardt, Christina B. 2014. *Safe Space: Gay Neighborhood History and the Politics of Violence*. Durham, NC: Duke University Press.

Hossain, S. Rajeeb. 2017. "Bangladesh Crackdown on Gay Men Is Another Gesture of Capitulation to Islamist Extremists." *Scroll*, May 29. https://scroll.in/article/838811 /fatal-error-bangladesh-crackdown-on-gays-is-another-gesture-of-capitulation-to -islamist-extremists.

Huq, Efadul. 2020. "Seeing the *Insurgent* in Transformative Planning Practices." *Planning Theory* 19, no. 4: 371–91. https://doi.org/10.1177/1473095219901290.

Kawasaka, Kazuyoshi. 2018. "Contradictory Discourses on Sexual Normality and National Identity in Japanese Modernity." *Sexuality and Culture* 22, no. 2: 593–613. https://doi.org/10.1007/s12119-017-9485-z.

Liow, Joseph Chinyong. 2016. "ISIS in the Pacific: Assessing Terrorism in Southeast Asia and the Threat to the Homeland." *The Brookings Institution*, April 27. https://www .brookings.edu/articles/isis-in-the-pacific-assessing-terrorism-in-southeast-asia-and -the-threat-to-the-homeland/.

Mahmud, Faisal. 2018. "Is Bangladesh Moving towards One-Party State?" *Al Jazeera*, April 4. https://www.aljazeera.com/features/2018/4/4/is-bangladesh-moving-towards -one-party-state.

Malik, Inshah. 2018. "Kashmiri Desire and Digital Space: Queering National Identity and the Indian Citizen." In *Queering Digital India: Activisms, Identities, Subjectivities*, edited by Rohit K. Dasgupta and Debanuj DasGupta, 180–94. Edinburgh: Edinburgh University Press, 2018.

Manalansan, Martin F., IV. 2004. *Global Divas: Filipino Gay Men in the Diaspora.* Durham, NC: Duke University Press.

Manalansan, Martin F., IV. 2005. "Race, Violence, and Neoliberal Spatial Politics in the Global City." *Social Text* 23, nos. 3–4: 141–55. https://doi.org/10.1215/01642472-23-3-4_84-85-141.

Manalansan, Martin. F., IV. 2014. "The 'Stuff' of Archives: Mess, Migration, and Queer Lives." *Radical History Review*, no. 120: 94–107.

Manalansan, Martin F., IV. 2015. "Queer Worldings: The Messy Art of Being Global in Manila and New York." *Antipode* 47, no. 3: 566–79. https://doi.org/10.1111/anti.12061.

Mbembe, Achille. 2001. *On the Postcolony.* Berkeley: University of California Press.

Miraftab, Faranak. 2009. "Insurgent Planning: Situating Radical Planning in the Global South." *Planning Theory* 8, no. 1: 32–50. https://doi.org/10.1177/1473095208099297.

Morgensen, Scott Lauria. 2009. "Arrival at Home." *GLQ: A Journal of Lesbian and Gay Studies* 15, no. 1: 67–96. https://doi.org/10.1215/10642684-2008-019.

Muñoz, José Esteban. 2019. "Introduction: Feeling Utopia." In *Cruising Utopia, 10th Anniversary Edition*, 1–18. New York: New York University Press.

Murray, Heather A. A. 2010. *Not in This Family: Gays and the Meaning of Kinship in Postwar North America.* Philadelphia: University of Pennsylvania Press.

Pilkey, Brent. 2014. "Queering Heteronormativity at Home: Older Gay Londoners and the Negotiation of Domestic Materiality." *Gender, Place & Culture* 21, no. 9: 1142–57. https://doi.org/10.1080/0966369X.2013.832659.

Puar, Jasbir K. 2017. *Terrorist Assemblages: Homonationalism in Queer Times.* 2nd ed. Durham, NC: Duke University Press.

Rahman, Shameema. 2008. "Bangladesh: Anti-Terrorism Ordinance Approved." Library of Congress. https://www.loc.gov/item/global-legal-monitor/2008-06-02/bangladesh-anti-terrorism-ordinance-approved.

Riaz, Ali. 2014. "Shifting Tides in South Asia: Bangladesh's Failed Election." *Journal of Democracy* 25, no. 2: 119–30.

Rivers, Daniel Winunwe. 2013. *Radical Relations: Lesbian Mothers, Gay Fathers, and Their Children in the United States since World War II.* Chapel Hill: University of North Carolina Press.

Roy, Siddharthya. 2017. "A Year of Bangladesh's War on Terror." July 6. https://thediplomat.com/2017/07/a-year-of-bangladeshs-war-on-terror/.

Rushbrook, Dereka. 2002. "Cities, Queer Space, and the Cosmopolitan Tourist." *GLQ: A Journal of Lesbian and Gay Studies* 8, no. 1: 183–206. https://muse.jhu.edu/article/12204.

Shakhsari, Sima. 2012. "From Homoerotics of Exile to Homopolitics of Diaspora." *Journal of Middle East Women's Studies* 8, no. 3: 14–40. https://doi.org/10.2979/jmiddeastwomstud.8.3.14.

Shakhsari, Sima. 2020. *Politics of Rightful Killing: Civil Society, Gender, and Sexuality in Weblogistan*. Durham, NC: Duke University Press.

Shanker, Adrian, ed. 2022. *Crisis and Care: Queer Activist Responses to a Global Pandemic*. Oakland, CA: PM Press.

Spurlin, William J. 2013. "Shifting Geopolitical Borders/Shifting Sexual Borders: Textual and Cultural Renegotiations of National Identity and Sexual Dissidence in Postcolonial Africa." *Studies in Ethnicity and Nationalism* 13, no. 1: 69–79. https://doi.org/10.1111/sena.12020.

Tongson, Karen. 2020. *Relocations: Queer Suburban Imaginaries*. New York: New York University Press. https://doi.org/10.18574/nyu/9780814769676.001.0001.

Vallerand, Olivier. 2013. "Home Is the Place We All Share: Building Queer Collective Utopias." *Journal of Architectural Education* 67, no. 1: 64–75. https://doi.org/10.1080/10464883.2013.767125.

Vider, Stephen. 2015. "'The Ultimate Extension of Gay Community': Communal Living and Gay Liberation in the 1970s." *Gender and History* 27, no. 3: 865–81. https://doi.org/10.1111/1468-0424.12167.

Vider, Stephen. 2021. *The Queerness of Home: Gender, Sexuality, and the Politics of Domesticity after World War II*. Chicago: University of Chicago Press.

Zaman, Fahmida. 2018. "Agencies of Social Movements: Experiences of Bangladesh's Shahbag movement and Hefazat-e-Islam." *Journal of Asian and African Studies* 53, no. 3: 339–49.

ETHAN FROME'S POLY PESSIMISM

Anarchist Non-Monogamy and the Question of Care

Holly Jackson

$\mathcal{I}$n 1897, the poet and social theorist J. William Lloyd imagined a future organized by what he called the new love ideal: "Around each pair of central lovers . . . will gather a group of side lovers, loving the central lovers and each other because of that love" (Lloyd 1897: 75). Indeed, he argued passionately that the bonds between non-monogamous lovers and their metamours would eventually replace the family as the building block of society. He describes an arrangement that might now be called a polycule: "Mary, who is the central love of John in family No. 1 is the side love of Robert who is the central love of Emma in family No. 2, who is a side love of Fred who is a central love of Isabel in family No. 3. Families in this system will become so mingled and inter-related that society will be like an interwoven garment, with every thread bound to every other by numberless ties" (75). This new sexual organization would not only transform private life, according to Lloyd, but also repair the damage of capitalist atomization more broadly, as polyamory would sustain greater individual freedom as well as community cooperation, creating a web of care for both children and adults far surpassing the isolated home. This brand of utopianism in which sexual freedom is imagined both to secure and express socialist transformation had figured prominently in US radical thought for at least seven decades by that time.[1]

Lloyd's *Free Comrade* was one of the periodicals published across the country at the turn of the twentieth century that regularly discussed marriage abolition and nonexclusive sex, along with *Lucifer, Word, Firebrand, Liberty, Free Society, Clothed by the Sun, Discontent*, and others.[2] They examined the role that multiple fathers might play in child rearing; they considered how a "comradeship

GLQ 30:4
DOI 10.1215/10642684-11331146
© 2024 by Duke University Press

contract" might govern the home life of unmarried partners with additional lovers; they described the architecture that might be appropriate for those arrangements; and they published poetry, serialized novels, and numerous editorials on the advantages and pitfalls of having multiple relationships.

A significant body of scholarship has established that a confluence of factors from the 1870s through the early twentieth century—including anti-Mormon and anti-Native legislation, the liberalization of divorce law, and the administration of citizenship to formerly enslaved African Americans—brought questions of sexual exclusivity and household composition to the fore, mandating monogamy as essential to white racial identity and American citizenship. As Nancy Cott (2000: 105), Bruce Burgett (2005: 77), and others have shown, landmark federal legislation criminalized unlawful cohabitation—including any relationship resembling marriage with more than one person—sometimes punishing offenders with disenfranchisement as well as jail time and fines. Katherine Franke (2015) notes that the enforcement of monogamy in the administration of citizenship rights to formerly enslaved people during Reconstruction contravened longstanding alternative practices for some, and the standardization of marriage was also a crucial tool in the settler project of making Native Americans "straight" (Rifkin 2011).[3] Sarah Barringer Gordon (1996: 339) has argued that the movement against Mormon polygamy "may well have been the single most successful nineteenth-century political legal and reform campaign."

But less attention has been paid to the explosion of counterdiscourses critiquing monogamy and advocating multipartner alternatives in this period. Clare Virginia Eby (2014) notes the widely read works by a transatlantic groups of academics, doctors, and journalists who proposed trial marriages, open marriages, and other revisions to the institution.[4] But leftists went further, taking the heightened attention to polygamy and other departures from the couple form in this moment as an opportunity to articulate an economic and political theory of critical non-monogamy and the abolition of the institution altogether. While the sexual and domestic practices of the Mormons bedeviled the federal government and profamily sentimentalists portrayed monogamy as freedom from polygamous bondage (Bentley 2002: 350), radical feminists countered with exposés of the unacknowledged non-monogamy of ordinary American marriage, debunking the norm rigorously upheld yet rarely practiced. As Victoria Woodhull (1871: 34) quipped: "I need not tell you that Mormonism is practiced in *other* places beside Utah." Francis Barry (1873: 4) claimed that mainstream marriage was not all that different from Mormon polygamy and demanded the abolition of both; in his view, the number of partners in these arrangements only determines whether one or more women will be subjugated. Sex radicals theorized a distinct version of nonexclusive love grounded in feminist politics and anticapitalist critique.

Attending to this anarchist discourse in the period most readily associated with the ascendancy of medical sexology suggests alternative histories of sexuality in which aberration was not exclusively located in identitarian interiority nor reduced to the single axis of object choice, but rather grounded in a critique of normative social and economic institutions.[5] Aaron Lecklider (2021) and Terrence Kissack (2008) have established that leftist print culture in the early twentieth century offered some of the earliest support for homosexuality, alongside its coverage of labor and class agitation, but it is important to note the prominence of non-monogamy in this strain of radical thought as well. It would suggest a political genealogy of sexual freedom connecting utopian socialism and other antebellum movements to the more recent history of queer liberation. Homosexuality and polyamory discursively coevolved to some degree, though the constructions of these deviations from the heteromonogamous norm differed importantly.

For examples of these early efforts both to destigmatize homosexuality and advance critical non-monogamy, we might look to antebellum free-lover Austin Kent (1857: 22), who insisted that people can experience both "lust" and "love" for "one or many" at the same time. Significantly, he also acknowledges the existence of "adhesiveness" between people of the same sex, noting that he himself had experienced a love that "passed the love of women" with two men (91). In the period of modern sexuality's emergence, Havelock Ellis's seven-volume series is best known for its treatment of sexual inversion, but he was an astute critic of monogamy as well. Indeed, the final volume closes, after chapters exploring varieties of transgender identification and sex play with urine, with a long essay disparaging monogamy and championing open marriage. He says the mainstream "conception of marriage" is "founded on a fiction" (1928: 515). Ellis states directly that "the promise of mutual exclusive and everlasting love is a promise that cannot be kept and should not be made. It cannot form a permanent basis of marriage" and "if it is taken seriously," it inevitably poisons and destroys it. Good marriages, he argues, last by "being shifted on to other foundations" (516). He charges that the movement to make divorce more accessible "unfortunately helped to narrow down and conventionalize the ideal of marriage, to fortify the old-fashioned romantic view," treating "the erotic element as though that were not only a highly important element but the actual sole content of marriage" and sexual infidelity as "an adequate reason for dissolving" a partnership (519). He scorns "little isolated family groups consumed by greedy absorption and cut off from all generous contact with the world" (518) and insists, on the contrary, that marriage should bring people "into a many-sided contact with the greater world, and that contact cannot be real and intimate if it excludes at the outset the possibility of other relationships" (529). Ellis presumably drew from firsthand experience of his own open marriage to queer intellectual Edith Lee, who was also a public thinker on alternative marriage.

Queer socialist Edward Carpenter was among the most impassioned advocates for sexual freedom in this period, and his influential *Love's Coming of Age* (1896) should be regarded not only as an early account of "homogenic" love but also as a classic work of poly utopianism. Carpenter imagines "a marriage, so free, so spontaneous, that it would allow of wide excursions of the pair from each other . . . and yet would hold them all the time in the bond of absolute sympathy, would by its very freedom be all the more poignantly attractive, and by its very scope and breadth all the richer and more vital—would be in a sense indestructible." He compares this open, committed relationship to two suns revolving, receding from each other only to return and "together blend their rays into the glory of one double star" (102–3). In a situation of such "sincere and natural a trust between man and wife," one partner's "friendship with a third person . . . might be hailed as a gain by both parties." Carpenter posits that it is possible "for married people to have intimacies with outsiders, and yet to continue perfectly true to each other and in rare instances, for triune and other such relations to be permanently maintained," coining a term for what we might now call a "throuple" (105).

This proved influential for J. William Lloyd (1902: 7), who claimed that reading Carpenter and Walt Whitman made him able to love men in the same way he had always loved women. But he notes that the important lesson to be gained from these sources is that no matter the object, sexual jealousy must be rejected: "It would appear that homogenic lovers are too often just as exclusive and jealous as the usual kind. When we once enlarge ourselves on this matter . . . we shall find . . . a whole world of love and lovers always ready and waiting for us. There is no reason why every kind of love that has ever been known to man should not be accepted. . . . Larger! Larger! Let us be more!—let us give and accept more!"

Moreover, these practices were not limited to homosexuals, Perfectionists, and the intellectual vanguard. Saidiya Hartman (2019) has illuminated the sexual "waywardness" and experimental intimacies of "ordinary" young Black women who are generally excluded from accounts of the "sexual modernists." Many working-class white Americans also practiced forms of "fluid marriage," as opposed to the exclusive and permanent ideal (Schwartzberg 2004). Indeed, mainstream newspapers covered so many bigamy cases that "the man with two

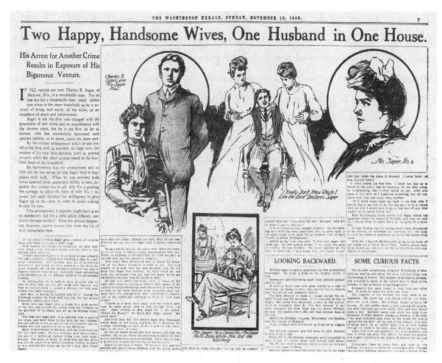

Figure 1. In the midst of a nationwide crackdown on non-monogamy, a range
of sources in the mainstream and at the margins offer glimpses of both poly
utopianism and poly pessimism. "Two Happy, Handsome Wives, One Husband
in One House." *The Washington Herald*. November 18, 1906.

wives" became a veritable stock character in the headlines of this period. Many
of these arrangements were exposed in the wave of trials for obscenity, unlawful
cohabitation, and gross indecency that sought to establish and enforce a heteromonogamous norm. Although media treatments of these cases should be regarded as
central to the implementation of sexual normativity, they nonetheless shed light on
the challenges of queer life in a society centered on the married couple. Mining
these bigamy cases for salacious content, journalists occasionally offer surprising
flashes of poly utopianism in their revelations of happy non-monogamous relationships unhappily brought under scrutiny.

For example, the *Washington Herald* (1906: 7) reported on the case against
Charles R. Sager under the headline "Two Happy, Handsome Wives, One Husband in One House" (fig. 1). Departing from the usual tone of these exposés, the
reporter emphasizes the "peace and contentment" of this "queer domestic life,"
and the article's illustrations highlight the benefits of having two women to share
domestic and care labor: one to do the washing while the other cares for the baby.

The wives arrived at the jail together daily to visit "their joint husband"; "Charlie is a good, kind man," they agreed, "and we shall surely stick to him through thick and thin." The reporters observe that he greets them both with kisses, and when they ask which one he will choose if he must, he responds, "Really, I don't know. I can't say." The article ends on a note of regret that such an agreeable domestic arrangement was a felony: "Sager's unique family is broken up, and he is not facing the future with any degree of enthusiasm."

As the newspapers were keen to illustrate, configurations beyond the couple have always been hiding in plain sight in American culture. Nancy Bentley and Elizabeth Freeman have noted that the dominant literary form of this period was also harnessed for the enforcement of monogamy in the face of manifold noncompliance. Bentley (2002: 344) has noted that antipolygamy activists carried out an impressive campaign of mass demonstrations and published a newspaper, the *Anti-Polygamy Standard*, but "probably the most important force in this grassroots movement," she argues, "was the antipolygamy novel, a popular subgenre that produced upwards of a hundred titles, a number of them bestsellers." Even beyond these baldly ideological works, she claims that "polygamy holds a . . . structurally important place in the history of the genre," specifically that "the novel has never tolerated it" (341). Though the novel may seem preoccupied throughout its history with bigamous threats of the kind featured in *Jane Eyre* and *Sister Carrie*, Bentley's argument suggests that such works ultimately shore up the monogamous norm. The anarchist sex radicals noticed this, too. In the *Adult*, American free-lover Lilian Harman reviewed English novels of the period like Grant Allen's *The Woman Who Did* (1895) and Thomas Hardy's *Jude the Obscure* (1895), complaining that their representations of freedom in love arrived at negative conclusions that did not reflect her happy experience of non-monogamy (Greenway 2009).

Freeman (2004: 639-43) also sees the realist novel as working to "contain the threat" of "proliferative affinities" in this pro-monogamy period but observes that the form is nevertheless "still shadowed by the exiled social form of plural marriage." Yet these literary shadows of multipartner desire and, more importantly, of critical non-monogamy or anti-monogamy remain largely unexplored.[6] There is indeed a tradition of works in which non-monogamous people might see their lives reflected, though the picture painted therein is not always a sunny one. These range, for example, from Herman Melville's *Pierre* (1852) to Carson McCullers's *Member of the Wedding* (1946), with a particular swell from the 1870s through the early twentieth century. Some of these works pair polyamory with other forms of sexual deviance and evoke the negative affects we have come to associate with queer literature, including mourning and hopelessness (Love 2007).[7]

However, while these ambivalent or even negative representations might seem to shore up monogamy by making alternatives seem not merely difficult but disastrous or tragic, it may be that their critiques are aimed instead at the systems that severely constrain nonnormative possibility. We might call this poly pessimism: a rejection of monogamy as a repressive institution, a desire for love and care beyond the familial matrix, but a despairing or critical awareness of the difficulty of alternatives under compulsory normativity that serves capitalist demands.

I turn now briefly to a hypercanonical example of a man with two wives in order to suggest not only the extent to which the consideration of these arrangements permeated the period but also to offer an alternate reading of the negative endings that often characterize the literature of non-monogamy. Critics have consistently read Edith Wharton's "novels about marital entrapment" in relation to her own disastrous marriage and eventual divorce. Some note her relationships with queer lover Morton Fullerton and longtime companion Walter Berry but also observe that she and her works are conservative on the issue of divorce, even more so than those of her contemporaries (Freeman 2003: 50). Though Wharton was far from a declared varietist, or advocate for freedom in love, we might consider her ambivalence about divorce alongside that of socialist critics of monogamous marriage at that time, including Francis Barry and Havelock Ellis, who felt that the surge of attention to divorce and demands for its greater accessibility ultimately shored up a false idea of marriage. Wharton debunked both marriage and its alternatives, emphasizing the limits of individual freedom in relation to coercive hegemonic institutions.

Many of Wharton's works interrogate the problems of marriage in ways that readings attached to traditional notions of "infidelity" are inadequate to describe. The stories "Souls Belated" (1899) and "The Reckoning" (1902) explicitly address experimental attempts to break out of traditional marriage into freer relations but both conclude that the social protections of marriage, however chafing, are indispensable (Lee 2008: 187). *The House of Mirth* (1905) goes further to suggest that marriage may be the only context that affords women the opportunity to enjoy multiple partners. Ned Van Alstyne remarks of Lily Bart, "When a girl's as good-looking as that she'd better marry; then no questions are asked" (Wharton 1905: 254). The unmarried Lily cannot risk the appearance of sexual impropriety, but Bertha Dorset and other married women's affairs are protected by a code of silence around marital non-monogamy. In presenting traditional marriage as a cover for sexual freedom, Wharton sends up the "disguised polygamy" of traditional marriage, as did critics like Elizabeth Cady Stanton and Karl Marx at this time.[8]

In *The Age of Innocence* (1920), arguably a realist elaboration of some of the questions suggested by the naturalist *Ethan Frome*, Wharton engages most directly with the mores of the elite New York scene, where she learned as a child the clearly delineated rules for dealing with the ubiquity of extramarital partners in an officially monogamous culture (Lee 2008). Newland Archer longs for a solution to his torturous love triangle that would not require him either to destroy his marriage or to debase his lover, eventually coming to realize that his wife and their entire community have assumed his involvement in a full sexual relationship that he has not actually dared to enjoy. Indeed, this novel presents a transnational range of perspectives on non-monogamy; we encounter both Ellen's aristocratic husband as a representative of European sexual ethics and her aunt Medora Manson's companion, Dr. Agathon Carver, the founder of the Valley of Love Community. Handing Archer his card, which is visually set apart from the rest of the novel's type, calling unusual attention to a seemingly minor character, Carver wonders "if this young gentleman is interested in my experiences" (Wharton 1920: 159). This moment seems to ask how Archer's predicament relates to sexual experiments on the radical fringe and whether it might be solved by joining a free-love community upstate, where perhaps his love for Ellen could be squared with his partnership with May. After all, he dreams of running away to some place where "categories" like "mistress" do not exist (293). Ultimately, Wharton romanticizes neither marriage nor extramarital relations, critical of both the traditional and emerging models of sexual morality that the novel's split historical setting indicates.

The monstrous ménage à trois revealed at the end of Wharton's *Ethan Frome* (1911), a blistering naturalist critique of monogamy and the particular class, racial, colonial, and regional considerations that shape it, suggests that the only imaginable alternative is an equally unlivable multiplication of care work and domestic tyranny—the expansion of marriage and the private home rather than its abolition. Though this novel may seem particularly phobic about multipartner possibilities, we might see it instead as astutely engaged with the same questions as the intragroup debates of anarchist varietists themselves.

In our initial introduction to Frome, we learn that he has a limp "checking each step like the jerk of a chain" (Wharton 1911: 4). Writing to Morton Fullerton about her own marriage in 1911, the year the novel was published, Wharton declared, "Isn't it awful to have a chain snaffled around one's neck for all time? . . . Oh, if only I were free—free—free!" (Eby 2014: xv). Varietists often referred to the "chains" of matrimony, including the novel *Chains*, serialized in the radical paper *Clothed with the Sun* in 1900–1901. Though what follows is the merest analytical sketch of *Ethan Frome*—a work overdue for a fuller and more expert revaluation focused on disability, among other issues—it offers a reading of the novel sensitive to the poly possibilities of the period as a way of breaking out of both conservative and liberal perspectives on marriage, affairs, and divorce to consider a fuller range of discourses on monogamy under capitalism and the questions it continues to raise.

Specifically, *Ethan Frome* is interested in the relationship between compulsory monogamy and the labor of care. As a younger man, Ethan could not leave the aptly named Starkfield, Massachusetts, because "somebody had to stay and care for the folks," specifically his sick parents. Romantic partnership initially promised to lighten the load of these responsibilities. But as his neighbor, Harmon, observes, "I guess it's always Ethan done the caring" (Wharton 1911: 7). Zeena nursed his mother devotedly, but after she died and they married, she insisted that her own health had been ruined. Indeed, Zeena's unreasonable demands for care over seven years of marriage have transformed the person he hoped would be a companion and a helpmate into "a mysterious alien presence, an evil energy secreted from the long years of silent brooding." In brief, "he abhorred her" (128).

The arrival of Mattie Silver, a poor relation of Zeena's who has come to work as her aide in exchange for room and board, is like "the lighting of a fire on a cold hearth" (36). We should note that even this promise of emotional warmth is presented in the language of housework. Though this three-person household seems potentially advantageous to all of them, once again the promise of distributed domestic labor is unrealized; it turns out that Mattie is unskilled at these tasks, and Ethan takes on her chores in addition to his own. Ethan and Mattie soon fall in love, but despite his miserable experience with marriage, he can only imagine their relationship in terms of marital norms. In this novel, family is something beyond duty and more akin to death, and as he surveys the Frome graveyard on his property, he thinks fondly, "We'll always go on living here together, and some day she'll lie there beside me" (55). This is the best outcome he can imagine—to be dead and buried together in the family plot—and it is ultimately what he gets.

Notably, Ethan exclusively calls her "Matt," even in moments of overheated romantic ejaculation: "Oh, *Matt!*" (158). This masculine pet name evokes a same-sex relationship to underscore the queerness of their extramarital connection. He is often saddened when he compares their situation to that of a newly engaged couple in town: "He felt a pang at the thought that these two need not hide their happiness" (84). He and Matt are in the closet because all unmarried people are queered by the marriage system.

Despite their relationship's illicitness, they yearn to experience it as a copy of marital normativity. When Zeena goes away overnight to see a specialist, Ethan and Mattie spend this rare interval of freedom playing at being just "like a married couple" (73). They perform an idealized domestic scene: she sews, he smokes in front of the fire, and they sit down to a homely dinner at a table set with the family's finest tableware. In the course of acting out this forbidden normativity, a house cat breaks a pickle dish that had been a wedding present for Zeena but which she never uses. "Oh Puss, you're too greedy!" Mattie exclaims (91).

Upon her return, Zeena furiously hints that the neighbors are starting to whisper about Ethan's relationship with Mattie and demands her immediate departure from the Frome household and replacement with a "hired girl" to do every "single thing around the house." The three of them have been living together in a situation that might have addressed their needs through shared resources, including affection and housekeeping, but Zeena is determined to separate the strands of care, labor, sex, and kinship that have become entangled in Mattie's increasingly ambiguous position in their home. Gutted by this news, Ethan hurriedly considers his options for ending his marriage. He is aware that divorce is more available than ever before. Indeed, a man his age in a nearby town "had escaped from just such a life of misery by going west with the girl he cared for" (143). But Ethan soon realizes that he has no money to travel and cannot afford to leave the farm or sell it, pay Zeena alimony, or support Mattie as a wife. Wharton seems to echo free-love novels such as *Hilda's Home* by Rosa Graul (1899: 71) in noting that more accessible divorce was still inaccessible to the poor because "like all laws it is for the moneyed class."

Ethan's confession of love to Mattie in what he thinks will be their final hour together is again framed as an ardent desire to perform for her the care work that is reserved for legitimate lovers only: "I want to do for you and care for you. I want to be there when you're sick and when you're lonesome" (Wharton 1911: 172). Despite the sincerity of his desire, there is very little Ethan can do for Mattie because there is no end to what he is required to do exclusively for Zeena. On a final sledding excursion that turns into a suicide pact, a violent crash accomplishes the goal of keeping them together forever, though severely injured. After the crash, Mattie is too altered and incapacitated to leave the Frome house or Starkfield after all since, as we are ominously told, she has nowhere else to go. Now Ethan must do for her and care for her, not because he loves her, but because she is family.[9]

As if the bonds of marriage and poverty were not enough, Ethan has added another link to the chain. He was clear from the beginning that loving Mattie meant caring for her materially, but the outcome of his new connection amounts to more constraint in love, not freedom. Rather than a romantic vision of interdependence, the final scene reveals the squalid living conditions of the man with two wives, none of them receiving adequate care. As a neighbor observes, "it's pretty bad, seeing all three of them there together" (192). The two squabbling women can no longer be distinguished; Mattie "has become a second Zeena" (Lee 2008: 380). Clearly this triune cannot afford the separate living quarters that most varietists agreed were necessary for freedom in love, along with the communization of domestic work. Though the addition of Mattie to this torturous marriage proffered a reprieve from domestic suffocation and want, by the end we can only agree with the neighbor: "It's a pity . . . that they're all shut up there'n that one kitchen. . . . It's horrible for them all" (194).

This conclusion seems a cruel punishment for Ethan and Mattie, who are guilty only of an unconsummated extramarital crush. Perhaps the novel's popularity has been due in part to its work as a morality tale, making the idea of living with two women—gaining a lover while keeping a wife—seem like a nightmare. The review of the novel in *The New York Times* (1911) noted that the story "on the face of it is a very sordid triangle," but ultimately "the effect is anything but sordid." We could read its unsparing conclusion as pro-monogamy propaganda, but Wharton's novel makes crucial points about the material obstacles to sexual freedom that were also advanced by the radical varietists of the time. Not only do lovers outside of marriage tend to replicate oppressive aspects of the institution, but new romantic attachments cannot provide liberation as long as care is privatized in the family. Monogamy may be a failure and a fraud, but capitalist conditions, including heteromonogamous norms, make it impossible to realize in practice the potential benefits of multipartner alternatives, especially for the poor, whose bare survival may depend on marital status. Polyamory holds out the hope for a more distributed model of care, increased personal freedom, and a plentitude of intimacies, but it may also entail the multiplication of compulsory private labor in a broader context of social punishment and economic austerity.[10]

The anarchist varietists were clear that the abolition of monogamous marriage could only be accomplished alongside the liberation of women and the workers of the world, but they were understandably stymied by the question of how these interlocking changes would unfold. For all his utopian imagining, Lloyd's (1888: 7) writings also reveal a strain of poly pessimism, acknowledging that the stigma and economic penalties of living a free life might bar working people from pursuing it:

> Here and there, in favored spots, favored individuals may realize the ideal
> of free-love and free homes but for the average poor man or woman, obliged

to labor ten or more hours per day to exist, and dependent upon the good-will of the community for even the permission to labor at all, with no spare means to defend against legal and illegal brutalities, and no division of labor to assist in its execution, it is clearly impossible.

Lloyd's new love ideal demanded that all domestic and care work be public and communal so that marital cohabitation would no longer be necessary: "The home is not a bake-shop, a restaurant, a laundry, a workshop of any kind; it is not a nurs-ery; in the future division of labor all these things will be outside of the home" (7). He longs for a time when "the consummation of love" will give "no legal power over the person, the pocketbook, or the arrangements of the home," but until then, free love will only be possible "in an isolated, momentary, fragmentary way" (7).

Indeed, he wondered whether it was any more ethical, under the existing system, to ask a woman to join an open relationship than it was to propose the bla-tantly offensive marriage relation. Routed by these two bad options, Lloyd declares in frustration: "The fact is there is no possible sexual relation which a thoughtful and kind man might not shrink from asking a woman to enter. Under the present system pain and degradation are certain for her, let her choose what she will, let her do what she may, or do nothing" (7). This tension in Lloyd's writings between a utopian investment in the transformative potential of free love and a despairing frustration with the social conditions under which it must be practiced is a defin-ing dynamic of poly theory and literature then as now. Lloyd's list of the labor that would need to be communized in order for the traditional family to be abandoned anticipates by 140 years Kathi Weeks's (2023: 448–49) "possibilities for a politi-cal project aimed at lessening the coercive forces that drive people into families and block their exits," including a guaranteed minimum income, affordable hous-ing, universal healthcare, and shorter working hours.

Women in anarchist circles also raised material critiques that challenged the association between sexual freedom and social liberation. A woman who signed herself "B" (1897: 7) observes that though she "hates marriage," freedom in love carried significant risks for working-class women at a time when birth control was not readily available. She claims that the majority of working men have enough difficulty supporting the children of one woman and that most women's health is compromised after having multiple births, which further hampered their ability to earn an independent living. She recounts the story of her marriage to a fellow radical who left her destitute to pursue new relationships and political community in Chicago while she was stuck in Omaha caring for their four children.

For these reasons, some argued that there was no point pursuing liberated love under capitalism. For example, W. H. Van Ornum (1898: 3) declared, "While freedom in sex relations is all important in an ideal society, it can never be attained, to any considerable extent, until economic freedom is first achieved." Others argued that a sexual revolution should be pursued first and would effectively set the scene for an anticapitalist uprising. In *Free Society*, alongside regular coverage of the lectures of Peter Kropotkin in Europe and labor actions in the United States, James S. Denson (1898) argued that there are plenty of socialists who, if they achieved their economic aims, would settle down into complacency with their conservative domestic lives. But "the man or woman who is freed from the bonds of sexual conventionality can never again willingly be content in the environments which our existing economic institutions provide" (3). Furthermore, he observes astutely that life in the atomized family unfits us for collective struggle. In his account, living differently trains one's revolutionary consciousness, and beginning with the reorganization of intimate relationships was the most direct way of bringing a new world into being. This sentiment echoes in Lauren Berlant's (2022: 32–33) observation that for sex radicals there is value in "actually pursuing an inconvenient self- and life-disturbance that would help or even force them to unlearn their unfulfilled ways of being in the world as it is" since revolutionary transition "involves leaps into insecurity."

A notable recent formulation of the connection between sexual freedom and social revolution that refuses the privatizing logic of expanded kin can be found in the Care Collective's 2020 manifesto (41–42), which looks to the language, ethics, and example of wayward sexuality as a model—but not a material basis—for flourishing beyond the family. Noting that "care at the scale of kinship . . . is all too often inadequate," they call instead for "promiscuous care," a set of more capacious, experimental, "indiscriminate" practices that would extend our responsibility beyond even the polycule, specifically and importantly to strangers. It is tempting to imagine that this is the ultimate outcome Lloyd (1888: 7) had in mind when he said that although his new love ideal could not be fully realized under the economic conditions of his time, "the first steps can be taken, and we are taking them."

Nineteenth-century expressions of critical non-monogamy in an array of cultural texts hold an important position in both the history of sexuality and the history of radical thought. Diverging from the medical discourses of sexuality, varietism or freedom in love was an anticapitalist project and a queer horizon theorized collectively out of experimental lived practices, not to join but to unseat socially acceptable forms of relation. In their analysis of both the gaps and the bridges between sexual freedom and social transformation, anti-monogamists and marriage abolitionists illuminate not only the sexual utopianism that connects the earliest waves of US socialism to more recent agendas for liberation, but also the calls for practical reorganization of home life and economies of care that this utopianism too often overshadows.

Notes

My thanks to Sari Edelstein, Britt Rusert, Lara Langer Cohen, Tori McCandless, and two anonymous reviewers for their crucial feedback on drafts of this essay.

1. This essay anachronistically intersperses the terminology of "polyamory," which the *OED* dates to 1992, with terms in use at the turn of the twentieth century, including "varietism" and "free love," in order to suggest a genealogy between antebellum utopian socialism and more contemporary theorizations and practices of critical non-monogamy. In referring here to earlier forms of radical sexual utopianism in the United States, I am thinking primarily of the socialist waves associated with Robert Owen and Charles Fourier, and to some extent Garrisonian abolitionist anarchism, but this genealogy is incomplete without sustained attention to Native American and Black histories of non-monogamy. See also Passet (2003) and Sears (1977). For earlier US settler battles over polygamy, see Pearsall (2019), and for decolonial theorizations of critical non-monogamy, see TallBear (2018).

2. See Longa (2010) for a bibliography of US English-language anarchist periodicals in this period.

3. Also see Coviello (2019: 2) on the "adjacent histories" of "erotic noncompliance" of the Mormons and Indigenous peoples.

4. See Eby (2014) on writers in this group, such as Elsie Clews Parson and Olive Shreiner. In England, too, "by the end of the 1890s marriage versus free love was a regular, if controversial, topic of debate in novels, plays and stories, newspaper articles and public meetings" (Greenway 2009: 161).

5. I offer the term "poly pessimism" to describe a strain of critical non-monogamy that departs from utopian discourses of sexual liberation and socialist liberation. My use of this term is not conceptually derived from Afropessimism or heteropessimism.

6. Freeman (2004: 627) offers a brief list of suggestions for further literary study. See Eby (2014) for readings of Theodore Dreiser, Upton Sinclair, and others in relation to varietism. Elsewhere I have written about a small selection of novels by active free-lovers offered in service of the cause, and forms other than the realist novel also allow for explorations of multipartner scenarios. Constance Fenimore Woolson's "Felipa" (1876) and Bayard Taylor's "Twin-Love" (1871) further suggest the representational

pairing of polyamory with homosexuality. Both Charles Chesnutt's "The Wife of His Youth" (1898) and Thomas Nelson Page's "Old Jabe's Marital Experiments" (1904) evince anxiety about Black bigamy, although from opposing ends of the ideological spectrum. On anti-monogamy, see Willey (2016).

7. Of course, there is good reason to approach discourses of non-monogamy cautiously; scholars have noted its associations in this period with white eugenics and Orientalism. Scholars of non-monogamy in this period have rightly emphasized that appeals to the science of reproduction placed some free lovers firmly in the racist, ableist camp of eugenics. Angela Willey (2016: 31) takes up Ellis at length and charges that advocacy for non-monogamy in this period, just as much as its normative counterpart, relied on "a discourse of sexual selection: where the stakes of heterosexual courtship are precisely the eugenic *quality* of the next generation." We should note as well that *Lucifer* became the *American Journal of Eugenics*, retaining its poly ethos but hitching its program to the national obsession with natural selection, which was a way to legitimize their frank discussion of sex and to argue for the social and scientific value of the freedom to choose multiple partners. But some strands of sex radicalism of the period aimed neither to scientize sexual alterity nor to optimize reproduction but rather to destabilize capitalism and its family forms in order to build a new society. On free love and eugenics, see also Hayden (2013).

8. According to *The Communist Manifesto* (Marx and Engels 1906: 41), "Bourgeois marriage is, in reality, a system of wives in common and thus, at the most, what the Communists might possibly be reproached with is that they desire to introduce, in substitution for a hypocritically concealed, an openly legalised community of women." Elizabeth Cady Stanton (1871: 71) described a form of "polygamy" in which "a man lives with one wife, whose children are his legal heirs, but who has many mistresses. This is everywhere practiced in the United States."

9. Though it is a site of horror in *Ethan Frome*, turning lovers into family is a long-standing poly-utopian trope still powerfully operative in recent media coverage of the Somerville, Massachusetts, statutes recognizing multipartner relationships. Importantly, this statute emerged in the early COVID-era context of society's contraction to "essential work" and household relationships. The *Boston Globe* (Barry 2020) announced that the city had "expanded its notion of family," and a representative of the Polyamory Legal Advocacy Coalition quoted in *The New York Times* (Goldstein 2023) stated that conservatives should be pleased that polyamorous people want to rely on private "care solutions" rather than "looking to the state." Though an intriguing precedent, we might regard this neoliberal advance warily, in part because "family," as Sophie Lewis (2022: 4) observes, is "the name we use for the fact that care is privatized in our society." Registering multiple sexual relationships with the government was not the liberation Lloyd (1897: 75) and his anarchist comrades had in mind. In his imagined poly utopia, by contrast, families would become permeable and ulti-

mately be surpassed. Indeed, he specified that networks of central and side lovers should be socially recognized, but not as "an *institution*, to be enforced by laws and petrified customs."

10. In contrast to the novel's distressing representation of constraint under the duties of multiplying domestic dependents, some contemporary critiques from the left suggest that non-monogamy does not go far enough in expanding the responsibilities that would undermine the autonomy and individualism vaunted under capitalism. Weeks (2023: 445) points to models of polyamory that value "relationships that are meant to minimize the challenges that complex interdependencies can pose to self-sovereignty."

References

B. 1897. "Open Letter to E. F. Reudenbusch." *Firebrand*, March 28, 7.

Barry, Ellen. 2020. "A City Gives Family Rights to Multiple-Partner Unions." *The New York Times*, July 5.

Barry, Francis. 1873. "Who Are Free Lovers?" *Woodhull & Claflin's Weekly*, April 5, 4.

Bentley, Nancy. 2002. "Marriage as Treason: Polygamy, Nation, and the Novel." In *The Futures of American Studies*, edited by Donald Pease and Robyn Wiegman, 341–70. Durham, NC: Duke University Press.

Berlant, Lauren. 2022. *On the Inconvenience of Other People*. Durham, NC: Duke University Press.

Burgett, Bruce. 2005. "On the Mormon Question: Race, Sex, and Polygamy in the 1850s and the 1990s." *American Quarterly* 57, no. 1: 75–102.

Care Collective. 2020. *The Care Manifesto: The Politics of Interdependence*. London: Verso.

Carpenter, Edward. 1896. *Love's Coming of Age*. Manchester: Labour Press.

Cott, Nancy F. 2000. *Public Vows: A History of Marriage and the Nation*. Cambridge, MA: Harvard University Press.

Coviello, Peter. 2019. *Make Yourselves Gods: Mormons and the Unfinished Business of American Secularism*. Chicago: University of Chicago Press.

Denson, James S. 1898. "Sexual and Economic Reform—A Question of Precedence." *Free Society*, April 24, 3.

Eby, Clare Virginia. 2014. *Til Choice Do Us Part: Marriage Reform in the Progressive Era*. Chicago: University of Chicago Press.

Ellis, Havelock. 1928. *Eonism and Other Supplementary Studies*. Vol. VII of *Studies in the Psychology of Sex*. 7 vols. Philadelphia: Davis.

Franke, Katherine. 2015. *Wedlocked: The Perils of Marriage Equality*. New York: NYU Press.

Freeman, Elizabeth. 2004. "The Whole(y) Family: Economies of Kinship in the Progressive Era." *American Literary History* 16, no. 4: 619–47.

Freeman, Kimberly A. 2003. *Love American Style: Divorce and the American Novel, 1881-1976*. New York: Routledge.

Goldstein, Meredith. 2023. "Somerville Celebrates Another First for Polyamorous People." *Boston Globe*, March 23. https://www.bostonglobe.com/2023/03/23/lifestyle/somerville-celebrates-another-first-polyamorous-people/.

Gordon, Sarah Barringer. 1996. "Our National Hearthstone: Anti-Polygamy Fiction and the Sentimental Campaign against Moral Diversity in Antebellum America." *Yale Journal of Law & the Humanities* 8, no. 2: 295–350.

Graul, Rosa. 1899. *Hilda's Home: A Story of Woman's Emancipation*. Chicago: M. Harman and Co.

Greenway, Judy. 2009. "Speaking Desire: Anarchism and Free Love as Utopian Performance in Fin de Siècle Britain." In *Anarchism and Utopianism*, edited by Laurence Davis and Ruth Kinna, 153–70. Manchester: Manchester University Press.

Hartman, Saidiya. 2019. *Wayward Lives, Beautiful Experiments: Intimate Histories of Social Upheaval*. New York: Norton.

Hayden, Wendy. 2013. *Evolutionary Rhetoric: Sex, Science, and Free Love in Nineteenth-Century Feminism*. Carbondale: Southern Illinois University Press.

Kent, Austin. 1857. *Free Love: Or, A Philosophical Demonstration of the Non-Exclusive Nature of Connubial Love*. Hopkinton, NY: Austin Kent.

Kissack, Terrence. 2008. *Free Comrades: Anarchism and Homosexuality in the United States, 1895–1917*. Chico, CA: AK Press.

Lecklider Aaron. 2021. *Love's Next Meeting: The Forgotten History of Homosexuality and the Left in American Culture*. Oakland: University of California Press.

Lee, Hermione. 2008. *Edith Wharton*. New York: Knopf Doubleday.

Lewis, Sophie. 2022. *Abolish the Family: A Manifesto for Care and Liberation*. New York: Verso.

Lloyd, J. William. 1888. "Love and Home." *Liberty*, November 10, 7.

Lloyd, J. William. 1897. "A New Love Ideal." *Lucifer*, March 10, 74–75.

Lloyd, J. William. 1902. [Untitled]. *Free Comrade*, October, P7.

Longa, Ernesto A. 2010. *Anarchist Periodicals in English Published in the United States (1833–1955): An Annotated Guide*. Plymouth, MA: Scarecrow Press.

Love, Heather. 2007. *Feeling Backward: Loss and the Politics of Queer History*. Cambridge, MA: Harvard University Press.

Marx, Karl, and Frederick Engels. 1906. *Manifesto of the Communist Party*. Chicago: Kerr and Co.

The New York Times. 1911. "Three Lives in Supreme Torture." October 8.

Passet, Joanne. 2003. *Sex Radicals and the Quest for Women's Equality*. Champaign: University of Illinois Press.

Pearsall, Sarah. 2019. *Polygamy: An Early American History*. New Haven, CT: Yale University Press.

Rifkin, Mark. 2011. *When Did Indians Become Straight? Kinship, the History of Sexuality, and Native Sovereignty*. New York: Oxford University Press.

Schwartzberg, Beverly. 2004 "'Lots of Them Did That': Desertion, Bigamy, and Marital Fluidity in Late-Nineteenth-Century America." *Journal of Social History* 37, no. 3: 573–600.

Sears, Hal D. 1977. *The Sex Radicals: Free Love in High Victorian America*. Lawrence: Regents Press of Kansas.

Stanton, Elizabeth Cady. 1871. "Marriage and Divorce." In *A History of the National Woman's Rights Movement for Twenty Years*, edited by Paulina W. Davis, 60-83. New York: Journeymen Printers Cooperative Association.

TallBear, Kim. 2018. "Making Love and Relations beyond Settler Sex and Family." In *Making Kin Not Population*, edited by Adele Clarke and Donna Haraway, 145–64. Chicago: Prickly Paradigm Press.

Van Ornum, W. H. 1898. "Note on Sex." *Free Society*, May 1, 3.

Washington Herald. 1906. "Two Happy, Handsome Wives, One Husband in One House." November 18.

Weeks, Kathi. 2023. "Abolition of the Family: The Most Infamous Feminist Proposal." *Feminist Theory* 24, no. 3: 433–53.

Wharton, Edith. 1905. *The House of Mirth*. New York: Charles Scribner's Sons.

Wharton, Edith. 1911. *Ethan Frome*. New York: Charles Scribner's Sons.

Wharton, Edith. 1920. *The Age of Innocence*. New York: D. Appleton.

Willey, Angela. 2016. *Undoing Monogamy: The Politics of Science and the Possibilities of Biology*. Durham, NC: Duke University Press.

Woodhull, Victoria. 1871. *And the Truth Shall Make You Free*. New York: Woodhull, Claflin.

"BUT ON SUNDAY, THEY ARE FREE"

Tomboy Domesticity and Home Time in *Sunday Beauty Queen*

Ariel M. Dela Cruz

𝒯he second scene in Baby Ruth Villarama's celebrated documentary *Sunday Beauty Queen* (2016) occurs after a beauty pageant, when it is time for queens and attendees alike to return home. A panning shot follows Rudelie Acosta, a Filipina[1] pageant competitor, as she wearily walks down a dimly lit street toward the house of her employer, where she has worked and lived as a domestic helper during her four years in Hong Kong. As she hastens further into the night, still in her high heels, the documentary's narrative text appears, reading: "After missing her curfew on the night of the pageant, Rudelie's employer terminates her. She has 14 days to find a new employer before she becomes an illegal alien" (Villarama 2016). Suddenly without shelter or employment, Acosta ventures across the city to meet Leo Selomenio, another Filipino domestic helper who was notified of Acosta's termination through a phone call from a friend during his[2] own commute home. Selomenio and Acosta join Judy Sison, a Filipina domestic helper and Selomenio's partner, as well as another unnamed Filipina domestic helper, in a small kitchen and living room. Upon their arrival, Selomenio reveals that the Philippine Consulate will often call him to pick up and care for terminated Filipino domestic helpers who are facing the threat of deportation by the Hong Kong government. He notes that every time this happens, he allows the recently terminated care workers to stay in his apartment. It is later explicitly revealed that the space that they gather in is the home of Selomenio, who is one of the few Filipino domestic helpers in Hong Kong who is permitted to live outside their place of employment.

The film's title, *Sunday Beauty Queen*, refers to the presence of "190,000 documented Filipino professional helpers in Hong Kong [who] live with their employers and work for 24 hours, six days a week. But on Sunday, they are free"

GLQ 30:4

DOI 10.1215/10642684-11331058

© 2024 by Duke University Press

(Villarama 2016). On Sunday many of these workers attend, assist with, and perform in Filipino beauty pageants for domestic helpers in Hong Kong, which Selomenio began organizing in 2008. Outside of these twenty-four hours, domestic helpers must abide by clause 3 of their standard employment contract (SEC), which states that foreign domestic helpers are required to live in the homes where they are employed. Clause 15 of the SEC, however, notes that on rare occasions domestic helpers are permitted to live outside of their employer's home, a process that requires approval from both their employer and the Hong Kong commissioner for labor (HKLD 2019). Thus, Selomenio and Sison, who were both afforded this opportunity, share a small apartment that is shown on three occasions during the documentary. Although the documentary's title references the weekly public spectacle of the beauty pageant, Selomenio's home also operates within the documentary as a site of domesticity that counters both the publicness of the beauty pageant and the domestic spheres that shape their working lives.

Within the contexts of white cisheteronormativity in the global North, the site of the domestic is often thought of as an apolitical and private entity, with social movements and spectacles outside the home instead imagined as public and political sites. However, as care workers, feminist scholars, and queer scholars such as Martin Manalansan (2008), Rhacel Parreñas (2001), and Robyn Rodriguez (2010) have argued, for Filipinos within the diaspora, the domestic has always been a site rife with political tensions and refusals. Dani Magsumbol (2022) writes that the ostensible "privacy" of the home in the global North only privileges families of employment who are protected beneath its realm. From poor working (and thus living) conditions, to financial and physical extraction, to other kinds of violence and abuse, the "private" home has operated and continues to operate as a site of precarity for the migrant domestic laborer. However, labor scholars like Ethel Tungohan (2013), Valerie Francisco-Menchavez (2018), and Conely de Leon (2016) also note how domestic migrant laborers continue to negotiate, resist, reshape, and refuse the violences of these so-called "private" and "apolitical" spaces, and to maintain modes of kinship, mothering, and care transnationally. In this way, the domestic is and always has been undergirded by racial, social, class, sexual, and gendered politics for domestic workers across the Filipino labor diaspora.

Scholarship of migrant domestic work often locates these violences and political negotiations within the home of the employer, but this article reorients us to a different domestic space where other modes of care and gender are being performed. Although the pageant stage offers a space for creativity, care, and beauty for domestic helpers amid the brutalities and violences of the home in Hong Kong, Selomenio's home acts as another domestic site that operates outside the space of employment yet still exists within the affective, political, geographic mappings of transnational care work. Within the documentary, Selomenio refashions his home to house and feed unjustly terminated caregivers, provide them with financial support and resources to seek better employment prior to deportation, create and house pageant materials, maintain romantic relationships, and further invest in networks of queer kinship and communities of care. Even though the domestic is often articulated as a transnational workplace or a purely private and feminized space removed from politics, in Selomenio's home, gender, care, and gendered care are collectively reimagined and reperformed.

Scattered throughout *Sunday Beauty Queen* are queer aesthetic and semantic markers that differentiate Selomenio from the other Filipino domestic helpers within the documentary, most of whom are cis Filipina women. Throughout the film, Selomenio's employers and other caregivers refer to him as "Daddy," and he usually dons polo shirts, T-shirts, and pants as part of his everyday wear. Though Selomenio could be read as a butch lesbian or transmasculine within normative conceptualizations of LGBTQ+ identities in the United States, within the context of Filipino sexualities he would be read as a tomboy. Scholars such as Jack Halberstam (2018), Evelyn Blackwood (2005), Franco Lai (2007), and Megan Sinnott (2008) have explored various tomboy embodiments in the United States, Indonesia, Hong Kong, and Thailand respectively, but these notions of tomboy mark a stark contrast to Filipino tomboys, who engage particular embodiments of class, race, gender, and sexuality. Kale Fajardo's (2014) groundbreaking work on tomboys and seafarers notes that this term differs from these other conceptions of tomboy, suggesting that the term refers to lower-class and working-class Filipino lesbians, gender nonconformists, female masculinities, and transmasculinities. As such, *tomboy*—which does not distinguish between gender and sexuality—is a racialized and classed gender-sexual formation that has enfolded within it various permutations of meaning.

Recognizing Selomenio not solely as a "butch lesbian domestic helper" (Piocos 2022: 1729) but as a tomboy domestic helper allows us to better understand the generative work of Selomenio and his home in *Sunday Beauty Queen*. In addition to examining tomboy as a particular Filipino gender-sexual embodiment, Gina Velasco (2022) has crucially placed tomboy and transness into conversation with one another to examine the traversing of gender identities and transnational sexualities across the Filipino diaspora. In this article, I add to Velasco's pairing of tomboy and transness by locating Selomenio, a tomboy domestic helper, within care work, a highly feminized mode of labor. As a transing analytic, "tomboy" unsettles and disaggregates normative configurations of class, race, gender, and sexuality, and it reassembles them to think beyond gender as simply an additive supplement to conversations on global care work.[3]

Just as tomboy unsettles and reentangles normative conceptions of gendered and racialized embodiment, tomboy domesticity is a term that can allow us to glean the ways in which tomboys dismantle transnational assumptions and givens about "home" within global care work. Tomboy domesticity, as I reveal through my reading of Selomenio within his home, is a reshaping of the domestic space by tomboys, shifting these spaces from being locations of violence and precarity into capacious sites of kinship, intimacy, mutual aid, solidarity, and care. My deployment of tomboy domesticity is about messing with and transing normative conceptions of home across the Filipino labor diaspora to make room for other figures, arrangements, intimacies, temporalities, and spatialities that emerge out of tomboy's foundational and ethical commitment to imagining otherwise. Tomboy domesticity is a way to think about how tomboys reconfigure the home itself into a transing site, a locus that is always in transit, both in the bodies that move through the space and in how it is continually reimagined and reshaped. Tomboys in *Sunday Beauty Queen* recognize how their embodiments provide them with fugitive access to certain kinds of freedom of home through particular modes of gender attribution and respectability politics. In response, they queer, rearrange, and mess with time, body, and space to perform alternative paradigms of domesticity.

Although there is generative work that centers the experiences of cis Filipinas and *bakla*[4] in care work scholarship, the queer subjectivities of tomboys are often invisibilized and erased. Selomenio's performances of care as a tomboy at home, then, are particularly important because of this erasure of tomboyness within representations of queer and trans life in media and scholarship. In particular, Robert Diaz (2018: 407) notes that the desires of tomboys are often consigned "to an elsewhere that cannot be imagined" despite *kabaklaan*'s[5] continual presence in Philippine popular culture and media. Inspired and galvanized by Selomenio's tomboy domesticity, this article is an attempt to glean those imaginings of elsewhere. Despite the presence of tomboys like Ice Siguerra and Jake Zyrus in popular culture as well as in Netflix's *Tiger King* (Goode and Chaiklin 2020) and *It's Showtime's* "That's My Tomboy!" (Vidanes 2013–2015; Velasco 2022), tomboyness is hardly centered as a critical site of examination. While I focus primarily on *Sunday Beauty Queen* within the scope of this article, tomboy domesticities and other representations of Filipino queerness, transness, and gender nonconformance exist and function in other spaces, particularly in other transnational spaces marked with the effects of marginalized labor and modes of racial capitalism. In sites with longer histories of gendered domestic labor, such as Toronto, tomboy domesticities have operated and continue to operate as spaces of care, kinship, and queer diasporic intimacy (Ramos 2018). Hence, I propose "tomboy domesticity" as a term that allows us to complicate our understandings of tomboys beyond frivolous and ancillary characters who operate solely as apolitical sidekicks to *bakla* and other cis people. To open space for these subjectivities, this article asks: what does Selomenio's control over his home space and time do for our understanding of care and the domestic? In this article, I will lay out for scholars of care work across the Filipinx diaspora how the work of tomboys shifts and transforms our understandings of gender, care, and gendered care and its political workings.

Utilizing both Allan Punzalan Isaac's (2022) notion of "Filipino time" and Martin Manalansan's (2014) work on the messiness of queer migratory lives as critical theoretical frameworks, I turn away from the stage and instead focus on what Stephen Vider (2019: 166) terms the "domestic archive" to think through "the ephemeral and embodied as well as the material" components of home. By focusing on the domestic (archive), I seek to excavate the mundane and quotidian performances of tomboy domesticity that allow us to read everyday Hong Kong domestic life differently. This article is divided into four parts. In the first section, I place Manalansan's conceptualization of "mess" and Isaac's notion of "Filipino time" into conversation with one another to further explore the political work of Selomenio's messy apartment in relation to tomboy domesticity. Afterward, I engage in close readings of two documentary scenes in which Selomenio's home is displayed within the documentary to explore how tomboy domesticity works against and refuses the hierarchical, violent, and extractive nature of institutionalized transnational migrant labor. These quotidian performances of care within the domestic allow for the emergence of queer diasporic intimacies that operate alongside and despite the violences that structure global care work. In *Sunday Beauty Queen*, Selomenio's control over his home space reframes the domestic as an archive of *kuwento* (stories), beauty, care, and desire, and it provides Selomenio with the capacity to be messy. Additionally, Selomenio's control over his home time—both on Sundays as well as after everyday work—shifts how care, sociality, rest, and kinship operate within the domestic. Overall, I argue that Selomenio's reshaping and reconfiguring of both domestic spaces and temporalities reorganizes the power dynamics that undergird modes of global care work.

"Magulo-Gulo Ang Bahay": Messing with Daddy's Home/Time

At the midpoint of *Sunday Beauty Queen*, Hazel Perdido, a Filipina domestic helper working in Hong Kong, calls for her "Mommy" and "Daddy" while standing

Figure 1. Perdido and Sison in the apartment while Sison replies, "The house
is so messy," in Villarama's (2016) *Sunday Beauty Queen*.

at a sliding door, gently gripping the bars of its cut-out panels. Slowly, footsteps
approach behind the door, and the reply "Wala si Daddy!" (Daddy's not here!) is
heard. After the resistant door is tugged open, "Mommy" is revealed to be Sison,
who lives with Selomenio or "Daddy." A tracking shot follows Perdido and Sison
into the apartment. Past the entrance is a small room, only big enough to fit a
refrigerator and sink with some counter space, a small table and couch, and two
shelves that house everyday appliances and paperwork. The table is cluttered with
pink satin sashes and a glue gun, and splayed across the couch are several plastic
bags and two cardboard boxes, each bursting with plastic-wrapped trophies and
tied loosely with lavender ribbons. Upon seeing this (dis)order of things, Perdido
teasingly shrieks, "Wow! Ito na ba ang mga sash and trophy ko? Wow! Kaloka!"
(Wow! Are these my sashes and trophies? Wow! Amazing!). As she heats up food
for her guest, Sison replies, "Magulo-gulo ang bahay!" (The house is a mess!),
before she continues to glue together the pageant materials that "Daddy" prepared
(fig. 1).

Selomenio and Sison's messy apartment harkens back to Manalansan's
groundbreaking and critical work on "mess" within and across the queer Filipinx diaspora.[6] Manalansan (2014: 99) takes up the term as a verb to think about
mess as "a route for funking up and mobilizing new understandings of stories,
values, objects, and space/time arrangements" in ways that refuse state-mandated
legibility and normative configurations of bodies, desires, spaces, and temporalities. Although this transnational labor force restricts how queer Filipino migrant
workers are able to move through time and space, Selomenio utilizes the queer

domestic to mess with, fragment, and rupture the arrangements of body, space, and time that violently structure his everyday working life. Additionally, the documentary's use of tracking shots reflect the nature of mess. By continuously following Selomenio and other workers throughout the documentary, the film's tracking shots highlight the ongoing presence of the state in their everyday lives and the ways in which the state continues to surveil domestic helpers as they unceasingly navigate labor precarity and extraction (Thompson and Bordwell 2019). The anxieties of these workers are further exemplified through the shaky camera that perpetually follows yet is never able to reach them. The unsteady tracking shot refuses to read the apartment or the bodies moving through it as static or fixed entities. Instead, Filipino domestic helpers persistently evade the shot's grasp, demonstrating their ongoing navigations within these structures, their collective desires to refuse the tracking and surveillance that marks their quotidian lives, and their messing up of normative conceptions of domesticity. Hence, Selomenio's apartment, while a physical archive of beauty pageants, is also an archive of feelings that houses the romantic intimacies and queer kinships that make up contractual labor time.

Because of the SEC's contractual obligations that force workers to occupy particular spaces and regulate their time away from work, it is equally important to consider how temporality shapes Selomenio's access to various domestic spaces and the access other live-in domestic helpers have to his home. In *Filipino Time*, Allan Punzalan Isaac (2022) explores how affective labor within global care work structures must be read alongside the generation of other chronicities and worlds imagined and materialized by those working within and against labor-time. Isaac succinctly articulates how migrant laborers, who are often articulated as "bagong bayani, or 'new national heroes,'" perform "refusal[s] to wallow" to demonstrate their complex imaginations and conjuring of other, more livable futures while simultaneously disrupting easy nationalist imaginaries of Filipino domestic workers as heroes or victims (96). Building on Isaac's work, I utilize tomboy domesticities to think about the countertemporalities, slippages, interruptions, and ruptures that tomboys create to disrupt contractual labor-time's violent grasp. Manalansan's and Isaac's works allow us to glean the ways in which tomboys utilize tomboy domesticity to mess with and take back the time that is used to police their mobilities and relationalities and to refashion contractual labor time.

Though Selomenio is often seen cleaning up and decluttering his employer's home, the messiness of his own apartment gestures toward the ways in which he messes up the space and time of domesticity within domestic migrant labor. However, the tidying up of his employer's house also offers us a way to think about the respectability politics Selomenio continually navigates and negotiates. When asked to describe Selomenio, Yoanna Leung, his employer's daughter, responds, "Now I know that Leo helps us and now we became like a good family. Something like that." Within his employer's domestic space, Selomenio performs respectability and comportment, which allows him to maintain his employment and provides him with access to housing outside of this space. Part of these respectability politics that undergird global care work include tropes of sacrifice, particularly in relation to the "abandoned" families care workers leave behind in the Philippines, as well as tropes of patronage and indebtedness to maintaining the families of their employers, who allow them to send remittances back home. Documentaries such as *Sunday Beauty Queen* often employ rhetorics of maternal sacrifice as the primary lens through which we can critique labor precarity and gendered inequities in labor migration.

Migrant care workers are often articulated within universalist and pragmatic tropes of sacrifice and patronage in the name of maintaining the nuclear family unit both abroad and in the Philippines. However, tomboy domesticities refuse these seemingly easy paradigms of maternal sacrifice. Instead, tomboy domesticities, like the ones Selomenio engages in, disrupt the "seemingly logical arrangement and natural symmetry of this rather static formula that reads as follows: domestic = family = heterosexual woman = care and love" (Manalansan 2008: 10). In what follows, I closely read two moments in *Sunday Beauty Queen* that feature Selomenio's home. Through these close readings, I assert that Selomenio's tomboy domesticities mess with home and time to exhibit modes of care that are alternatives to those that figure Filipino caregivers as national heroes within the diasporic imagination. These refashionings of home resist these moralizing tropes and offer us other narratives of tomboy life and care and their political workings.

"Bakit Hindi Niya Ako'y Tinawag?"

I return to Acosta's termination once again because it provides the context for the first appearance of Selomenio's home in *Sunday Beauty Queen*. Acosta sits in front of a bunk bed covered in colorful pillows and decorative blankets and explains that after arriving home during her day off but "past curfew," her employers asked her to return to work. After stating that she would work at six o'clock the next morning, she was met with refusals and demands to work immediately. To these rebuttals, Acosta replied, "Ma'am, that's not right. That's illegal," and she threatened to call the police if they were asking her to work during her time off. As mentioned above, despite the requirement to have no less than twenty-four hours off from work weekly, employers like Acosta's often restrict Filipino domestic helpers' time during their day off by setting curfews, stating that they fear for their domestic helpers' well-being and safety, which they are responsible for. In such a moment of distress and catastrophe, Acosta and other Filipino domestic helpers immediately travel to Selomenio's home as a site of refuge.

The criticality of Selomenio's space in moments of crisis is not only significant to this moment; his home has historically been a sought-after site for terminated Filipino domestic helpers. As other care workers present in the home chime in with similar accounts of being told to suck it up and deal with it, Selomenio turns to the camera and recounts his experiences supporting other terminated Filipino domestic helpers. He expressively says:

> Kahit na wala ka na matirhan, wala na pa silang maggagawa. Tatawagan pa ako ni Ma'am "May bakante? Kukunin mo na itong naterminate dito? Punta ka dito, may problema siya." Pupunta ako doon sa consulate! Tapos iuwi ko yung naterminate. Ako magpakain, ako magpapamasahe. May shelter sila pero . . .

> (Even if you have nowhere to go [for shelter], [the consulate] can't do anything about it. Ma'am will call me and say, "Is there still a vacant spot? Will you come over to pick up someone who was terminated? Come here, she has a problem." I'll go to the consulate! Then I'll bring home the person who was terminated. I'll feed her, I'll give her transportation money. [The consulate] has a shelter but . . .).

Selomenio's comment is both a response to visitors' accumulated workplace experiences and a spotlight that draws attention to the state's failures to care for Filipino domestic helpers, the state's reliance on Selomenio's labor of care, and an ethical practice of tomboy domesticity that seeks to reimagine what care could look like amid the state's carelessness.

In this scene, it is clear that the Philippine Consulate's constant disposal of the Filipino domestic laborer through termination requires and desires that same Filipino affective labor. The consulate is not just attentive to terminating domestic helpers spontaneously; it is equally vigilant in asking Selomenio to engage in the affective, physical, and material support that it does not have the bandwidth or capacity to engage in. Despite the consulate's creation of a shelter for Filipino domestic helpers, it is still Selomenio's home that terminated Filipinos must turn to; otherwise they are met with inaction and lack of shelter. As such, the Philippine Consulate's failure and overreliance on Selomenio demonstrates how state-sanctioned violence is happening on multiple scales. First, Filipino affective labor is continually required to maintain the nation while repeatedly reinforcing their disposability. Second, in addition to caring for and about Hong Kong citizens and their homes, Selomenio is also necessary for caring about and for other domestic helpers. As he notes, Selomenio routinely makes his way to the consulate to house, feed, and help seek further employment for these terminated domestic helpers. These extractive experiences mark the everyday contours of the institutionalization of transnational migrant labor. Outside of his hours of work, during his home time, the consulate forces Selomenio to continue to service others in the name of collective care.

Curfews set by employers as well as the failures of the consulate illuminate how the home operates as a site of corporeal, temporal, and spatial regulation on multiple scales within migrant care work. The supposed "care" of Hong Kong employers and the consulate produce precarious living and working conditions for domestic helpers, but Selomenio refuses to reproduce this kind of care. Although the consulate assumes he is responsible for taking care of other caregivers, his performance of this care operates outside the logics of labor-time and instead functions as a necessary practice of collective survival. These desires for collective support and survival are central to care workers engaging in transnational domestic labor. In her book *The Labor of Care*, Valerie Francisco-Menchavez (2018) examines the "communities of care" that domestic migrant laborers engage in transnationally, through which care is exchanged between migrant workers. The institutionalization of care relies on verticalities and linear trajectories of bodies performing and receiving affective labor, namely Filipina women moving to the global North to care for and about their employers. However, Francisco-Menchavez notes that communities of care are multidirectional, rhizomatic, and horizontal, and they allow migrant laborers to take care of each other and receive support.

Here, Selomenio's tomboy domesticity materializes as a recognition of his different, and in many ways privileged, living conditions and a refusal to gatekeep his access to an alternative paradigm of home space and home time. When he says he takes the terminated caregiver home to feed them, Selomenio notes that he brings this caregiver not to *his* home, but simply "home." The home he brings them to is a space in which this caregiver need not rely on the state or perform any labor to be worthy of care, shelter, food, and financial support. In stating this, Selomenio makes a direct comparison between the ethics of his home and those of the consulate's shelter. Selomenio's home space blurs the lines of private and public; it is a site of constant transit that allows other caregivers to receive care in a home space in which their bodies are not governed by labor regulations. As such, tomboy domesticity allows Selomenio and other Filipino migrant caregivers to refuse, negotiate, and reshape the domestic spaces that continue to dispose of, dehumanize, and fail them. As part of this negotiation, tomboy domesticities mess with narratives of body that not only associate performances of care with femininity and operate in a linear, cisheternormative model of time, but also exist solely in service of labor-time. In other words, tomboy domesticities utilize their control over home time and space to provide room for other kinds of embodiments, desires, longings, and pleasures that cannot exist within the nuclear domestic spaces that constellate transnational migrant labor.

Within tomboy domesticity, the navigation of termination, shelter, and emotional pain is a collective issue; it is felt wholly and fully among them all. Selomenio's desire to shelter friends and other strangers who are domestic helpers, to make his way to the consulate, and to further provide them with access to (his) home provides them with corporeal security and releases them from the physical and emotional control that employers often utilize to extract from their workers. Immediately following Acosta's testimony, an unnamed Filipino domestic helper teases her by saying she was not careful enough, eventually critiquing how care workers are often made to regulate their emotions to appease their employers, with Selomenio and others present vehemently agreeing. Through their *tsismis* (gossip) and *kuwentuhan* (storytelling), caregivers are able to mock the malicious abuse of their present and former employers, tease each other, complain about eating scraps after serving food to their employers, and laugh over topics unrelated to work, all while sharing a meal in the same home at the same time. In a labor force that is undergirded by transactional, hierarchical, and extractive "care," or perhaps more accurately, violence under the guise of care, Selomenio reimagines what care can look like within these same spaces. His desire to perform alternative modes of care reiterate that he is aware of the kinds of "care" that structure the Filipino labor diaspora, its institutionalization of care, the failures of the consulate, and the violence of the domestic helper's employer. These kinds of "care" rely on white supremacist and capitalist cisheteropatriarchy, wherein care is unidirectional, bioessentialist, ableist, racist, transactional, and hierarchical. This kind of "care" normalizes individuality, precarity, violence, and carelessness. Thus, Selomenio's messy care is not a replication of the so-called care that structures this labor diaspora, but a refusal of it.

While others are only free on Sundays, Selomenio is allotted more time at home, or home time, because he is one of the few domestic helpers with the capacity to live in a space outside his employer's home. This domestic temporality is used within domestic migrant labor to maintain the nuclear family unit, but Selomenio reshapes and reconfigures these temporalities of home time to center collective pleasure, devastation, and survival. Because other domestic helpers are only free on Sundays, Selomenio provides them with a space of diasporic return, an apartment to come home to outside the boundaries of their living and employment spaces. With control over his home time and home space, Selomenio messes with the domestic to invite other domestic helpers over to *tsismis*, laugh, commiserate, listen, and express their experiences as care workers in Hong Kong. The documentary's opening phrase, "But on Sunday, they are free," can also be deployed here to examine how Selomenio's tomboy domesticity allows for collective experiences of fugitive freedom. I articulate these as *fugitive* freedoms and not simply "freedoms" to note that these performances of care as well as these caregivers, tomboy or not, continue to operate within the conditions of global care work. Despite and alongside this, tomboy domesticities allow him to reshape, reimagine, and open up his own domestic space to provide a space of refuge, knowledge exchange, and storytelling for domestic helpers who have experienced the violence of the domestic within institutionalized care work.

"Kabisig Chick-Boy"

Despite its appearance earlier in *Sunday Beauty Queen*, Selomenio provides a small tour of his home after the documentary showcases his employer for the first time. During this introduction, we see a number of objects strewn across his apartment, including a *balikbayan* box outside the apartment and an archive of past beauty pageants that Selomenio has organized. Additionally, his domestic archive opens space for other ephemeral moments to occur, including Selomenio's own oral histories and images of Selomenio counting tickets for the next pageant, modes of embodied performance that Diana Taylor (2007: 24) refers to as the "repertoire." While counting tickets on his couch, he speaks to the camera, saying:

> Ang una unang pageant namin is "Beauty and the Best." Yung babae: Beauty. Yung les: Best. Ay hindi! Hindi pala yung "Beauty and the Best" una una, Chick-Boy pala! "Kabisig Chick-Boy!" Para mga les.[7] (Our very first pageant was "Beauty and the Best." The girls: Beauty. The les: Best. No wait! Beauty and the Best was not the first after all, it was Chick-Boy![8] "Chick-Boys Arm in Arm!" For the les.)

Following his messing up of the memory, he outlines how the money earned at the pageant is shared among Filipino domestic helpers, to aid either those who need it in Hong Kong or who need resources to send back to the Philippines. It becomes clear that the pageant is more than a public spectacle in Hong Kong; it is also a crucial part of Selomenio's home space and home time. What does it mean to bring the stage, the trophies, and the sashes into the private space? What does it mean to bring the pageant and beauty to the living room?

Beyond the realm of the aesthetic, beauty functions within the Filipino diasporic context as a political practice and locus that offers us ways to think about the power dynamics that situate global care work. Genevieve Clutario (2023) notes that beauty is more than a site of pleasure and celebration; it is also a political site embedded with political influence, regulation, empowerment, and refusal. In this way, my uptake of beauty does not flatten it to an aesthetic desire but instead grapples with the significant political role that beauty has played in regime-building and imperialism in the Philippines and transnationally. Read alongside Clutario's work, Selomenio's messy historical tracing of his beauty pageant organizing reflects the reorganization of time that informs tomboy domesticity, and it orients us toward the political power of his Sunday labors. The context of tomboy domestic migrant labor in Hong Kong marks his body as an undesirable entity within the national imagination. However, his dis/organizing asserts his own conceptualization of beauty. Even though tomboy domestic helpers are consistently elided from the global city, the labor force, and queer and trans representations, Selomenio's first iteration of beauty is linking arms with other tomboys through the disorder and reorder of time. In doing so, Selomenio reimagines beauty, temporality, and the domestic while gesturing toward the political significance of tomboy-tomboy relationalities.

After Selomenio receives the call about Acosta's termination, he gets off his bus and waits on the roadside with another unnamed tomboy caregiver who was commiserating with Selomenio about physical pain during work hours (fig. 2). Most work about tomboyness centers on butch-femme relationships and relationalities, but this moment shows Selomenio as a recipient of care through the regard and attendance of the unnamed tomboy domestic helper, obfuscating scholarly and colloquial assumptions that tomboy relations solely operate between tomboys and femmes. Here, both the pageants and the domestic articulate tomboys as both beauty and the best. These intimacies embody what Hil Malatino (2019: 656) has described as a "t4t [trans-for-trans] praxis of love," which "is antiutopian, guiding a praxis of solidarity" that includes "small acts that make life more livable in and through difficult circumstances." In this sense, these intimacies between tomboys, which we might call "t4t" to mean "tomboy-for-tomboy," demonstrate tomboyness's ethical commitment to collective survival and endurance.

Figure 2. Selomenio and another
unnamed tomboy domestic helper
riding a bus after a pageant in
Villarama's (2016) *Sunday Beauty
Queen*. Selomenio receives a
call notifying him of Acosta's
termination.

In seeking and providing support for each other on Sunday, these tomboy care workers transform the domestic into a site of desirability and longing.
Selomenio's conception of beauty and his provision and acceptance of alternative
modes of care also reveal other kinds of relations that are central to negotiating
employment and social life in Hong Kong. These tomboy domesticities allow for
other conditions of possibility and intimacies to emerge *between* tomboys. Selomenio refuses the undesirability and abjection that marks domestic migrant labor
while also recuperating a different kind of beauty in service of a new politic of care
that centers a collective movement through these spaces. These t4t intimacies are
not solely located in the home. The tomboys' conversation about physical pain during and after work on the bus ride home, and their act of waiting with each other
on the side of the road, demonstrate the spilling over of tomboy domesticities into
the global city. In *Sunday Beauty Queen*, these t4t intimacies allow for tomboy
domesticities to emerge outside sites of dwelling, providing senses of care, safety,
and home between tomboys within the domestic and elsewhere.

Additionally, tomboy domesticities are not limited to the homes of live-out
caregivers; they can also be enacted within spaces of live-in employment. Although
Selomenio now has control over his home space and time, he recounts the precarious
working conditions he had to endure prior to working with his current employer. In
his previous place of employment, he fulfilled the live-in requirement as most other
domestic helpers are made to do. There, he was made to sleep on a foam mat on the
floor in front of the refrigerator, where his sleep constantly disturbed by employers
getting up for water and late-night snacks. He also noted how he, much like other
caregivers, was given scraps and leftovers, and family pets were often treated better
than he was. These events led him to cry and scream out of his employer's window,
"Hoy! Kayong mga taga-Hong Kong kayo ang sasama ng mga ugali!" (Hey! You
people from Hong Kong have bad manners!).

Selomenio's emotional eruption demonstrates how tomboy domesticity not
only operates for those who have access to homes outside their workplaces but also

seeks to mess up these sites of violence. In the very home where he is being controlled and surveilled, Selomenio messes up its respectable order. As mentioned above, Filipino migrant workers must perform a particular mode of respectable citizenship wherein they must control and internalize their frustrations so as to not disturb the nuclear family and regulatory processes that are crucial to Hong Kong domestic life. At the windowsill, Selomenio reconfigures and messes with these regulations to refuse and critique the violences of care he experiences within the very space that he experiences them. In this way, tomboy domesticities mess up the domestic in privileged living spaces outside of work, the global city, and they mess with and clutter domestic workspaces themselves. Through messing with and cluttering domestic (work)spaces, tomboys open space, however fugitive, for resistance and refusal. Tomboy domesticities in this scene are echoing sonic reverberations with no clear point of arrival that plead for and demand another way of living.

Conclusion

Throughout *Sunday Beauty Queen*, Selomenio messes with, ruptures, and fractures assumed notions of tomboy, time, and home. The care work that structures his everyday working life continues to extract his time and labor, but he continuously reconfigures his access to and control over home time and space to reorganize the very constructions of power that structure global care work. These reorganizations and clutterings open space for desire, intimacy, safety, and storytelling. Moreover, despite living with Sison as Mommy and Daddy, Selomenio's home is not simply the replication of butch-femme aesthetics. The messy apartment also acts as an archive, storage space, workspace, and a site of refuge, support, imagination, and resistance to the violences of the homes Filipinx caregivers labor within, expanding our notions of feminized forms of care and of tomboy masculinities. At and outside his messy home, Selomenio engages in tomboy domesticity to refuse the respectability and legibility that provided him with access to that space. I argue that tomboy domesticity functions as a commitment to rupture that allows for alternative modes and practices of home, temporality, gender, care, and gendered care. Tomboys utilize their capacity to control home space, home time, and time off to reimagine alternative modes and conditions of living and caring within the domestic. Thus, tomboy domesticity allows Selomenio to establish an alternative domestic space that messes with time, space, and body to refuse the violences of care within migrant domestic labor.

Because Sundays are the only days when care workers are free, it is the only day when they can go to the beauty pageants. This also means that Sundays are the only days when domestic helpers can visit Selomenio's house. It is on those

Sundays that they glimpse and taste fleeting senses of fugitive freedom. Unlike the institutionalization of care, Selomenio's everyday practice is untethered to notions of capital exchange, morality, and purity. Instead, he engages in a necessary and messy practice that does not seek perfection but is simply meant to be done. Tomboy domesticity carves out a time and space for the practice of and investment in the obliteration of (institutionalized) care, for the necessary and unfamiliar attempt at imagining elsewhere and otherwise. It is a practice that does not know the next step, but it recognizes that a step has to be made. It is leaning into something, not knowing if it will be beautiful or the best, but sure it will be messy.

Notes

I wish to thank the special issue coeditors, Lauren Gutterman, Martin F. Manalansan IV, and Stephen Vider, as well as my anonymous reviewers, for their generous insights and support. I am also deeply indebted to Rejoice Abutsa, Christine Balance, Joanmarie Bañez, Robert Diaz, Gina Goico, Allan Punzalan Isaac, Ferdie Lopez, Dani Magsumbol, Stef Martin, Mariana Mora, Imogen Tam, and the members of the 2023 Cornell Migrations Summer Institute who have all cared for, nourished, read, and helped strengthen this article. This article draws on research supported by the Social Sciences and Humanities Research Council. All translations are my own unless otherwise noted.

1. I utilize Filipino/Filipina throughout this article because it is utilized by figures within the film as well as the filmmakers. In doing so, I want to reflect the ways in which care workers in Hong Kong articulate their experiences, relations, and themselves.
2. I utilize he/him/his pronouns for Selomenio to reflect the way he is referred to in the subtitles of the documentary. Although *siya* is the nongendered pronoun used in Tagalog, the documentary's subtitles translate Selomenio's pronouns to he/him/his. I read this as a curated choice on the part of the filmmakers and utilize it as part of my reading of Selomenio.
3. Here, I want to especially thank Minh Vu for helping me think through theorizing "tomboy" within a trans studies framework.
4. This Tagalog term is used to describe several embodiments and identities including Filipino gay men and trans women who are usually lower class or working class.
5. This is not to say that *kabaklaan* (queerness) and tomboyness are mutually exclusive. As the forthcoming work of Robert Diaz shows, Selomenio is a figure through whom we can understand *kabaklaan* and tomboyness as not incommensurate.
6. Kale Fajardo (2014: 119) also theorizes about "gulo" in relation to tomboys, particularly as a mode of "political disorder and gender trouble" in Manila during the Marcos regime. While Fajardo provides a critical and significant contribution through the framing of "gulo" as a form of public and political disruption, I focus more here

on Manalansan's notion of "mess" to think about the clutter of Selomenio's diasporic apartment.

7. Here, Selomenio refers to himself and other tomboy caregivers as *mga les* (lesbians). Although Selomenio identifies himself and other caregivers as *mga les*, I read Selomenio too as tomboy, particularly because the term has enfolded into itself various meanings, behaviors, desires, and embodiments, including *les*.

8. A flirtatious, charming person who attracts many women.

References

Blackwood, Evelyn. 2005. "Transnational Sexualities in One Place: Indonesian Readings." *Gender & Society* 19, no. 2: 221–42.

Clutario, Genevieve Alva. 2023. *Beauty Regimes: A History of Power and Modern Empire in the Philippines, 1898–1941.* Durham, NC: Duke University Press.

de Leon, Conely. 2016. "Family Separation and Reunification among Former Filipina Migrant Domestic Workers and Their Adult Daughters in Two Canadian Cities." In *When Care Work Goes Global: Locating the Social Relations of Domestic Work,* edited by Mary Romero, Valerie Preston, and Wenona Giles, 139–58. New York, NY: Routledge Press.

Diaz, Robert. 2018. "Biyuti from Below: Contemporary Philippine Cinema and the Transing of Kabaklaan." *Transgender Studies Quarterly* 5, no. 3: 404–24.

Fajardo, Kale Bantigue. 2014. "Queering and Transing the Great Lakes: Filipino/a Tomboy Masculinities and Manhoods across Waters." *GLQ: A Journal of Lesbian and Gay Studies* 20, nos. 1–2: 115–40.

Francisco-Menchavez, Valerie. 2018. *The Labor of Care: Filipina Migrants and Transnational Families in the Digital Age.* Champaign, IL: University of Illinois Press.

Goode, Eric, and Rebecca Chaiklin, dirs. 2020. *Tiger King.* A Goode Films Production.

Halberstam, Jack. 2018. *Female Masculinity: 20th Anniversary Edition with a New Preface.* Durham, NC: Duke University Press.

HKLD (Hong Kong Labour Department). 2019. *Know Your Obligations. Be a Responsible and Smart Employer. A Handbook for Employing Foreign Domestic Helpers.* https://www.fdh.labour.gov.hk/res/pdf/Handy_Guide_FDHs_eng.pdf.

Isaac, Allan Punzalan. 2022. *Filipino Time: Affective Worlds and Contracted Labor.* New York, NY: Fordham University Press.

Lai, Franco. 2007. "Lesbian Masculinities: Identity and Body Construction among Tomboys in Hong Kong." In *Women's Sexualities and Masculinities in a Globalizing Asia,* edited by Saskia E. Wieringa, Evelyn Blackwood, and Abha Bhaiya, 159–79. New York, NY: Palgrave Macmillan US.

Magsumbol, Dani. 2022. "A Political Economy of Emotions." *Alon: Journal for Filipinx American and Diasporic Studies* 2, no. 2: 125–28.

Malatino, Hil. 2019. "Future Fatigue: Trans Intimacies and Trans Presents (or How to Survive the Interregnum)." *TSQ: Transgender Studies Quarterly* 6, no. 4: 635–58.

Manalansan IV, Martin F. 2008. "Queering the Chain of Care Paradigm." *Scholar & Feminist Online* 6, no. 3: 10. http://sfonline.barnard.edu/immigration/manalansan _01.htm.

Manalansan, Martin F., IV. 2014. "The 'Stuff' of Archives: Mess, Migration, and Queer Lives." *Radical History Review*, no. 120: 94–107.

Parreñas, Rhacel. 2015. *Servants of Globalization: Migration and Domestic Work*. Redwood City, CA: Stanford University Press.

Piocos III, Carlos M. 2022. "The Queer Promise of Pageantry: Queering Feminized Migration and the Labor of Care in *Sunday Beauty Queen* (2016)." *Feminist Media Studies* 22, no. 7: 1729–44.

Ramos, J. B. 2018. "Life Reflections of a Filipino Elvis." In *Diasporic Intimacies: Queer Filipinos and Canadian Imaginaries*, edited by Robert Diaz, Marissa Largo, and Fritz Pino, 67–80. Evanston, IL: Northwestern University Press.

Rodriguez, Robyn Magalit. 2010. *Migrants for Export: How the Philippine State Brokers Labor to the World*. Minneapolis, MN: University of Minnesota Press.

Sinnott, Megan. 2008. "The Romance of the Queer: The Sexual and Gender Norms on Tom and Dee in Thailand." In *AsiaPacifiQueer: Rethinking Genders and Sexualities*, edited by Fran Martin, Peter Jackson, and Mark McLelland, 131–48. Champaign, IL: University of Illinois Press.

Taylor, Diana. 2007. *The Archive and the Repertoire: Performing Cultural Memory in the Americas*. Durham, NC: Duke University Press.

Thompson, Kristin and David Bordwell. 2019. *Film History: An Introduction*. 4th ed. New York, NY: McGraw Hill Education.

Tungohan, Ethel. 2013. "Reconceptualizing Motherhood, Reconceptualizing Resistance: Migrant Domestic Workers, Transnational Hyper-Maternalism, and Activism." *International Feminist Journal of Politics* 15, no. 1: 39–57.

Velasco, Gina. 2022. "'That's My Tomboy': Queer Filipinx Diasporic Transmasculinities." *Alon: Journal for Filipinx American and Diasporic Studies* 2, no. 1: 67–73.

Vidanes, Bobet, dir. 2013–2015. *It's Showtime*. ABS-CBN Entertainment.

Vider, Stephen. 2019. "Public Disclosures of Private Realities: HIV/AIDS and the Domestic Archive." *Public Historian* 41, no. 2: 163–89.

Villarama, Baby Ruth. 2016. *Sunday Beauty Queen*. TBA Studios. https://youtu.be/TB _bwb7K-7E?si=cZEXqFAZnuLTRVYE.

"STOP AIDS EVICTIONS!"

Discrimination, Rent Regulation, and New York City's Housing Crisis (1985–1988)

Maggie Schreiner

*M*ichael Brown received a notice of eviction from his home of eight years in March 1985, just two months after his lover, Robert Hayes, had died of AIDS after an extended hospital stay. Hayes was the only tenant named on the lease, and the landlord chose to deny Michael Brown a lease renewal for their one-bedroom apartment in the Chelsea neighborhood of New York City.[1] Brown fought his eviction, both through the courts and through grassroots political organizing in his neighborhood. His campaign to stay in his home became the center of an unprecedented collaboration between New York City's long-established tenant movement and newer gay rights organizations. Working under the umbrella of the nascent Chelsea AIDS Committee, activists brought knowledge acquired in the traditional tenant movement into new gay and lesbian organizations. This collaboration was a result of Chelsea's history as a center of both militant tenant organizing and neighborhood-based gay and lesbian activism. In Chelsea, gay and lesbian residents joined the housing movement as low-income tenants, while also participating in neighborhood activism reflecting their concerns as gay and lesbian residents. Michael Brown's eviction case brought these two local organizing traditions into direct collaboration.

This article brings together work highlighting the political agency of tenants to challenge and change their living conditions with work examining the role of housing and care during the AIDS epidemic. Following Ronald Lawson and Stephen Barton's study locating the role of women in New York City's tenant movement, historians Roberta Gold and Tamar Carroll have demonstrated the centrality of women's leadership in neighborhood and citywide housing organizing (Carroll 2015; Gold 2009; Lawson and Barton 1980). However, the role of sexuality and

GLQ 30:4
DOI 10.1215/10642684-11331114
© 2024 by Duke University Press

of gay and lesbian tenants and activists in New York City's housing movement remains largely absent in historical studies.

Recent works have examined the role of housing and care during the AIDS epidemic to show how advocates simultaneously expanded definitions of home and family while also pursuing a legal standard for protection premised on middle-class, heteronormative norms of economic interdependence and monogamy (Bhaman 2021; Esparza 2022; Vider 2021a). This article contributes to this scholarship by resituating gay and lesbian advocacy for housing during the early AIDS crisis within a long trajectory of New York City tenant activism, demonstrating the role of coalition building, mentorship, and cross-movement collaboration. Following the example of Carroll's *Mobilizing New York*, this article traces neighborhood-based coalition building across boundaries of sexuality and gender (Carroll 2015: 20). It first uses reports produced by the New York City Commission on Human Rights during the early 1980s to consider the challenges gay and lesbian tenants faced in finding and retaining affordable housing. It then discusses the campaign to prevent Brown's eviction within the political context and activist traditions of Chelsea and New York City, before considering the hidden legacies of Brown's case.

Homophobic Discrimination in Housing

Tenants in the early 1980s faced a variety of challenges in locating and keeping affordable housing in New York City. Over the previous fifteen years, the city's rent regulation system had been weakened, and over one million apartments moved from the more stringent system of rent control into the weaker rent stabilization system. During the 1970s, many New York City neighborhoods were impacted by the mass abandonment of housing stock that landlords deemed no longer profitable (Starecheski 2016: 47). In addition to building abandonment, low-income city residents faced the withdrawal of city services as the federal, state, and municipal governments all responded to the city's fiscal crisis by implementing austerity (Phillips-Fein 2017: 207–8). Additional threats in some neighborhoods included gentrification through luxury redevelopment, the new "brownstone" movement, conversion of rent-regulated apartments to owner-occupied cooperatives, hospital and university expansions, and the conversion of single-room-occupancy hotels to middle-class housing (Holtzman 2019: 890; Lawson and Naison 1986). The erosion of the rent control system and the systematic conversion of low-income housing to middle-income housing dramatically reduced the availability of affordable apartments and caused significant increases in rental prices throughout the city.

For gay and lesbian tenants, the lack of affordable housing was compounded by homophobic discrimination by landlords, neighbors, and city officials. Over the course of the 1980s, the New York City Commission on Human Rights issued at least five reports documenting discrimination against gays, lesbians, and people with AIDS.[2] In November 1981, the commission submitted a report to the New York City Council in support of the "Gay Rights Bill" campaign to extend human rights protections based on sexual orientation. The report documented cases of discrimination in employment, housing, and public accommodations based on a small-scale survey of thirty-five gay men and lesbian women. Of these thirty-five people, eight reported having been evicted or denied housing due to their sexual orientation (NYCCHR 1981).

Following this survey, the commission launched the Gay and Lesbian Discrimination Documentation Project to record a growing number of complaints regarding discrimination related to sexual orientation and AIDS. Within two years, sexual orientation discrimination was the most common form of complaint brought to the commission. An early report (NYCCHR 1986a) observes that "these figures become more impressive when one remembers that gay men and lesbians tend not to report discrimination. One obvious reason for this is that many gays and lesbians are aware that their civil rights are not protected." Although the Commission on Human Rights received and documented reports of sexual orientation discrimination, the commission did not have jurisdiction to investigate or respond to these reports before 1986, given their purview to enforce the New York City Human Rights Law (4). But the explosion of complaints that accompanied the early AIDS epidemic spurred the commission to document cases of discrimination related to sexual orientation and AIDS, even though these cases were beyond their formal investigative scope.

Housing-related complaints represented approximately 12 percent of the discrimination complaints received between 1983 and 1986.[3] The reports summarize each complaint, which demonstrate a wide scope of harassment, violence, eviction, and denial of apartment rentals experienced by gay men, lesbians, and people with AIDS. The reports include numerous instances of landlords refusing to rent apartments to gays and lesbians, verbal harassment by landlords and neighbors, and physical violence. There are reports of people with AIDS being physically thrown out of apartments by neighbors and landlords, and of heat and hot water being turned off in apartments occupied by people with AIDS. Reports from social workers document evictions of people with AIDS during hospitalizations, and in one instance the eviction of a multigenerational family the day after a family member with AIDS returned home from the hospital (NYCCHR 1986a: 44).

Although many of these cases were beyond the commission's jurisdiction, staff attempted informal mediation and resolution of cases, which they were not able to pursue through formal legal channels. Case summaries frequently noted the commission's jurisdictional limits, often in light of the intersecting forms of discrimination that gay and lesbian tenants experienced. In one case, a gay Latino couple were refused a lease renewal following landlord harassment on the basis of both their sexual orientation and their race. When contacted by the commission, the landlord stated that she was not homophobic, but she thought that gay people "should all be burned." The commission's summary of the complaint says, "We advised them that if they felt their nationalities were part of the problem, they could file a housing complaint on that basis alone. However, the landlady's focus on their gayness almost guaranteed the failure of their complaint, since gay housing issues are not jurisdictional" (NYCCHR 1986a: 54). In this case, the commission's informal resolution process was effective, and the couple were offered a lease renewal, although the report is silent about whether the couple continued to experience harassment from their landlord.

262 West 22nd Street

When Michael Brown contemplated eviction from his Chelsea apartment, he was likely aware of both the limited housing stock available to low-income residents in New York City and the pervasive homophobic discrimination he might face from potential landlords and neighbors. His status as the surviving partner of someone who had died of AIDS would have further increased his vulnerability to discrimination, as well as verbal and physical violence, in his search for new housing.

Following the death of his partner, Robert Hayes, in 1985, Brown wrote his landlord to request a new lease. In his letter, Brown made a powerful emotive claim to his home. Not only was the apartment his residence; it was where he had made a home for eight years with his lover Hayes. The letter reveals Brown to be a savvy and informed tenant: not only had he sought out legal advice prior to writing the landlord, he connected with the Chelsea Coalition on Housing, his neighborhood tenant union. Brown sent the letter via certified mail, likely reflecting advice from the Chelsea Coalition on Housing to establish a legal record of his communication with the landlord.

Over a month later, Brown received a reply from his landlord's legal representative. The letter, in formal language, stated that Brown did not have any rights to remain in the apartment and was expected to vacate within ten days: "The fact that you resided with [Hayes] prior to his death, as you claimed in your letter, does not extend to you the protections of a rent-stabilized tenant of record."[4] Brown probably wasn't surprised by the landlord's response to his letter. His landlord, the company Two Associates, with Bruce Kafenbaum as its principal, had taken ownership of 262 West 22nd Street three years earlier, in 1982, paying $128,300 ("Mortgage for 262 West 22nd Street, NY NY" 1982). The Chelsea apartment building was Bruce Kafenbaum's first purchase as Two Associates, though within the next five years he went on to buy an additional forty-nine buildings in Manhattan, Brooklyn, and the Bronx for over $24 million.[5] After purchasing the Chelsea apartment building where Hayes and Brown lived, Kafenbaum immediately attempted to evict all of the building's rent-regulated tenants. In an affidavit filed with the New York Supreme Court, Brown stated that the "landlord tried to evict all the tenants for no good reason, but the tenants banded together, and with the help of the Chelsea Coalition on Housing, were able to save our homes."[6]

Although the tenants were able to remain in their homes, conditions in the building on West 22nd Street remained far from ideal. Brown's affidavit depicts a building in very poor condition: during the winter of 1984–1985, tenants lacked heat and hot water so frequently that Brown called a city hotline to log the conditions "once or twice a week," and public hallways were continuously filled with garbage and construction debris, such that the landlord was issued a violation by the New York City Department of Sanitation. Brown also noted numerous incomplete repairs, including a broken front door lock, holes in the walls, and loose live electrical wires in his apartment.[7] This denial of essential services and repairs matches the pattern of behavior of landlords who were "milking" their buildings until they could be torn down and replaced, or until buildings were empty of low-income, rent-regulated tenants and could be gut-renovated and rented to wealthier tenants.

As rent-stabilized tenants, Brown and Hayes paid $161 per month for their one-bedroom apartment in 1985. This was significantly lower than the median rent in the city, which was $325 in 1984 (Stegman 1988: 59). Kafenbaum believed that the fair market (i.e., unregulated) value of the apartment's rent was $1,000 per month that same year.[8] This significant difference between the actual and the desired monthly rent probably explains Kafenbaum's aggressive tactics against the tenants of 262 West 22nd Street, as well as his decision to evict Brown following Hayes's death. While the rent stabilization system likely would have stymied Kafenbaum's desire to legally rent the apartment for $1,000 per month, an empty apartment would have allowed him to increase the rent through a 10 percent vacancy increase, as well as through capital improvements to the apartment in the form of major renovations, which could be applied to a legal rent increase. And if

Kafenbaum wanted to increase the rent illegally, that would be more easily accomplished with a new resident than with Brown, an experienced and assertive tenant organizer.

Renters in apartment buildings throughout Chelsea were experiencing similar landlord behavior during the early 1980s. *Tenant*, a monthly newsletter from a citywide tenant union, the Metropolitan Council on Housing, described Chelsea as "a neighborhood in crisis" due to an upsurge in landlord violence, particularly against long-term elderly and gay residents (Lehman 1982). After over a decade of redevelopment and gentrification, Chelsea in the 1980s remained a mixed-income neighborhood of working class and middle-income residents, including a long-standing Latinx population and a shrinking number of merchant seamen and their families. Chelsea's gay and lesbian population had grown throughout the 1970s, as lower-income gays and lesbians were priced out of the West Village and moved to the neighborhood immediately to the north (Tom Duane, pers. comm., February 16, 2023). In the late 1970s, residents formed the Chelsea Gay Association (CGA), which claimed to be the first gay and lesbian neighborhood association in the country (*CGAN* 1979). In addition to facilitating a robust series of social events, the CGA organized political responses to relevant local issues.

The CGA responded to abusive landlord tactics by supporting tenant unions in targeted buildings and hosting community meetings. In January 1979, the CGA voted to support tenants at 233 West 15th Street, and the organization provided contact information in their newsletter for people who were interested in joining the campaign (*CGAN* 1979). Two years later, the CGA hosted a "Housing Forum" presenting perspectives from tenants, landlords, and legal representatives (*CGAN* 1981: 1). Kafenbaum took ownership of 262 West 22nd Street a few months after this meeting, and Brown and Hayes connected with this wave of local tenant organizing in Chelsea as they and their neighbors fought to stay in their homes.

"Stop AIDS Evictions!"

Michael Brown challenged the eviction notice that he received from Kafenbaum's lawyers. Brown was represented by Russell Pearce at the Chelsea Legal Aid Society and was supported by the Chelsea AIDS Committee, an organization that emerged in response to his case. Inspired by the lawyers of the 1960s civil rights and antiwar movements, Pearce had started working at Chelsea Legal Aid in the early 1980s. A significant element of his work focused on eviction prevention, anti-gentrification legal advocacy, and AIDS in Chelsea and the neighboring West Village. Pearce described Chelsea as "ground zero of AIDS and the gentrification war" (pers. comm., February 24, 2023). At the time, there was no established legal defense for people who were facing eviction following the death of their partners, and Pearce was uniquely positioned to challenge Brown's eviction by drawing the connections between gentrification, eviction, and AIDS.

In December 1985, Justice Helen Freedman issued her first ruling on Brown's case, stating that while she was "extremely sympathetic to the defendant's unfortunate plight," she was constrained by a recent court interpretation of the Rent Stabilization Law that denied family members lease renewals.[9] In this ruling, Justice Freedman referred to *Sullivan v. Brevard Associates*, which concerned two sisters who cohabited in an apartment. The New York Court of Appeals ruled that the sister who was not named on the lease was not permitted to remain in the apartment after the leaseholding sister moved out. The ruling in *Sullivan v. Brevard* meant that only the person who had signed the lease had the right to a lease renewal in a rent-stabilized apartment. The ruling had significant implications for all renters in New York City, not just those in same-sex relationships.

Justice Freedman stayed Brown's eviction until March 31, 1986, maintaining his monthly rent at $161 until he vacated the apartment. In her ruling, Justice Freedman urged legislative action to ensure surviving spouses would not become homeless. The same week, the New York Division of Housing and Community Renewal (DHCR), the state agency that oversaw the rent stabilization and rent control programs, issued an emergency operational bulletin aiming to stem a feared tide of evictions from rent-stabilized apartments following the *Sullivan v. Brevard* decision. The emergency bulletin defined "immediate family," who must receive lease renewals, and "non-immediate family in continuous habitation," who must be offered first right of refusal for new vacancy leases in rent-stabilized housing.[10] Although the new DHCR definitions did not acknowledge same-sex relationships, Pearce successfully moved to stay the initial judgment and reargue the case.

In the interim, Pearce contacted Tom Duane, then the Democratic Party district leader and an established tenant organizer in Chelsea, and asked him to organize publicly on behalf of Brown. Duane spearheaded the creation of the Chelsea AIDS Committee, which quickly moved to organize a demonstration at Brown's apartment at 262 West 22nd Street (Katz 1989: 33) (fig. 1).[11] The demonstration was planned for late March, when Justice Freedman's second ruling was expected and when Brown faced potential eviction.

Duane drew on a multigenerational tradition of militant tenant activism in Chelsea. He had moved to the neighborhood in the late 1970s, drawn by the growing gay community, the vibrant activist scene, and the affordable rent. He paid $175 a month for a studio with a bathroom in the apartment, which he emphasized

Figure 1. Flyer for the Chelsea
AIDS Committee demonstration
at Michael Brown's apartment
in March 1986 (Housing
Subject Files, Lesbian Herstory
Archives).

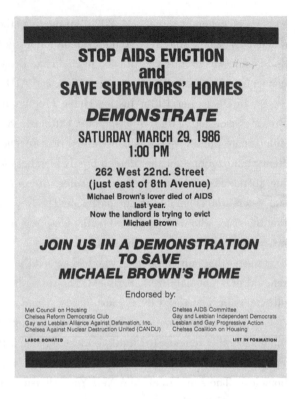

was "very important!" (pers. comm, February 16, 2023). He showed up to demonstrations held by the Chelsea Coalition on Housing, and he began to learn about tenant organizing from the movement's elders, in particular Jane Wood. A founder of the Chelsea Coalition on Housing, Wood had moved to New York City in 1930 and joined the American Labor Party, where she learned about poor tenement conditions in Chelsea during her door-knocking rounds. A petite older woman, Wood was known to stare down landlord thugs and police to prevent evictions. Wood became a citywide tenant leader as a cofounder of the Metropolitan Council on Housing in 1959, and a core organizer of Operation Move-In, a squatters' campaign in 1970 (Gold 2014: 96, 192).

In founding the Metropolitan Council on Housing, Wood joined with a network of female tenant organizers such as Jane Benedict, Frances Goldin, and Esther Rand in New York City's largely women-led tenant movement. Historian Roberta Gold has argued that tenant organizing provided a space to cultivate women's leadership, based not on claims of political legitimacy as mothers but on an understanding of women's ability to intervene in the inherently political realm of housing. In the 1960s and 1970s, tenant organizing connected a generation of Old

Left female tenant leaders such as Wood with young second-wave feminists (Gold 2009: 387).

The 1970 squatters' campaign, Operation Move-In, served as a significant moment for building intergenerational connections within New York City's tenant movement. During the summer of 1970, tenant unions and radical organizations such as the Black Panther Party, the Young Lords, and I Wor Kuen moved families into vacant apartments. In Chelsea, the Chelsea Coalition on Housing supported fifty Puerto Ricans in moving into a building on West 15th Street slated for luxury conversion (Gold 2009: 397–98). The campaign captured the imagination of young feminists, who began to learn from the older generation of female tenant organizers. A decade later, as a growing number of gay and lesbian tenants made their homes in Chelsea, Jane Wood began to mentor this new generation of tenants who were experiencing the violent gentrification of Chelsea, and soon the added challenges of the emerging AIDS crisis. As the tenant movement had brought feminist organizers into the movement in the early 1970s, Wood trained an emerging generation of gay tenant activists in Chelsea as they faced the dual threats of gentrification and AIDS in the early 1980s (Tom Duane, pers. comm., February 16, 2023).

The Chelsea AIDS Committee began to grow rapidly, becoming the center of a city- and statewide coalition of gay rights and tenant organizations. A flyer for the March demonstration, titled "Stop AIDS Evictions and Save Survivors' Homes," included endorsements from Democratic clubs, gay rights organizations, and housing organizations ("Stop AIDS Evictions and Save Survivors' Homes" 1986). The demonstration, attended by over two hundred people, revealed the strong connections between the Chelsea AIDS Committee and the housing movement (*Tenant/Inquilino* 1986: 7). Deborah Glick, president of the Gay and Lesbian Independent Democrats (GLID), addressed the rally, connecting the unique issues of gay and lesbian tenants with the larger tenant movement. Her remarks were summarized in a GLID newsletter: "Glick spoke on the need for increased activism to protect tenants from the greed of landlords. She criticized Mayor Koch for creating a city where landlords and developers are given a free hand through tax abatements. She called for justice for Brown and called on lesbians and gays to rally to his cause" (Taylor 1986: 1, 4). Leaders of the citywide tenant movement also addressed the demonstration, including Susan Mufson, a board member of the Metropolitan Council on Housing, and Jane Wood, a cofounder of the Chelsea Coalition on Housing. Wood remembered Hayes, Brown's partner, in her speech: when the Chelsea Coalition on Housing organized the building in 1982, "Robert

Figure 2. Tom Duane speaks at the rally in front of Michael Brown's apartment
building in March 1986 (Metropolitan Council on Housing records, Box 56,
Tamiment Library and Robert F. Wagner Labor Archives, New York University).

Hayes was one of the best fighters," she said, and she urged the rally to picket the
landlord in his memory (Gelbert 1986).

Tom Duane, anticipating a negative ruling from Justice Freedman,
announced the formation of an eviction defense watch to physically defend Brown
from eviction by city marshals (see fig. 2). Eviction defense had emerged as a tactic
of the New York City tenant movement fifty years earlier, during the Great Depression. Following evictions by city marshals, Communist Party–affiliated organizers began to move furniture from the street back into apartments, while neighborhood residents attempted to physically prevent marshals or police from repeating
evictions. The tactic was employed thousands of times across the city in the early
1930s, and it became a standard method used by the city's tenant organizations in
the following decades (Lawson and Naison 1986: 101).

Only seven people signed up for the Chelsea Coalition on AIDS eviction
watch, but the volunteer list demonstrates the engagement of tenant organizers
with the issue of AIDS-related evictions. One of the volunteers was Jane Wood,
who would have had personal memories of the Communist Party–led eviction
defenses of the Depression era. In addition to Wood and Metropolitan Council on
Housing board member Susan Mufson, the list also included Michael McKee, a

former Metropolitan Council on Housing organizer and founder of the New York State Tenants Legislative Coalition, now New York State Tenants and Neighbors ("Eviction Watch Volunteers from 3/29/86 Rally" 1986). McKee had founded the Chelsea Gay Association with Duane in the late 1970s, and their advocacy on behalf of Brown built upon close to a decade of neighborhood organizing in Chelsea (Duane 2018).

Eviction Creates Homelessness

Justice Freedman's second ruling on Michael Brown's case came three weeks after the demonstration at his apartment building. The ruling confirmed the validity of the DHCR bulletin and granted Brown the right to remain in his apartment through a vacancy lease, overturning the earlier decision. The Chelsea AIDS Committee demonstration, which received substantial press coverage, had dramatically increased the case's visibility. Brown's lawyer Russell Pearce recalled, "I personally believe even though we did great litigating, that she ruled in our favor because of Tom Duane's demonstrations, which were on the news every weekend. She knew it might be a ceiling to her career if she didn't rule in our favor because of what Tom was doing" (pers. comm., February 24, 2023).

In her ruling, Justice Freedman struggled to square the DHCR definition of "family" (which did not acknowledge same-sex relationships), new civil rights protections granted to gay and lesbian New Yorkers by City Hall, previous court decisions that denied formalized relationships between same-sex partners, and the evidence of the close and loving relationship between Brown and Hayes. The ruling granted Brown a *vacancy* lease (given to nonimmediate family), not a lease *renewal* (given to immediate family such as surviving husbands and wives). Justice Freedman's ruling referenced "severe repercussions" that might result from recognizing common-law relationships but also noted that "to find that he is not a surviving spouse does not mean that Brown should not be deemed to be a family member for purposes of entitling him to a vacancy lease.... There is no rational reason to exclude persons in Brown's situation from being classified as a family member, when in fact, the relationship was much closer than that of most family members."[12] For Brown, the ruling meant that he had won the right to remain in his apartment—but with the 10 percent rent increase of a vacancy lease given to nonimmediate family members.

A 10 percent rent increase, which brought his monthly rent to $177, was possibly a financial burden for Brown. Due to Hayes's death, Brown was no longer sharing his rent with another person. The court heard substantial evidence about the poor conditions of the apartment, which would be unlikely to be borne by tenants with the financial means to rent an apartment in better condition. Additionally, the court heard that Brown and Hayes had lived in the small one-bedroom apartment with Hayes's mother for two years while she was dying of cancer. For a brief time, Hayes's sister also lived with the couple.[13] The doubling up of family members in a small, decrepit apartment is evidence that Brown and Hayes did not have financial resources to cushion personal or family emergencies. Finally, Brown found legal representation through Chelsea Legal Aid, which indicates that Brown was receiving some form of public assistance since he was eligible for legal aid (Russell Pearce, pers. comm., February 24, 2023).

Brown's respite from eviction lasted for twelve months. His landlord appealed Justice Freedman's ruling, and the following spring the appellate division of the New York Supreme Court decided in the landlord's favor. The court issued a narrow ruling on the legal authority of the DHCR and did not comment on Brown's right to remain in the apartment as Robert Hayes's surviving partner (Johnson 1987). The court struck down the interim DHCR regulations and upheld an earlier court decision that denied family members the right to continued residency in apartments following the death or departure of the named tenant.[14] A request by Brown's lawyers to appeal to the New York Court of Appeals was denied.

Public interest in Brown's case seems to have dissipated over the course of his legal fight to remain in his home. Although the media reported widely on the final court decision, in 1987 his case didn't spark the outpouring of support that he had experienced a year earlier. And seemingly, the eviction defense watch had disbanded; Brown was evicted from his home on West 22nd Street in January 1988, almost exactly three years after Hayes's death. An update in the March 1988 issue of *GLID News* noted that two months later, Brown was still searching for somewhere to live. The update urged readers to "hope this hero of our community is not forgotten," but archival traces of Brown disappear after this brief mention (Duane 1988). Whether Brown found stable and affordable housing or entered long-term homelessness is unknown.

The year of Brown's eviction, the Partnership for the Homeless estimated that there were five thousand homeless people with AIDS in the city, a number that included both people living in congregate shelters and over three thousand people living on the streets, in subways, or in parks. The same year, the city provided a scant forty-four supportive housing beds for people with AIDS (ACT UP New York 1988). GLID reported hearing from a surviving partner facing eviction once per week; the advocacy organization Gay Men's Health Crisis reported receiving one such call per day.[15] Housing instability for people with AIDS and their family members was not without consequence: a 1986 study titled "AIDS Shelter Project" concluded that 26 percent of people with AIDS were homeless. For gay men with AIDS who were also intravenous drug users, the same study found that a staggering 85 percent were homeless within six months of diagnosis (Gottfried 1986: 10). In the early days of the AIDS crisis, the lack of treatment options combined with the fragile health and susceptibility to infection of people with AIDS meant that inadequate housing or homelessness could rapidly become a death sentence.

The explosion of homelessness among people with AIDS and their family members was not inevitable; rather, it was the result of policy decisions. Landlords' ability to pursue financially opportunistic evictions was a significant factor in Brown's loss of housing. New York City's rent regulation system prioritized the property rights of landlords, not Brown's right to remain in his home of eight years. Even Brown's brief legal victory was premised upon a form of second-class citizenship: he won the right to a vacancy lease for "nonimmediate" family members, with the accompanying financial penalty of a 10 percent vacancy increase. Although studies on the differentiation of citizenship benefits premised upon sexuality have primarily focused on the federal government, following the example of Margot Canaday's *Straight State*, Brown's case demonstrates how state-level courts also inscribed second-class citizenship for gays and lesbians (Canaday 2009; Bell 2018).

Brown's Hidden Legacies

As the 1980s progressed, grassroots advocates, including those in ACT UP New York, increasingly focused on the growing issue of homelessness, while the fight against AIDS-related evictions occurred increasingly in the legal realm. Brown's case presaged a flood of legal cases challenging evictions from surviving partners. "John Edwin Hoffer fought his eviction following the death of his partner David Perez, only to die himself while waiting on a motion to appeal. . . . Patrick Hennisse died of AIDS twelve days after marrying his wife Candy Systra, who was evicted despite a legal marriage because she had not lived in the shared apartment for more than two years" (Bhaman 2021: 95). Some simply sought enough time to die in their own homes. Artist David Wojnarowicz requested a stay of eviction from the apartment he had shared with photographer Peter Hujar as his own health declined (96).

During these years, Tom Duane used a strategy from the Chelsea Coalition on Housing to keep tenants in their apartments. The New York Supreme Court had issued a narrow ruling in Brown's case, which did not set legal precedent for future eviction cases premised on the death of the tenant of record. This meant that Housing Court judges had discretion in deciding individual cases. Susan Cohen and Bobbi Berlin from the Chelsea Coalition on Housing taught Duane about the judicial appointment and election system in the state of New York, and Duane, as Democratic district leader, quickly became very good at picking strong candidates and getting those candidates elected to civil court (Tom Duane, pers. comm., February 16, 2023). Duane began to attend eviction proceedings, and he recalled that "the judges might take notice that I was sitting there" and soon "judges just stopped ruling on the cases and they just waited. They were going to wait until these cases went up to the Court of Appeals," the state's highest court (pers. comm., February 16, 2023). For tenants, the result of these instances of judicial discretion was that their eviction proceedings were stayed, and they could remain in their apartments for the time being. Women from the Chelsea Coalition on Housing had taught Duane how to identify a bad landlord, organize tenants, and when necessary, employ courtroom strategies to delay evictions.

The first of the AIDS eviction cases to be heard by the state of New York's highest court, the Court of Appeals, resulted from Miguel Braschi's decision to contest his eviction following the death of his partner, Leslie Blanchard, in 1986. The court case, known as *Braschi v. Stahl Associates Co.*, concerned their rent-controlled Midtown Manhattan apartment. However, unlike Brown, Miguel Braschi would not face homelessness if he lost his eviction case. Braschi was heir to the $5 million estate of his partner, who was a celebrity hair colorist. The estate included an art collection and a one-hundred-acre country home in New Jersey (Esparza 2022: 80). Reflecting the increasingly high profile of AIDS-related eviction cases, and the growing engagement of the gay and lesbian legal advocacy community, Braschi was represented by William Rubenstein from the American Civil Liberties Union's (ACLU's) National Lesbian and Gay Rights Project. The Association of the Bar of the City of New York, the Legal Aid Society, and New York City's Corporation Counsel all submitted amici briefs, in addition to those submitted by AIDS advocacy groups.[16]

In 1989, the court ruled that Braschi should be recognized as a spouse under the New York City Human Rights Law, the first recognition of same-sex partnerships in the state of New York.[17] Initially, the consequences of the Braschi case were limited by the fact that Braschi's apartment was rent controlled, a system that governed just over one hundred thousand apartments at the time of the ruling. However, the *Braschi* decision required the DHCR to promulgate new regulations that would have a wider impact. Negotiations with the DHCR brought the ACLU lawyers into the room with Brown's Legal Aid lawyer Russell Pearce (who, by 1989, had become the chief counsel for the New York City Commission on

Human Rights), as well as Tom Duane, gay tenant organizer Michael McKee, and representatives from the Met Council on Housing and Legal Aid Housing. Pearce recalled that "the tenant leaders wanted more expansive . . . kinds of configurations of family" that would protect the maximum number of tenants from eviction (pers. comm., February 24, 2023). While Braschi's lawyers were not initially planning to push for expansive regulations, tenant advocates convinced the ACLU and DHCR to adopt a broad definition of family for the purposes of apartment succession rights: "It was all these things, it was, you were out to your family, your names were on the mailbox, your magazine subscriptions, joint checking account, the superintendent [knew], all these different things. . . . Except for they couldn't ask about sex. I love that. . . . It was really just if you said you were family, you were family; people thought you were family, you were family" (Duane 2018).

Historians Salonee Bhaman and René Esparza have argued that the *Braschi* case, reflecting the ACLU's legal strategy emphasizing the couple's economic interdependence and monogamous relationship, produced a definition of family premised upon middle-class heteronormativity (Bhaman 2021; Esparza 2022). Stephen Vider has proposed an alternative reading of the ACLU's legal strategy as a "universalist argument . . . [that] Braschi and Blanchard should be treated as a family because they behaved like a family" (Vider 2021b: 258). While Duane's description of the resulting regulatory changes gestures toward the heteronormative exclusivity of economic nonessentials like magazine subscriptions, it simultaneously points to a moment where tenant advocates pushed the state to adopt a definition of family based on wide range of behaviors. This universalist definition of family benefited not only same-sex partners but also others in nontraditional or nonintimate relationships. It was a victory that reflected the successful legal arguments of the ACLU and the presence of tenant advocates in the subsequent negotiations with the DHCR. These advocates, originally brought together in Brown's defense, approached the negotiations with a commitment to keeping as many people as possible in their homes.

Brown's case does not have the legal significance of *Braschi v. Stahl*; the outcome of his case was not happy or precedent setting. Brown lost his case and was evicted. However, attention to the two-year fight for Brown's home reveals collaboration, mentorship, and coalition-building between the city's tenant movement and gay and lesbian neighborhood activists. This collaboration made AIDS-related evictions a high-profile political issue and brought advocates into communication and collaboration, and ultimately into regulatory negotiations following the *Braschi* ruling. Brown's case demonstrates how gay and lesbian activists during the early AIDS crisis were guided by New York City's long tradition of tenant advocacy.

Notes

Thank you to Anne Valk, Roberta Gold, Michele Mitchell, Sarah Covington, and the journal's editors and reviewers for feedback on earlier drafts of this article. I would also like to thank archivists from the New York City Municipal Archives, the LaGuardia and Wagner Archives, and the New York State Library for facilitating this research. Additional thanks to Tom Duane and Russell Pearce for discussing Michael Brown's case with me.

1. Entes, Clifford A. 1985. "Letter from Clifford A. Entes to Michael Brown," March 26. *Two Associates v. Michael Brown*, 127AD2d173 (1986). New York State Library. Hereafter, *TAMB*.

2. For more on the history of the New York City Commission on Human Rights and their role in combating housing discrimination, see Benjamin 1974; Varela 1996; Schill 1996; and Grigolo 2019.

3. Sexual orientation–related housing discrimination complaints constituted 10.9 percent of the total from November 1983 to October 1985, while AIDS-related housing discrimination complaints accounted for 12.9 percent of the total collected between November 1983 and April 1986 (NYCCHR 1986b: 9; 1986a: 6).

4. Entes. 1985. "Letter from Clifford A. Entes." *TAMB*.

5. Property information for Two Associates is available through the Automated City Register Information System, maintained by the New York City Department of Finance. Two Associates property holdings were determined by reviewing mortgage and deed information for property transactions listing Two Associates as a principal party between 1966 and 2022.

6. Brown, Michael. 1985. "Affidavit of Michael Brown in Support of Cross-Motion and in Opposition to Motion," pp. 7–8. *TAMB*.

7. Brown. 1985. "Affidavit of Michael Brown," pp. 5–7. *TAMB*.

8. Kafenbaum, Bruce. 1985. "Affidavit of Bruce Kafenbaum in Support of Motion," p. 156. *TAMB*.

9. Freedman, Helen E. 1985. "Decision of Justice Freedman," p. 19. *TAMB*.

10. New York State Division of Housing and Community Renewal. 1985. "Emergency Operational Bulletin 85-1, Succession - Right to Renew a Lease in a Rent Stabilized Housing Accommodation." *TAMB*. For more on the debate around the interim DHCR regulations, see the detailed discussion in Esparza (2022).

11. Tom Duane was elected to the city council in 1991 after revealing his HIV-positive status during the campaign, and he served in the New York Senate from 1999 until 2012. Duane was the first openly gay member of the New York Senate.

12. Freedman, Helen E. 1986. "Decision of Justice Freedman." *TAMB*.

13. Pearce, Russell. 1985. "Affirmation of Russell Pearce in Support of Cross-Motion and in Opposition to Motion." *TAMB*.

14. New York Supreme Court, Appellate Division. 1987. "Opinion of the Court." *TAMB*.
15. Frederick A. O. Schwarz, Jr., Corporation Counsel of The City of New York. 1986. "Amicus Curiae, New York City Commission on Human Rights." *TAMB*.
16. New York Court of Appeals. 1989. "Opinion of the Court." *Braschi v. Stahl Associates Co.*, 74 N.Y.2d 201 (1989). New York State Library. Hereafter, *BSA*.
17. New York Court of Appeals. 1989. "Opinion of the Court." *BSA*.

References

ACT UP New York (AIDS Coalition to Unleash Power). 1988. "How's Ed Doing?," October 20. Box 29, folder 24, ACT UP New York Records 1969, 1982–1997, MssCol 10. Manuscripts and Archives Division. New York Public Library.

Bell, Jonathan. 2018. "Rethinking the 'Straight State': Welfare Politics, Health Care, and Public Policy in the Shadow of AIDS." *Journal of American History* 104, no. 4: 931–52.

Benjamin, Gerald. 1974. *Race Relations and the New York City Commission on Human Rights*. Ithaca, NY: Cornell University Press.

Bhaman, Salonee. 2021. "'For a Few Months of Peace': Housing and Care in the Early AIDS Crisis." *Radical History Review*, no. 140: 78–106.

Canaday, Margot. 2009. *The Straight State: Sexuality and Citizenship in Twentieth-Century America*. Princeton, NJ: Princeton University Press.

Carroll, Tamar W. 2015. *Mobilizing New York: AIDS, Antipoverty, and Feminist Activism*. Chapel Hill: University of North Carolina Press.

CGAN (Chelsea Gay Association Newsletter). 1979. "CGA Update." March 3-4.

CGAN (Chelsea Gay Association Newsletter). 1981. "Calendar." November 1.

Duane, Tom. 1988. "District Leader's Report." *GLID News*, March 3.

Duane, Tom. 2018. "Tom Duane." Interview by Steven Palmer. Stonewall Oral History Project. LGBTCenterNYC. April 3. https://youtu.be/sGu1UB5bPBs.

Esparza, René. 2022. "'We Lived as Do Spouses': AIDS, Neoliberalism, and Family-Based Apartment Succession Rights in 1980s New York City." *Journal of the History of Sexuality* 31, no. 1: 1–31.

"Eviction Watch Volunteers from 3/29/86 Rally." 1986. Tom Duane papers, LGBT Collection, Box 150012, Folder 7. LaGuardia and Wagner Archives, La Guardia Community College, City University of New York.

Gelbert, Bruce-Michael. 1986. "N.Y. Activists Fight Eviction of PWA's Survivor." *Gay Community News*, April 12, n.p.

Gold, Roberta. 2009. "'I Had Not Seen Women like That Before': Intergenerational Feminism in New York City's Tenant Movement." *Feminist Studies* 35, no. 2: 387–415.

Gold, Roberta. 2014. *When Tenants Claimed the City: The Struggle for Citizenship in New York City Housing*. Urbana: University of Illinois Press.

Gottfried, David. 1986. "Report on Gay and Lesbian Issues for the Village Independent Democrats." Tom Duane papers, LGBT Collection, Box 150012, Folder 7. LaGuardia and Wagner Archives, La Guardia Community College, City University of New York.

Grigolo, Michele. 2019. *The Human Rights City: New York, San Francisco, Barcelona.* London and New York: Routledge.

Holtzman, Benjamin. 2019. "'Shelter Is Only a First Step': Housing the Homeless in 1980s New York City." *Journal of Social History* 52, no. 3: 886–910.

Johnson, Kirk. 1987. "Homosexual's Lover Loses Housing Bid." *New York Times*, April 10.

Katz, Sandor. 1989. "Will Gays Really Fly in New York Politics?" *Outlook*, August 21, 32–35.

Lawson, Ronald, and Stephen E. Barton. 1980. "Sex Roles in Social Movements: A Case Study of the Tenant Movement in New York City." *Signs: Journal of Women in Culture and Society* 6, no. 2: 230–47. https://doi.org/10.1086/493794.

Lawson, Ronald, and Mark D. Naison. 1986. *The Tenant Movement in New York City, 1904–1984.* New Brunswick, NJ: Rutgers University Press.

Lehman, Eric. 1982. "Housing Discrimination Rampant for New York Lesbians and Gays." *Tenant/Inquilino*, February 1982. TAM 173, Metropolitan Council on Housing records. Tamiment Library and Robert F. Wagner Labor Archive, New York University.

"Mortgage for 262 West 22nd Street, NY NY." 1982. Document # FT_1560000010856. New York City Department of Finance, Office of the City Register.

NYCCHR (New York City Commission on Human Rights). 1981. "Report of a Survey by the New York City Commission on Human Rights on Instances of Discrimination among Gay Citizens in New York." Council Member Miriam Friedlander Legislative Files, Box 051443, Folder 7. LaGuardia and Wagner Archives, La Guardia Community College, City University of New York.

NYCCHR (New York City Commission on Human Rights). 1986a. "Gay and Lesbian Discrimination Documentation Project: Two Year Report on Complaints of Sexual Orientation Discrimination, November 1983-October 1986." New York City Municipal Archives.

NYCCHR (New York City Commission on Human Rights). 1986b. "Report on Discrimination against People with AIDS, November 1983–April 1986." New York City Municipal Archives.

Phillips-Fein, Kim. 2017. *Fear City: New York's Fiscal Crisis and the Rise of Austerity Politics.* New York: Metropolitan Books, Henry Holt and Company.

Schill, Michael H. 1996. "Local Enforcement of Laws Prohibiting Discrimination in Housing: The New York City Human Rights Commission." *Fordham Urban Law Journal* 23, no. 4: 991–1030.

Starecheski, Amy. 2016. *Ours to Lose: When Squatters Became Homeowners in New York City.* Chicago: University of Chicago Press.

Stegman, Michael A. 1988. "Housing and Vacancy Report: New York City, 1987." City of New York Department of Housing Preservation and Development. New York City Municipal Archives.

"Stop AIDS Evictions and Save Survivors' Homes." 1986. Tom Duane papers, LGBT Collection, Box 150012, Folder 7. LaGuardia and Wagner Archives, La Guardia Community College, City University of New York.

Taylor, Dave. 1986. "Gay Eviction Thwarted." *GLID News*, May, 1–4.

Tenant/Inquilino. 1986. "Chelsea AIDS Case Rally," May. TAM 173, Metropolitan Council on Housing records, Box 67. Tamiment Library and Robert F. Wagner Labor Archive, New York University.

Varela, Marta B. 1996. "The First Forty Years of the Commission on Human Rights." *Fordham Urban Law Journal* 23, no. 4: 983–90.

Vider, Stephen. 2021a. *The Queerness of Home: Gender, Sexuality, and the Politics of Domesticity after World War II*. Chicago: University of Chicago Press.

Vider, Stephen. 2021b. "What Happened to the Functional Family?" In *Intimate States: Gender, Sexuality, and Governance in Modern US History*, edited by Margot Canaday, Nancy F. Cott, and Robert O. Self, 257–79. Chicago: University of Chicago Press.

QUEER LIMITROPHIC DWELLING

Miguel A. Avalos

Introduction

*O*n a cold Thursday morning during my fieldwork for this article, I stopped at a pedestrian bridge that rises above several vehicle lanes on the Mexican side of the San Ysidro port of entry (SYPOE) into the United States. The vehicles below me meandered toward the immigration inspection booths in the distance, and a single row of yellow-painted concrete highway dividers separated the expeditious SENTRI lanes from the slower ReadyLanes and general lanes. I saw parked cars next to the highway dividers belonging to border vendors that dwelled between the vehicle lanes. They sold souvenirs, newspapers, and breakfast items like burritos, tamales, coffee, and *champurrado*. I heard a cacophony of car horns, loud music, screeching brakes, and the occasional motorcycle speeding toward the front of one of the general lanes to the dismay of immobile car owners. I caught snippets of people's conversations as they walked behind me toward the pedestrian queue or saw them out of the corner of my eye, trying to get a glimpse of the queue. "¡Tres, cuatro horas!" (Three, four hours!) I heard someone exclaim. I turn to my left and saw a man with a backpack and a lunch bag hanging from his left shoulder. He must have seen the pedestrian queue seeming to serpentine into four different lanes as he walked toward me. The beginning of one queue looped backward into the end of another until there was insufficient space to accommodate all pedestrians on the main path. The fourth queue slowly made its way up a ramp and onto a bridge several meters behind me. The man paid no attention to me as he likely thought about the ordeal he was about to undertake.

At approximately 11 a.m. later that day, I walked up the ramp leading up to the second bridge and began waiting in the fourth queue, despite hoping the overall queue wouldn't be as long as earlier that morning. About an hour and a half later, my feet and lower back begin to ache, and I focused more on these

GLQ 30:4
DOI 10.1215/10642684-11331098
© 2024 by Duke University Press

bodily pains and on constantly shifting my weight from one leg to the other than on writing down observations. I was still not at the second bridge's ramp. I checked the day's temperature on my phone: 80 degrees Fahrenheit with a clear sky and a powerfully bright midday sun. I was sweating, and I saw people's faces shimmering with sweat, some flapping their shirts to cool down as they walked past me and toward the end of the fourth queue. Others flagged down border vendors selling cold bottles of water or food like tacos, breakfast burritos, and tortas, eating while waiting in line. A man in front of me held a black umbrella and, under its shade, told his friend, "Lo cansado no es el trabajo, lo cansado es esto" (Work is not tiring; *this* [waiting in line] is tiring). I agreed silently and thought of other conversations with people waiting in line who compared transborder commuting to hiking or working out. I glanced over to the barely moving vehicle queues, still thinking of the man's statement, and reflected on my history of transborder commuting and how much I had hated doing it when I was younger.

I have a history of moving between two countries and transborder commuting. Both entail a state of displacement, albeit different in terms of the temporal rhythm of everyday life. Between the late 1990s and early 2000s, I completed kindergarten in Tijuana; moved with my family to Orange County, California; then to San Diego County; and finally back to Tijuana. During our return to Tijuana in the 2000s, I attended elementary school in San Diego and transborder commuted back to Tijuana Monday through Friday with my father. This routine followed a rhythm different from my classmates in San Diego. My mornings began with a knock on my bedroom door at three or four a.m. and a lethargic walk to the bathroom downstairs. I then took a quick shower and got ready for school, still half asleep, angry, and hoping to sleep more in the car's backseat. However, I could not sleep because of my father's constant acceleration and braking, attempting to match the ebb and flow of the vehicle queue so as not to let another vehicle cut in front of our car or to capitalize on another's distraction by switching into their faster lane. While awake, I completed unfinished homework, read books, or stared at border vendors delivering food up and down the corridors between the vehicle queues. Sometimes, I tried to get my father to buy us some churros or sweets. My attempts were often unsuccessful because I usually ate breakfast at school to save time and money. If we were late because of long wait times, we would stop by a nearby Burger King in San Ysidro to purchase food. After school, I walked to my aunt's apartment, about five minutes away, and waited there for my parents to pick me up around five p.m. Following some small talk with my aunt, we would leave for Tijuana. Together, the narratives above provide a small glimpse of the daily work transborder commuters undertake to dwell in the US-Mexico borderlands and call that place home.

My experiences of relocating between Mexico and the United States, transborder commuting, and waiting at ports of entry reflect what Gloria E. Anzaldùa (2002: 1) theorizes as "dwelling in nepantla." Nepantla describes a subjectivity (e.g., *la mestiza*) and a space (i.e., a bridge), naming a liminal subject position in a constant state of displacement between two or more worlds (Anzaldúa 2002). To dwell in nepantla means constantly moving between worlds such that displacement has "become a sort of 'home'" that is homelike and unhomelike simultaneously (1). Nevertheless, homes do not exist independently outside the subject; they are social, material, affective, and symbolic objects produced through dwelling and conditioned by power embedded in historical processes (Blunt and Dowling 2006; Young 1997). Thus, dwelling in the US-Mexico borderlands, a liminal and constantly shifting space, requires transborder commuters to adopt a queer perspective toward everyday practices, *queering* both home and dwelling.[1]

This essay's analyses form part of a broader project on the home that examines transborder commuters' affective, material, and nonlinear temporal experiences—what I call "helical temporalities of home and belonging." In this article, I examine transborder commuters' life-making or "queer tactics," which allow them to navigate and survive the "disruptive situations" (Moussawi 2020) produced by the US-Mexico border regime (USMBR) and racial capitalism. I propose the concept of "queer limitrophic dwelling" to capture how commuters spatially decentralize their homes in Tijuana by drawing on transborder kinships and by making queer use of objects and spaces to produce ephemeral and mobile dwelling spaces across San Diego, Tijuana, and the SYPOE. Crucially, I mobilize the terms *limitrophe* and *dwelling* to highlight the US-Mexico borderlands' capabilities to nourish and preserve life, even momentarily, despite ongoing border militarization and violence. Drawing on twenty-one months of ethnography and interviews with transborder commuters in the San Diego-Tijuana border region, this article contributes to queer, feminist, and transnational scholarship that reconceptualizes home and dwelling as messy, dynamic, relational, and coconstitutive (Ahmed et al. 2003; Manalansan 2018).

Home: An Interdisciplinary Perspective

Domesticity, privacy, and intimacy—usually associated with the white, middle-class, heterosexual family home—developed between the sixteenth and eighteenth centuries among bourgeois families in northern Europe (Rybczynski 1987). This development transformed the once-public medieval home into a more private, familial space for the heterosexual nuclear family by cultivating a domestic atmosphere distinct from the outside world (Rybczynski 1987). These historical legacies of empire greatly conditioned hegemonic US discourses and images of the ideal home, portraying the suburban home as the ideal site for the white hetero-sexual nuclear family and a haven from the workplace (Blunt and Dowling 2006).

Feminist scholars have shown how Euro-American notions of domestic-ity are foundational to Western imperial projects, inextricably linking domestic politics to imperial expansionism (Stratford 2019). During the nineteenth cen-tury, white middle-class women wrote extensively about domesticity while playing an increasingly prominent role as magazine editors, curating writings for other women regarding the home, marriage, and beauty (Stratford 2019). These accounts of domesticity argued that the white, Christian, middle-class home could serve as a "civilizing" tool in service to US imperialism by redefining "dwelling" in accordance with Euro-American standards (Kaplan 1998). Domestic politics were entwined with imperial possibilities such that, for example, a clean home—the responsibility of white women—meant a healthy white citizenry *and* a healthy set-tler nation (Stratford 2019). These nineteenth-century discourses on US domestic-ity linked the Euro-American home and women's role in it with US nation-building domestically at a time when the United States expanded geopolitically (Kaplan 1998). US domesticity would assuage US racial anxieties by becoming the thresh-old of assimilation, granting racialized and ethnic communities conditional inclu-sion if they aspired and adhered to these normative standards (Kaplan 1998).

Aspiring to or adopting the Euro-American ideal of home became a marker of a minoritized group's exclusion from or inclusion within the US settler nation and its hierarchy of racialized citizenship. For example, mainstream political mobilizations for gay and lesbian marriage equality among white and middle-class gays and lesbians have adopted a homonormative framework, excluding racially minoritized and sexually nonnormative subjects from US society and domesticity (Duggan 2003; Ferguson 2005). Euro-American articulations of home continue to be "imagined [as] 'better,' more socially appropriate and an ideal to be aspired to," despite their unreachability for minoritized communities (Blunt and Dowling 2006: 99). Thus, home becomes linked to aspirational affects, defining what con-stitutes the "good life," often understood through the ideal home (e.g., a suburban house).

Queer Limitrophic Dwelling: A Theoretical Outline

US-Mexico borderlands scholarship tends to analyze this region through Agam-ben's (2008) notion of "the state of exception" or Mbembe's (2003) concept of

queer tactics by asserting that they also arise from a subject's queer use of spaces and objects while messing up the "proper" ways of being upheld by the state (e.g., citizenship, home). By approaching home and dwelling through the lenses of queer use (Ahmed 2019) and mess (Manalansan 2018), waking up early and sleeping in one's car become visible as queer tactics that, breaking with normative ideas of where and when to sleep, become productive life-making tactics.[3] Moreover, transborder commuter's accounts, including mine, reveal how sleeping in one's car *produces* decentralized homes that, while not affording the same levels of privacy, allow them to negotiate and survive multiple temporalities like port of entry time, work time, or school time.

For transborder commuters who own a vehicle, this mode of transportation often becomes a momentary mobile dwelling with the necessary accoutrements to get ready for work, sleep, or even attend class at a moment's notice. These instances exemplify what Bissel and Gorman-Murray (2020: 2) refer to as "mobile dwelling," highlighting how "different practices of mobility have given rise to a range of unique sites of dwelling." For example, Lizbeth's use of her car shifts based on context, playing different roles in her commute depending on the wait-time information she receives from border Facebook groups and Google Maps:[4]

> Por ejemplo, si yo entro a las once . . . me levanto a las cinco en punto. Entonces estoy viendo que "oh, la línea esta rápida, avanza muy bien, entonces me puedo quedar otra hora dormida y ya me voy más, con más calma." Pero si dicen no, que la línea esta horrible, yo ya tengo un paquete de emergencias para alistarme en el carro y ya me alisto me arreglo, me lavo los dientes, pero todo.

> (For example, if work starts at 11 [a.m.] . . . I wake up at 5 [a.m]. So, I'm seeing that "oh, the line is fast, it's moving well, so I can sleep another hour and I'll leave more calmly." But, if they say "no," that the line is horrible, I already have an emergency package to get ready in the car and I get ready, I brush my teeth, everything.)

Lizbeth notably mentions the possibility of getting ready for work in her car while waiting at the SYPOE, demonstrating another queer tactic involving the decentralization of home through dwelling practices. In the United States's dominant imaginary, the Euro-American home is often construed as the private sphere par excellence, locatable through an address, and assumed to be static (Blunt and Dowling 2006). Yet, as Anne-Marie Fortier (2001: 118) argues, such dominant understandings objectify home as a place "where things and subjects stand still" rather than something more processual and ephemeral. Transborder commuters live in material conditions wherein they constantly negotiate the Euro-American idea of home, most notably regarding privacy and fixity, because adhering to this ideal would be detrimental to their livelihoods and survival. Although the privacy afforded by transborder commuters' mobile dwelling may be less than that available in an apartment or house, it allows them to reliably meet essential commitments like working in San Diego. This trade-off is crucial in facilitating queer limitrophic dwelling, that is, the decentralization of home across Tijuana, San Diego, and the SYPOE, rendering the queer use of one's vehicle as a productive life-making or queer tactic.

Waiting is often considered a passive activity, yet transborder commuters like Lizbeth use lengthy wait times at ports of entry as a resource. As mentioned earlier, Lizbeth makes sure she has "an emergency package to get ready in her car," which she uses while waiting in the vehicle queues:

> Me pongo a escuchar música o me maquillo o hago las cosas que no puedo hacer aquí en la casa como alistarme. . . . A veces la línea estuvo tan fea que, si tuve que hacer mi clase por Zoom, en vez de llegar a la clase.

> (I listen to music or do my makeup or things I can't do here at home like get ready. . . . Sometimes the line was so bad that I even had to attend class via Zoom, rather than attending [in person].)

When Lizbeth believed she could not attend her in-person class on time, she attended via Zoom. This queer tactic highlights technology's role in transforming the vehicle into a mobile classroom and dwelling, foregrounding the relationship between material culture, home, and dwelling. In this respect, Sara Bonfanti (2020: 40) argues that "what turns any dwelling into someone's home place is the way" transnational subjects circulate and apply meaning to domestic material culture. Transborder commuters create ephemeral homes by circulating domestic material culture (e.g., emergency packages) *and* the queer use of different objects and spaces in tandem and on the move. These quotidian dwelling practices often occur outside of one's static home, especially in transborder commuting, emphasizing my interlocutors' decentralization of home, often contingent on commuting conditions and their temporal obligations.

Transborder commuters' "emergency packages" vary greatly. Noemi, a thirty-one-year-old Mexican American woman with dual citizenship, discusses what she keeps in her vehicle and how she prepares for transborder commuting.

Yo ya dejo todo listo un día antes. En mi carro . . . ya tengo todo ahí listo porque yo sé, ósea, yo ya, en la mañana, yo ya sé que no mas agarro mi lonche y ya me subo al carro, pero yo ya me bañé. . . . En el carro traigo mi vida, ósea, todo. Como mi ropa del trabajo esta planchada adentro de mi carro como para yo cruzar la línea y me cambio en el trabajo y todo, ósea, yo tengo todo en mi carro. Y yo me levanto como a las 2 y media.

(I leave everything ready the day before. In my car, I already have everything there ready because I know, like, in the morning, I already know I can just grab my lunch and get in my car, but I've already showered. . . . In my car I have my life, like, everything. Like my ironed work clothes are inside my car so that when I cross, I can change at work and everything, like, I have everything in my car. And I wake up at 2:30 a.m.)

Whereas Lizbeth may brush her teeth in her vehicle, Noemi prepares the items needed the day before transborder commuting.[5] In addition to contesting the relation between home and privacy, it is essential to highlight how preparing and using these emergency packages during or after transborder commuting is a form of domestic labor, effacing the line between the home and different public spheres (e.g., work, classroom). Indeed, feminist scholars have demonstrated how the private and public spheres are interdependent—their normalized separation faltering during times of emergency such as the COVID-19 pandemic—or unattainable for minoritized communities (Kay 2020; Blunt and Dowling 2006). Lizbeth's and Noemi's queer tactics demonstrate this interdependence by creating and using emergency packages that enable them to conduct quotidian dwelling practices, meet their educational or labor commitments, and use wait times resourcefully. In this way, queer limitrophic dwelling becomes visible as a collection of life-making or queer tactics allowing them to negotiate dwelling in nepantla as transborder commuters traveling between Tijuana and San Diego.

Transborder commuters' mobile dwellings are not limited to their vehicles; they often draw on their social networks and nonresidential places to cocreate temporary dwellings in San Diego. For example, Noemi says she has always lived in Tijuana but often stays at friends' places in San Diego, mainly when she is tired and does not want to commute. However, she also finds other resources:

Si, y luego también . . . pago la membresía de un gimnasio para ir a bañarme. Empecé cuando entré a la universidad en el año 2012. [Saque la membresía] porque cruzaba muy temprano, me quería bañar antes de dormirme a la casa de quien me iba quedar a dormir. Entonces para no molestar o incomodar me bañaba en el gimnasio y luego ya me iba ya lista para descansar. Y también como a veces me quedaba mucho tiempo en la universidad, ocupaba como un refresh o algo así y me iba a bañar. Pero después descubrí que la universidad tenía regaderas y ahí me bañaba.

(Yes, and then also . . . I pay for a gym membership to go take a shower. I started when I first attended a university in 2012. I took out a membership because I crossed very early, I wanted to take a shower before sleeping in the house I was going to stay in [that day]. So, to not bother or inconvenience anyone, I showered at the gym and then I was ready to rest. And, since I stayed at school for a very long time, I needed like a refresh or something like that and so I went to take a shower. Later I discovered that the university had a shower and I showered there.)

Noemi draws on her social networks—or, more specifically, transborder kinships—and nonresidential places like gyms to conduct different quotidian dwelling practices, which becomes part of a repertoire of queer tactics used by transborder commuters. She produces a relational, ephemeral, and decentralized network of dwelling spaces where she can rest or shower instead of dealing with the SYPOE's temporality and the fatigue of transborder commuting. In this way, queer limitrophic dwelling, through these life-making or queer tactics, becomes the process through which transborder commuters transgress normative ideas associated with home and dwelling, producing different material understandings of each to meet their daily needs and commitments. For example, Noemi's home cannot be reduced to a singular address; it may include multiple addresses and spaces with no address (e.g., her vehicle). Transborder commuters' narratives force us to consider home and dwelling as coconstitutive and multirelational phenomena that, while often used interchangeably, have different material functions.

The notions of dwelling and limitrophe involve subjectivity, nourishment, and power.[6] Drawing on Heidegger ([1951] 2012), dwelling represents a place *and* a practice where the subject's internal and external worlds meld and gain meaning (Harrison 2007). However, Young's (1997) feminist critique of Heidegger's gendered conception of dwelling reveals how he undertheorized dwelling's preserving function because of its association with women's homemaking practices (i.e., domestic labor). Nevertheless, domestic labor, including transborder commuters' queer tactics, endow "things with living meaning, arranging them in spaces [to] facilitate the life activities of those to whom they belong" (151). To dwell is to build (e.g., worldmaking) *and* to preserve and nourish the subject and the material and imaginative dimensions of home (Long 2013). Given the above, I use the term *limitrophe* to consider the US-Mexico borderlands' capabilities to nourish and maintain life, even if momentarily, while also being a space of ongoing border violence—a paradoxical tension often omitted in contemporary narratives of this region. The root *trophe*, as in the terms "trophocyte" or "trophobiont," evokes nourishment, support, and growth, providing a conceptual link to dwelling as a preserving and life-making practice.

Some dwelling spaces transborder commuters create do not necessarily provide shelter or privacy. Jose, a twenty-eight-year-old Mexican American man working as a car salesperson, shares how commuting during high school meant that he occasionally remained in San Diego rather than returning to his home in Tijuana:

> There were some times where I stayed with my girlfriend over here because I just didn't want to deal with it. And then there was a few times where I was part of the school band and at a certain hour there were no more buses, so if I stayed on this side too late, I knew I was going to have to walk five miles home. So I just decided, screw it, I'm gonna take a nap at the park. Not the best idea I've ever had; it's super cold, and at one point the sprinklers turned on. That was not fun.

As Jose points out, if he stayed on the US side too late, there would be no bus service to take him to the SYPOE, so in this situation it was always a possibility that he would have to stay overnight, even though he didn't want to do it. He further mentions that he prepared and "learned from the first time . . . kinda layered up, bring clothes in my backpack." This account illustrates how transborder commuters who rely on public transportation also harness their transborder kinships and public spaces to produce momentary mobile dwellings. Like Lizbeth and Noemi, Jose's life-making or queer tactics blur the line between the private and the public spheres, demonstrating their interdependency, especially for transborder commuters navigating multiple temporalities under conditions of constant displacement (i.e., "dwelling in nepantla"). As such, Jose's account interrogates the Euro-American assumptions that homes must be private, comfortable, or in fixed locations, characteristics often unattainable for minoritized communities, especially in border regions. Transborder commuters' homes emerge through their life-making or queer tactics, producing mobile dwellings. Queer limitrophic dwelling is an ongoing practice that builds, preserves, and sustains transborder commuters' livelihoods through decentralized and ephemeral homes in the face of the USMBR's violence.

It is crucial to consider the role of a US address vis-à-vis queer limitrophic dwelling's material dimension. Esmeralda, a thirty-year-old Mexican woman working for a diversity, equity, and inclusion consulting firm, describes the importance of having a US address, especially when transborder commuting for school:

> It was [in high school], like so many of the people there lived in T. J. so it was super illegal to do, you couldn't live in Tijuana and cross, go to school there. It was forbidden by the school, but people still did it. And I didn't have an address in [the United States] so I remember my dad paid this lady to let us use her address. So, I used her address for a bit and then she's like "Oh now I want five hundred dollars a month." And my dad is like "What? She's not even living with you." So, he said no and then she called the school and told them that I wasn't living there and that I was just using her address. So then they were going to kick me out, but I was one of the only people registered to go to college, so then they were just like, "Just kidding! Just bring us another address!"

Transborder commuters complicate renderings of homes as private, immobile, and even locatable through an address. For example, Esmeralda notes how she needed an address to attend high school in San Diego because she did not want to attend school in Tijuana while residing there. Moreover, she foregrounds how this queer tactic was "super illegal to do" and "forbidden by the school." Having an address makes subjects spatially legible to the state, serving as normative surveillance technology and a method for distributing access to rights and privileges to denizens within its territory. In the United States, for example, one needs an address to open a bank account or obtain a driver's license. However, as Esmeralda's account demonstrates, one need not reside at the address one uses to obtain or access certain services. Her use of the woman's address is a queer tactic insofar as it subverts the assumption that an address refers to one's place of residence, transgressing the school's proscription against such practices. In this way, transborder commuters' desires propel them to find ways to be nominally present in the United States without necessarily being physically present, to bring desired experiences (e.g., education) closer.

Lizbeth, Noemi, Jose, Esmeralda, and other transborder commuters share similar material conditions and experiences despite their differing relations to power. This tension provides a glimpse of the affective and temporal dimensions of queer limitrophic dwelling tied to Ahmed's (2006) phenomenological approach to "orientation." Orientation refers to a subject's inherited directedness, their proximity to objects, and how they inhabit space and time (Ahmed 2006). For example, a "migrant orientation" may refer to "the lived experience of facing at least two directions: toward a home that has been lost, and to a place that is not yet home" (10). While productive, the migrant subject seems to move linearly between their "lost home" and "yet-to-be home" such that one home is eventually succeeded by the other in a stagelike progression. A transborder orientation, on the other hand, may require us to rethink the lost and yet-to-be home as experienced simultaneously and ephemerally, forcing us to consider instead the *helical temporalities* of home, dwelling, and belonging while highlighting the USMBR's role in producing a transborder orientation.

Border regimes condition transborder, migrant, and diasporic orientations, especially toward home and dwelling, but at US land ports of entry, proximity and distance are temporalized rather than spatialized. In other words, long wait times at ports of entry function like the significant distance that some diasporic communities negotiate through social relations or the circulation of material cultures between their multiple homes. This translation function may explain the commonalities *and* the differences between how transborder commuters and diasporic communities produce and experience ephemeral yet rooted transnational homes (see Hernandez 2023). Moreover, the USMBR delimits the proximities border residents and transborder commuters inherit and what types of objects are available to them through temporal sequestration (Avalos 2022). Queer limitrophic dwelling is a process *and* a set of life-making or queer tactics that help transborder commuters negotiate multiple temporalities and temporal sequestration. Transborder commuters persevere and dwell in the US-Mexico borderlands, a place often viewed through the lens of death.

Coda

The onset of the COVID-19 pandemic in 2020 forced me to think about home, perhaps because I could not leave the Midwest and return home to San Diego. I contemplated the many times my family and I had moved and when I left home for my undergraduate and graduate studies. I remembered the pain of constantly moving homes and how I had reviled transborder commuting and the work it took, but I did not have the language to name it. I gravitated toward scholarship on transnational migration and diasporic communities as well as queer and feminist scholarship on home and dwelling because the narratives and theoretical frameworks resonated with me but could not fully explain what I experienced. I found a gap in the literature, a place where my history and experiences and those of other transborder commuters could fit. At this time, I also turned to bell hooks's (1991: 11) article "Theory as Liberatory Praxis," in which she argues that "to name our pain, to theorize from that location" is a means of recovering one's voice *and* an act of collective healing for those who have been historically minoritized in the United States.

Queer limitrophic dwelling captures how transborder commuters *queer* Euro-American ideas of home, dwelling, and domesticity. This concept demonstrates how they navigate multiple temporalities and survive normalized conditions of displacement and mobility occasioned by US land ports of entry and racial capitalism. I have shown how transborder commuters decentralized their homes in Tijuana by drawing on transborder kinships and by making use of several life-making or queer tactics at the SYPOE and across San Diego. Crucially, transborder commuters adopt a queer perspective towards home and create ephemeral mobile dwellings to fulfill their commitments, such as work or to attend school. Thus, I show how dwelling is an ongoing process that simultaneously builds, preserves, and nourishes one's home, subjectivity, and livelihood. Queer limitrophic dwelling also underscores the need to foreground the role of border regimes in scholarship on transnational homes, especially in border regions, where cross-border mobilities might occur with a higher frequency, and port of entry temporalities take precedence over other temporalities. Moreover, it also pushes scholars to consider normativity vis-à-vis dwelling practices, expanding our understanding of material articulations of home and its association with privacy and a stable location (e.g., an address). While theorized from the San Diego-Tijuana borderlands, queer limitrophic dwelling can help scholars understand mobile populations' articulations of home and their dwelling practices as ongoing, historical processes enmeshed in power structures.

Taking my cue from Manalansan's (2014: 96) question of what makes a home queer if we approach home via affect and contingent "processes, behaviors, and situations" rather than solely through the lens of sexual identity, this article shifts our focus from examining the practice of dwelling within a fixed understanding of home to foregrounding queer dwelling practices in spaces within a limitrophe or borderland. It also shifts where qualitative analyses begin, from discrete identity categories to practices and material conditions that shape subjects and are shaped by subjects' practices.

Notes

I want to thank Ghassan Moussawi, Jessennya Hernandez, Soraya Cipolla, and Aparajita Santra for their helpful feedback on earlier versions of this essay. Additionally, I want to thank the Humanities Research Institute at the University of Illinois for their generous financial support. I also want to thank my interlocutors who shared their personal experiences for this essay and my dissertation. All translations are my own unless otherwise noted.

1. Following Moussawi and Vidal-Ortiz (2020), I use "queer" as a lens and method that analytically centers power relations, practices, normativity, and nonsexual terrains while decentering Euro-American forms of knowledge production. It foregrounds the *coconstitution* of structures of domination, how they produce normativity, and how minoritized subjects navigate and resist them (Moussawi and Vidal-Ortiz 2020).

2. Many of my interlocutors self-identified as "Mexicano/a," "Latino/a," or "Hispanic" while also noting that they were US citizens. I use the term Mexican American to capture this ambivalence.

3. I use "queer tactics" and "life-making strategies" interchangeably to highlight transborder commuters' queer and material dwelling practices as being productive and nourishing.

4. Through what Avalos and Moussawi (2023: 15) call "digital transborder kinships" found in these border Facebook groups, Lizbeth can access live information on SYPOE wait times, best transit routes, and general commuting information provided by other transborder commuters.

5. I refer to practices that help transborder commuters prepare for and navigate the physical, mental, and affective toll of transborder commuting as "waiting work."

6. Housing studies scholars have productively disentangled the theoretical differences between home and dwelling (see Coolen and Meesters 2012; Karjalainen 1993). However, this scholarship's conceptual disambiguation seldom considers the interplay between subjectivity, dwelling, home, and power.

References

Agamben, Giorgio. 2008. *State of Exception*. Chicago: University of Chicago Press.

Ahmed, Sara. 2006. "Orientations: Toward a Queer Phenomenology." *GLQ: A Journal of Lesbian and Gay Studies* 12, no. 4: 543–74. https://doi.org/10.1215/10642684 -2006-002.

Ahmed, Sara. 2019. "Queer Use." In *What's the Use? On the Uses of Use*, 197–229. Durham, NC: Duke University Press.

Ahmed, Sara, Claudia Castañeda, Anne-Marie Fortier, and Mimi Sheller. 2003. "Introduction: Uprootings/Regroundings: Questions of Home and Migration." In *Uprootings/ Regroundings: Questions of Home and Migration*, edited by Sara Ahmed, Claudia

Castañeda, Anne-Marie Fortier, and Mimi Sheller, 1–19. London: Bloomsbury Academic.

Anzaldúa, Gloria. 2002. "Preface: (Un)Natural Bridges, (Un)Safe Spaces." In *This Bridge We Call Home: Radical Visions for Transformation*, edited by Anzaldúa and AnaLouise Keating, 1–5. New York: Routledge.

Avalos, Miguel A. 2022. "Border Regimes and Temporal Sequestration: An Autoethnography of Waiting." *Sociological Review* 70, no. 1: 124–39. https://doi.org/10.1177/00380261211048884.

Avalos, Miguel A., and Ghassan Moussawi. 2023. "(Re)Framing the Emerging Mobility Regime at the US-Mexico Borderlands: COVID-19, Temporality, and Racial Capitalism." *Mobilities* 18, no. 3: 408–24. https://doi.org/10.1080/17450101.2022.2109986.

Bissell, David, and Andrew Gorman-Murray. 2020. "Mobile Dwelling." *Applied Mobilities* 5, no. 1: 1–5. https://doi.org/10.1080/23800127.2020.1716453.

Blunt, Alison, and Robyn Dowling. 2006. *Home*. New York: Routledge.

Bonfanti, Sara. 2020. "(Im)Materiality." In *Ethnographies of Home and Mobility: Shifting Roofs*, edited by Alejandro Miranda Nieto, Aurora Massa, and Sara Bonfanti, 39–65. New York: Routledge.

Coolen, Henny, and Janine Meesters. 2012. "Editorial Special Issue: House, Home and Dwelling." *Journal of Housing and the Built Environment* 27, no. 1: 1–10. https://doi.org/10.1007/s10901-011-9247-4.

Díaz-Barriga, Miguel, and Margaret E. Dorsey. 2020. *Fencing in Democracy: Border Walls, Necrocitizenship, and the Security State*. Global Insecurities. Durham, NC: Duke University Press.

Duggan, Lisa. 2003. *The Twilight of Equality? Neoliberalism, Cultural Politics, and the Attack on Democracy*. Boston: Beacon Press.

Ferguson, Roderick A. 2005. "Race-ing Homonormativity: Citizenship, Sociology, and Gay Identity." In *Black Queer Studies*, edited by E. Patrick Johnson and Mae G. Henderson, 52–67. Durham, NC: Duke University Press.

Fortier, Anne-Marie. 2001. "'Coming Home': Queer Migrations and Multiple Evocations of Home." *European Journal of Cultural Studies* 4, no. 4: 405–24. https://doi.org/10.1177/136754940100400403.

Gopinath, Gayatri. 2018. *Unruly Visions: The Aesthetic Practices of Queer Diaspora*. Durham, NC: Duke University Press. https://doi.org/10.1215/9781478002161.

Harrison, Paul. 2007. "The Space between Us: Opening Remarks on the Concept of Dwelling." *Environment and Planning D: Society and Space* 25, no. 4: 625–47.

Heidegger, Martin. (1951) 2012. "Building, Dwelling, Thinking." In *The Domestic Space Reader*, edited by Chiara Briganti and Kathy Mezei, 21–26. Toronto: University of Toronto Press.

Hernandez, Jessennya. 2023. "Queer Space Making across Greater Los Angeles: Reimagining Urban Autonomy through Collective Care." *Gender, Place & Culture*, October, 1–23. https://doi.org/10.1080/0966369X.2023.2265583.

hooks, bell. 1991. "Theory as Liberatory Practice." *Yale Journal of Law and Feminism* 4, no. 1: 1–12.

Kaplan, Amy. 1998. "Manifest Domesticity." *American Literature* 70, no. 3: 581–606. https://doi.org/10.2307/2902710.

Karjalainen, Pauli Tapani. 1993. "House, Home and the Place of Dwelling." *Scandinavian Housing and Planning Research* 10, no. 2: 65–74. https://doi.org/10.1080/02815739308730324.

Kay, Jilly Boyce. 2020. "'Stay the Fuck at Home!': Feminism, Family, and the Private Home in a Time of Coronavirus." *Feminist Media Studies* 20, no. 6: 883–88. https://doi.org/10.1080/14680777.2020.1765293.

Long, Joanna C. 2013. "Diasporic Dwelling: The Poetics of Domestic Space." *Gender, Place & Culture* 20, no. 3: 329–45. https://doi.org/10.1080/0966369X.2012.674932.

Manalansan, Martin F., IV. 2014. "The 'Stuff' of Archives: Mess, Migration, and Queer Lives." *Radical History Review*, no. 120: 94–107. https://doi.org/10.1215/01636545-2703742.

Manalansan, Martin F., IV. 2018. "Messy Mismeasures: Exploring the Wilderness of Queer Migrant Lives." *South Atlantic Quarterly* 117, no. 3: 491–506. https://doi.org/10.1215/00382876-6942105.

Márquez, John D. 2012. "Latinos as the 'Living Dead': Raciality, Expendability, and Border Militarization." *Latino Studies* 10, no. 4: 473–98. https://doi.org/10.1057/lst.2012.39.

Mbembe, Achille. 2003. "Necropolitcs." *Public Culture* 15, no. 1: 11–40. https://doi.org/10.1215/08992363-15-1-11.

Moussawi, Ghassan. 2020. *Disruptive Situations: Fractal Orientalism and Queer Strategies in Beirut.* Philadelphia: Temple University Press.

Moussawi, Ghassan, and Salvador Vidal-Ortiz. 2020. "A Queer Sociology: On Power, Race, and Decentering Whiteness." *Sociological Forum* 35, no. 4: 1272–89. https://doi.org/10.1111/socf.12647.

Rybczynski, Witold. 1987. *Home: A Short History of an Idea.* New York: Penguin.

Salter, Mark B. 2008. "When the Exception Becomes the Rule: Borders, Sovereignty, and Citizenship." *Citizenship Studies* 12, no. 4: 365–80. https://doi.org/10.1080/13621020802184234.

Stratford, Elaine. 2019. *Home, Nature, and the Feminine Ideal: Geographies of the Interior and of Empire.* Lanham, MD: Rowman & Littlefield.

Young, Iris Marion. 1997. *Intersecting Voices: Dilemmas of Gender, Political Philosophy, and Policy.* Dilemmas of Gender, Political Philosophy, and Policy. Princeton, NJ: Princeton University Press.

DISGENDERED

Imagining Homeless Kinships and Futures during the Great Depression

Cody C. St. Clair

*N*o future exists in homelessness, so it seems. To put this another way: under modern regimes of neoliberal racial capitalism, homelessness indexes an extreme vulnerability to premature death, to use Ruth Wilson Gilmore's (2022: 107) well-known definition of racism. Recent studies of homeless mortality in the United States estimate that homeless life expectancy is roughly thirty years lower than the national average.[1] Homeless life appears as stolen life, futures truncated by the immiserations of racial capitalism wherein the pursuit of accumulation and profit necessitates "relations of severe inequality" and "the unequal differentiation of human value" (Melamed 2015: 77). Stolen homeless life is the result of annihilatory logics baked into the last half century's politics of urban renewal and neoliberal austerity. As geographer Don Mitchell (1997: 305) declares in his seminal essay on antihomeless legislation, "By in effect annihilating the spaces in which the homeless must live, these laws seek simply to annihilate homeless people themselves." Racializing logics—"the division of humanity into 'worthy' and 'unworthy' forms" (Melamed 2015: 80)—give shape to this eliminationism, conceiving of homeless persons as a subhuman danger to the health and wealth of the nation-state.[2]

Dominant discourses on homelessness conceive its temporalities as directly opposed to those of the nation, understood here as the tripartite configuration of the state, the market, and civil society, three institutions in which homeless persons stand as surplus life, existing in near-absolute exclusion as agential subjects. The materiality of homeless immiseration forecloses futures and ends lives prematurely; in addition, the housed public sees homeless life as devoid of futurity and thus as unfit for the future-focused orientation of democratic citizenship.[3] As

GLQ 30:4

DOI 10.1215/10642684-11330994

© 2024 by Duke University Press

the production of homeless life, eviction and dispossession evacuate the body of its legible histories and futures, reducing it to its present embodiments of placelessness, dirtiness, begging, panhandling, scavenging, and squatting. The state, market, and civil society, in turn, deem these embodiments as dangerous, targeting the homeless for incarceration and death. When a population is dubbed futureless—with temporalities out of step with the market, civil society, and the heteropatriarchal home, as well as with embodiments unassimilable into gendered property relations—policies of eradication easily follow.

Scholars often spotlight how neoliberalism has produced contemporarily specific conditions of homeless immiseration and uniquely brutal antihomeless legislation, but the broader problem of homeless nonfuturity extends further back in time, at least to the Great Depression and the foundation of the New Deal welfare state. In highly simplified terms, the narrative of twentieth-century US political economy and poverty is as follows: the laissez-faire overaccumulation and extreme economic inequalities of the Progressive era precipitated the 1929 stock market crash and the resultant economic depression while also enlivening a militant labor movement and spurring demands for a social welfare state that would protect against future economic volatility and mass unemployment. These demands coalesced into multiple waves of relief, reform, and public works legislation that we today refer to collectively as the New Deal and its political descendent, the Great Society's "war on poverty." Beginning in the Nixon era and crystallizing under the Clinton administration, the rise of neoliberalism saw the dismantling of the New Deal order, the "end of welfare as we know it," and the transformation of the war on poverty into the "war against the poor" (Wacquant 2009: 49), the most bloodthirsty policies of which were and still are used against the homeless.[4] A customary rehearsal of this narrative comes from Leonard Feldman (2004: 2) when he declares that the war on poverty's "politics of compassion" during the 1960s and 1970s transformed into "a new war against the homeless" in the 1990s as municipalities deployed increasingly carceral tactics against homeless life. This account is accurate in some respects: the Clinton administration's passage of workfare and tough-on-crime legislation, for instance, has devastated Black, Latinx, Indigenous, and working-poor communities.[5] However, when looking at a longer history of antihomeless sentiment, this "new" war appears less as a break with the past than as an intensification of oppressive tactics long used by local governments to surveil and manage the homeless. When examining the Great Depression and New Deal eras from the perspective of those experiencing housing deprivation, we find stories that illustrate historical continuity with the neoliberal era, exposing a war against the homeless that long precedes the most horrifying examples at the turn of the millennium.

In US history, the Great Depression stands out foremost as an era of unparalleled economic hardship and mass unemployment that inaugurated our contemporary homeless crisis. When the federal government conducted a homeless census in 1933, it produced a conservative estimate of 1.2 million unhoused persons (Crouse 1986: 48). Ninety years later, estimates are unnervingly similar: in 2023, the executive director of the United States Interagency Council on Homelessness testified before the US Senate that no fewer than 1.2 million people suffer homelessness each year (Olivet 2023: 3). Depression-era cultural production, both shaped by and respondent to this unprecedented economic crisis, showcased an identifiably modern figure of the homeless subject, one who was not strictly the male vagrant of eras past but which now encompassed large numbers of women, children, and entire families. With its numbers growing and its faces changing, homelessness became a source of public panic and extensive sociological inquiry (DePastino 2003: 200–209). National and local newspapers devoted daily attention to evictions, detailing both mundane and sensational human-interest stories of how local municipalities were dispossessing civilians (St. Clair 2022: 502–7). Hollywood responded with melodramatic depictions of urban and migratory homeless life in such films as *Hallelujah, I'm a Bum* (1933), *Wild Boys of the Road* (1933), *One More Spring* (1935), *Modern Times* (1936), and *Girls of the Road* (1940). Likewise, representations of homelessness suffused US literary culture, not only in celebrated texts like John Dos Passos's *U.S.A.* (1937) and John Steinbeck's *The Grapes of Wrath* (1939) but also in a fervent proletarian literary culture that produced lesser-known works like Thomas Kromer's *Waiting for Nothing*, Edward Anderson's *Hungry Men*, Nelson Algren's *Somebody in Boots*, and H. T. Tsiang's *The Hanging on Union Square*. All published in 1935, these novels underscore homelessness as a condition of rightlessness where the homeless body's relation to the nation becomes reduced to and defined by the right to be dispossessed.

In what follows, I argue that the Depression stands as a wellspring of poetry and prose that imagines the stolen life of homelessness otherwise, that reads the embodiments and relationalities of homeless dispossession as an abolitionist horizon, cutting across the structural, epistemic violence of urban sociology, charity organizations, welfare bureaucracy, and the carceral state as well as practicing radical alternatives of relating to housing and of building coalitions. Arguably influenced by discourses on subproletarian pathology, myriad Depression-era writers regarded the homeless as bereft of futurity, the condition of unhoused immiseration conceived of as a state of social death that marked the homeless as kinless. This vein of Depression-era literature—found in the poetry of Thomas McGrath, the blues lyrics of Memphis Minnie, and the fiction of Edward Newhouse, Erskine Caldwell, and Meridel Le Sueur—conceives of homelessness as a *disgendering* experience in which the homeless body becomes an aberration from the heteropatriarchal gender binary. Depression-era literature, I maintain, illustrates how the social and juridical processes of disgendering target homeless women for incarceration, sterilization, and child theft and condemns homeless men's kinship and domesticity as an eradicable threat to social well-being. Alongside this literature, I locate a countercurrent that explores how, in the face of manifold economic, racialized, and gendered subjections, homeless persons continue to build kinships and collective futures that, albeit restrained by social death, manifest through and exceed their bare existence. In particular, I examine Philip Rahv's poem "Homeless but Not Motherless" (1934) and Le Sueur's novel *The Girl* (ca. 1939), finding in both a recognition not only of the disgendering violence of eviction but also of the potentialities for forging kinship across homeless exclusions from labor, housing, family, and civil society. Both texts envisage queer kinship and domesticity—as represented, in Rahv, by a homeless mother-son tramping duo and, in Le Sueur, by a community of homeless women squatting in an abandoned warehouse—as modalities of radical political belonging and comradeship that, I argue, open onto horizons of liberation.

Disgender

Eviction and homelessness are *disgendering* experiences in which the homeless body becomes an aberration from heteropatriarchy's schema of binary gender. Building on Hortense Spillers's (1987: 68) concept of "ungendered" flesh within the context of Black enslavement, this article's concept of *disgender* refers not only to ungendering as a "loss of gender" but also to the coterminous experience of being utterly gendered. In this sense, I derive two distinct etymological meanings of *dis-*, denoting reversal and removal as well as completeness and intensification. In her landmark essay, Spillers writes of the captive Black body's ungendering, arguing that enslavement dispossessed these bodies of kinship relations (and therefore of gender relations) such that the heteropatriarchal social signifiers of gender do not adequately capture Black lived experience. I contend that a comparable, though nonequivalent, racialized-gendered dispossession occurs in homeless embodiments across race.[6]

Disgender produces contradictory gender embodiments in the homeless body, a paradox that fluctuates between and encompasses both the *hyper* and the *hypo*. Feldman (2004: 11) explains a comparable phenomenon where he finds the homeless body as "always double," as embodying both sides of binary oppositions, such as sacred/profane and free/unfree. Interpreting the homeless body as a reservoir of paradoxical symbolic excess, Samira Kawash (1998: 319–20) describes a scene in a crowded subway car where a homeless body, "folded impossibly small," "immobile, [and] absolutely nonthreatening," is surrounded by empty seats "as though an invisible cordon has been established around this body signaling some danger." A scholar of Fanon, Kawash draws a parallel between the social productions of the homeless body and the Black body, recalling a comparable scene in *Black Skin, White Masks* (Fanon 2008: 92) where the Martinican philosopher describes how the racial epidermal schema triples the Black body's socioaffective reach in public space. The homeless body becomes both small and big, docile and dangerous, contradictions that racialize this body and its embodiments in public spaces, targeting it and subjecting it to state-sanctioned and extralegal violence.

My designation of the homeless body as a racialized embodiment—one that can but does not necessarily overlap with dominant epidermal taxonomies—builds upon Jodi Melamed's (2015: 81) discussion of the "racialized status" of the vagabond, a historic precursor to the modern social category of the homeless. Most of my archive's homeless characters are (probably) white, inasmuch as one presumes that an absence of explicit details about either skin color or racial-ethnic identity presupposes white skin and whiteness. Save for Memphis Minnie, a Black American blues singer, and Phillip Rahv, a Jewish Ukrainian writer, my archive's authors are also white vis-à-vis an early-twentieth-century racial schema. Still, I understand the political-economic production of homelessness itself as a racializing process that contravenes the social production of whiteness, which in the field of critical race studies often serves as shorthand for the cultural, economic, and political advantages "of having white or light colored skin" (Wray 2006: 5). Without denying the white skin of these authors and their respective characters, I maintain that this common conceptualization of whiteness does not sufficiently explain the racial and gendered embodiments of their homeless characters. If, as Lisa Cacho (2012: 17) writes, "race is the methodology of social value"; if as Melamed elaborates, the goal of racial capitalism is to produce and exploit *race* as the unequal distribution of human value for the purposes of expropriation and accumulation; if, as Gilmore (2022) identifies, the conditions of expropriation—this production and exploitation of unequal human value—create group-specific susceptibility to premature death; and if, under white supremacy, whiteness constitutes a political-economic category of prime valuation, then irrespective of epidermal taxonomy, homeless life, as surplus life targeted for premature death, is at odds with whiteness.

The material conditions of dispossession and immiseration produce the violent paradoxes of disgender. As such, disgender is not proportional to the more

generalized contradictions of gender that exist within all bodies under heteropatriarchal racial capitalism. Instead, disgender names a specific exclusion from
the social protections of gender that concurs with a subjection to the violence of
gender. Excluded from the right of entry that heteropatriarchal gender provides
into the life-sustaining relations of kinship and domesticity, homeless subjects are
subjected to the violence that produces and maintains these institutions. To be
homeless is not only to be "outside housing," writes Craig Willse (2015: 2); to be
homeless is also "to be very much caught inside this monster [of housing] that
distributes life chances and death likelihoods." To be disgendered is not only to
be evicted from heteropatriarchal kinship and domesticity but also to be trapped
within the political-economic force field that reproduces heteropatriarchal gender.
In the context of homeless women, Stephanie Golden offers a telling example of
disgender's violent operations. Detailing an appalling story of men urinating on
the heads of homeless women squatting beneath an elevated subway platform,
Golden (1992: 5) asks, "What could these men have seen when they looked at
those women to feel free to commit an act so breathtakingly vicious? . . . In a society that has always professed to respect women, often limiting their actions in the
name of protecting them," Golden writes, homeless women are conversely "hidden away at the margins of the city and treated like stray dogs." Golden finds
that the violence perpetrated against homeless women marks them as undeserv-
ing of protection—ungendering them as "unprotected female flesh" (Spillers 1987:
68)—not only because they are seen as subhuman nonwomen ("stray dogs") but
also because they are women, seemingly docile targets for gendered humiliation.
Gendering and ungendering "speak the same language" (Spillers 1987: 78). During the 1930s, such disgendering logics were used endlessly to describe the homeless woman in such terms as: a "masculine-minded travesty upon her sex" (Maxwell 1929: 292); "innocent depravity" (Vorse 1933: 356); and simultaneously prey
and predator, "hunted by railroad detectives, police, and degenerate men" while
also "liv[ing] a predatory and polyandrous existence" (Minehan 1934: 316, 335).
The era's breathless reportage on homeless women bespeaks how the paradoxes
of disgender further reified the gender binary, solidifying domestic ideologies of
women's protection in and by the home.

The discourse of disgender understood the homeless man as simultaneously
hypermasculine and hypomasculine, predator and prey. In the United States, the
notion that homeless men are pathologically savage and sexually violent dates as
far back as Reconstruction. In Francis Wayland's *Papers on Out-Door Relief and
Tramps* (1877: 11), he argues that the homeless tramp's "reign of terror" on civil
society consists of acts "worse than murder": "The innocent little maiden," "the

farmer's wife," and "the aged couple" were "alike the victims of [the tramp's] homicidal or licentious violence." Using language reminiscent of settler-colonial logics for the eradication of Indigenous nations, Lee O. Harris (1878: 269) imagines a US countryside in his novel *The Man Who Tramps* where homeless men, as "ravenous wolves and skulking savages," stalk and rape "wives and daughters" with impunity. Unbeholden to the "sacredness of family ties, the love of mother or wife, or child," the homeless man was a "depraved savage" (Wayland 1877: 10), living "a purely masculine life of self-directed indolence," lacking "the sexual self-government and moral incentives" of labor and family life (DePastino 2003: 27). As Skid Row sociologists Howard Bahr and Theodore Caplow (1973) write, the homeless man "is a man out of control" (58), disaffiliated from the "bonds that link settled persons to a network of interconnected social structures" (5). Yet, arguments about the inherent failed masculinity of homeless men equally abounded. For journalist William Slocum (1949: 63), the homeless man was the mama's boy "who had stayed home with Mother while the older brothers went out and got themselves set in business." As Slocum writes, "the doting mother" is to "blame for thousands who seek escape on Skid Row" (64), revealing a belief that overdomestication produced weak men who, as a result, failed in the capitalist marketplace, suffered chronic unemployment, and fell into homeless poverty. Both being too far from heteronormative domesticity and being too close to it were to blame for homeless men's gender troubles.

The era's disgendering logics conceived of the homeless body as teeming with contradictions that positioned both homeless men and women "as symbols of gender disorder" and "family breakdown" (DePastino 2003: 202), as renegades from the mandates of heteropatriarchal kinship. What Todd DePastino calls the "hobo panic" (216) of the 1930s was foremost a gender panic, an anxiety that homeless women would controvert the myth that masculinity is the property of men (Reckless 1934: 175). The flip side to the anxieties of homeless women was a panic about homeless masculinity infilled with a contradictory rhetoric of both excess and insufficiency, as writers like Cliff Maxwell (1929) and William Reckless (1934) feared that the gender embodiments of both homeless men and women signaled more broadly that men were losing their masculinity while women were unrightfully usurping it. While such logic was oversimplistic, it reflected, albeit fretfully, the material reality of homeless disgendering, evincing how the history of homeless dispossession is a history of queerness: of bodies violently excluded from, navigating the peripheries of, and cutting through the orbit of heteropatriarchal gender and kinship.

Kinlessness and the Right to be Dispossessed

In Depression-era representations of homeless life, to be disgendered—to be subjected to the violence of heteropatriarchal gender while being simultaneously excluded from its tenuous systems of privatized kinship and care—is to experience a form of death, a foreclosure of futures imaginable under the dominion of private property. Such is the affective landscape of homeless disgender and death that we find in Thomas McGrath's "poem to be nameless" (1940: 19–20), which intuits how, under a political-economic regime of private property, *home* and *future* become materially coextensive such that one cannot meaningfully exist without the other. To use Willse's phrasing (2015: 3), McGrath's poem theorizes the home as a biopolitical "technology that makes live and lets die," precipitating "possibilities for life and experiences of near death." Reflecting on both the material and metaphysical conditions of homeless immiseration, McGrath's (1940: 19–20) genderless persona is overcome with a sense of ontological annihilation that extends both forward and backward in time:

> the lilac lanes
> echoed once with our footsteps and now no more
> wake to our laughter or the sensuous air
> lave us with warmth or wet or weft of spring.
> .... look on the stones for our names.
> .... you do not remember our names.
> the marks on the trees are ours. in cornerstones
> some notes have been left lost no more
> of us remains but the dead words and the air
> turns the paper to ashes. in never spring
> we will return now. . . .
> .... our names
> were thick in the morgues. . . .
> we were always homeless. . . .
> we were exiles from tomorrow.

These lines' spatiotemporal distortions speak to feelings of eradication that absorb homeless life. The spring that the speaker remembers and longs for exists as both mythic past and impossible future ("never spring"), leading them to conclude that their homeless compatriots are "exiles from tomorrow." The poem then figures this condition of exiled futurity as a relation to the nation-state, to "the princely exultant names" printed in the newspapers that the homeless use for warmth ("wrapped in the proud names / we slept over ventilators"), an image that decries how the future of the nation—the modes of production and consumption that mythically secure its future—necessitates the futurelessness of homeless dispossession and immiseration (19).

In "poem to be nameless," the *lessness*es begin to pile up. Futurelessness bequeaths namelessness ("our useless names"), a condition of social illegibility, something that has no kin or kind to give it a history and future (20). Namelessness becomes kinlessness. The speaker feels his homelessness as a state devoid of love—"we had names. / one was for love. we lacked it"—where "names for love" connotes kinship as not only genealogy but also intimacy, sexuality, companionship, and caregiving (19–20). In the absence of love's affective bonds, the speaker's only means of affinity resides with and in lifeless objects: "the park benches knew us." "Our useless names" thus signals namelessness as a condition of reified anonymity. Homelessness evacuates one's subjectivity of its embodied particularities, becoming a condition of "bare genealogy" wherein the names of homeless persons do not function within the logics of gender, bloodline, or kinship (Bentley 2009: 271). This notion is mirrored in the nameless anonymity of the poem's speaker, whose voice feels genderless and whose depictions of homeless life markedly deviate from the tradition of staunchly masculine hobo poetry.[7] In its futurelessness, namelessness, and genderlessness, the homeless body becomes kinless, dispossessed not only of the kinship bonds that created and sustained it but also of any right to make new kin.

Kinlessness—a condition of rightlessness wherein one is dispossessed of any claim to the maintenance and production of kin relations—exemplifies the disgendering violence of homelessness. Depression-era writers of homeless life foreground kinlessness as constitutive of homeless immiseration, as legitimating their exclusion from socially privatized care networks as well as the destruction of homeless encampments, state-sanctioned child theft, and sterilization. This is not to say that the homeless lack kinfolk, be they consanguineous, affinal, or affiliative. For instance, Edward Newhouse's novel *You Can't Sleep Here* (1934) explores the modalities of fraught domesticity and kin-making that homeless men undertake in a New York City Hooverville, including how they come to build and share their dwellings as well as how the shanty town supplies them with a minimal sense of participation in the city's broader economic and political circuits. Still, the kinship forms that the homeless do build are constantly under threat of "breach" (Spillers 1987: 74)—the right to be dispossessed—by the state, the market, and civil society. At the novel's end, the city, at the behest of the Chamber of Commerce, demolishes the Hooverville, declaring the inhabitants' claims to their land and kinship illegitimate and deviant. The homeless men are merely "playing house" (Newhouse 1934: 160), a telling analogy that recognizes their domesticity as functionally comparable to the bourgeois home but figures it as a queer forgery that unlawfully circumvents the heteropatriarchal relations of private property. Further, the Chamber of Commerce decrees the encampment to be "a nuisance" to business, "a harmful influence on children" (evoking the threadbare anxieties around hobohemia as a geography of queer sexual enticement), and "bad for real estate values all around" (210–11).[8] This threat of breach—and its eventual execution—traces the kinlessness of homelessness.

Lizzie "Memphis Minnie" Douglas's 1936 blues song "Out in the Cold" represents homeless kinlessness as the exclusion from socially privatized care. The song opens with Douglas's abrupt eviction from her home as she croons, "I dreamt a dream last night I never dreamt before. / And when I woke up this morning, my trunk was setting outdoors." Singing on the street in the eviction's aftermath, the singer implies that she was evicted not only in the morning after she awoke but also during the night while she was dreaming: "That was me last night, hoo, hoo, you drove from your door" (Garon and Garon 2014: 270). This paradox suggests that the very act of her dreaming—perhaps of something utopian, beyond racial-gendered capitalism—is what gets her evicted. In its referent's vagueness, the "you" who evicted Douglas reads as possibly being not just her lover or family but also larger social actors—white landlordism and Jim Crow—that violently exclude her from the multiple protections of home as property, domesticity, womanhood, and citizenship. This choice to situate dreaming—the reproductive labors of both sleep and utopian desire—as the impetus for her eviction reads as a proleptic rebuttal to Gaston Bachelard's ([1958] 1994: 6) claim in *The Poetics of Space* that "the house shelters daydreaming." Although he ignores the unequal (read: classed and racialized) access to sanctified homemaking, Bachelard proffers a materialist understanding of dreamwork as an essential activity of domestic labor. Therefore, Douglas's song illustrates how her Black dreamwork—her domestic reproductive labor and her utopian longings—is unprotected by the home and constitutes a violation (of heteropatriarchal racial capitalism) that sanctions her eviction. In this act of dreaming—in those ecstatic interjections of "hoo, hoo" that both locate and cut through the moment of eviction—Douglas imagines an unspoken world of possibilities for Black and poor women's embodiments, which the eviction crushes by producing her body as unprotected ("my feets are near about froze") and kinless ("won't nobody open the door") (Garon and Garon 2014: 270).

In other Depression-era cultural texts, homeless kinlessness takes the form of pre- and postnatal severing of relations between parent and child through incarceration, child removal, and sterilization. These writers underscore how homeless persons are de facto disgendered from the sanctity of "the American family" that formed the supposed heart of the New Deal order.[9] Erskine Caldwell's 1933 short story "Slow Death" deftly illustrates the subjection of homeless families to a state of kinless breach and the prolonged conditions of immiseration that precipitate homeless mortality. The story focuses primarily on the character of Dave, a homeless man who is struck and fatally injured by a motorist who refuses to aid him. The titular slow death begins with Dave's starvation wages and then with a mass layoff that results in his wageless debt to a landlord who, in the dead of winter, removes the house's doors and windowpanes. With nowhere to go, Dave's family squats in a decaying, rain- and windswept house: "Two of the children died before January was over. In February his wife went. . . . Dave did not know whether his daughter had died. . . . The last time he had seen her was when a policeman came and took her away one morning, leaving Dave sitting in a corner of the windowless house" (Caldwell 1933: 28). Kinlessness surfaces when the conditions of homeless immiseration render kinship illegible within the heteropatriarchal, privatized terms of the home and family. Emphasizing this exclusion, "Slow Death" opens with images of homeless disgender as Caldwell uses animalistic imagery to describe the lifeways of shanty town residents living beneath a bridge, calling their makeshift dwellings "dog houses" and recounting how, "when babies were born, people leaned over the railings above and listened to the screams of birth and threw peanut shells over the side" (28). This representation of homeless life as subhuman sets the stage for the landlord's, the motorist's (as a symbol of civil society), and the state's eliminationist treatment of Dave's family. Excluded from the protections of the heteronormative nuclear family, Dave's family is still subject to its hegemony, their exclusion naturalized into a mark of individual failure and pathology that, in turn, legitimates the landlord's brutal eviction methods and the state's forced separation of Dave from his daughter. All of these various meanings of homeless kinlessness congeal into the symbol of Dave's "bum's blood" as both an imagined pathology of abjection justifying dispossession and death—"They don't want bum's blood on the goddam pretty upholstery"—and as the fleshy materiality of immiseration: "I had felt his heart beating as though I had held it in the palm of my hand" (29). Bum's blood is the opposite of the bloodline, of the heteronormative foundation of kinship ties through blood relation. Bum's blood is a negative pedigree that dissolves the lineal tissue that supposedly connects past and future generations, thus giving cause to the state of breach and bare genealogy that permits the neglect and death of homeless life.

In *The Girl* (ca. 1939), Meridel Le Sueur figures this negative pedigree and pathologization of homeless bodies within the context of eugenics discourses that understood homelessness in cultural terms, anticipating the neoliberal era's "culture of poverty" discourse, and that targeted these bodies for medical subjugation.[10] From the novel's beginning, the threats of sterilization and child theft loom for the unnamed homeless protagonist and the women who surround her: "I was lucky to have Clara showing me how to wander on the street and not be picked up by plainclothesmen and police matrons. They will pick you up, Clara told me, and give you tests and sterilize you. . . . Girl, [Amelia] said to me as I helped her, Girl I had six children. Yes six, and I saw in her eyes they were all gone" (Le Sueur [1978] 2022: 1, 10). This threat of sterilization and child removal persists until the novel's final chapters when the girl, pregnant, is institutionalized in a welfare maternity home: "She should be tested for sterilization after her baby is born. In our opinion sterilization would be advisable" (171).

Le Sueur based this section of *The Girl* on "Sequel to Love" (1935), a brief testimonial from a homeless woman facing sterilization, which the author published in a communist literary magazine. In this narrative, a first-person speaker, Margaret, tells of her present incarceration at the Faribault State School and Hospital in Minnesota, a "place where they keep the feeble-minded" (Le Sueur 1977: 11). Recounting how the state has already taken away one of her children, Margaret explains how Faribault refuses to release her until she submits to sterilization, a common eugenic practice that sought to control the reproductive capacities of poor and homeless women, whom many social scientists and medical professionals racialized and disgendered as undesirably hyperfertile.[11] As Margaret details, the sterilization and child theft intend her alienation from body and kin: "Workers ain't supposed to have any pleasure and now they're takin' that away . . . and they're afraid I'll have another baby" (11). Here, "pleasure" correlates kinship and kin-making with sexuality—"I like men. I ain't got any other pleasure but with men"—as well as with reproduction and child-rearing—"Pete and me sure had a cute kid, but we'll never see it no more"—leading Margaret to conclude, "They don't want us to have nothin'. Now they want to sterilize us so we won't have that," with *nothin'* capturing this double dispossession of kinship and sexuality (13). As Molly Ladd-Taylor (2017: 166) explains, Le Sueur represents the sterilization of homeless women "as the embodied violence of [racial] capitalism," in which some forms of kinship and kin-making are deemed unworthy of investment and are subjected to eradication, foreclosing the futures that the homeless strive to build under conditions of disgendered privation.

Impossible Kinships

But futurelessness and kinlessness are not the last words on homelessness. In this article's archive, each text invests in the impossible collectivities and futures that manifest through and beyond the conditions of bare genealogy. McGrath (1940: 19) speaks of the love he feels for the forgotten, nameless names of his homeless compatriots—"I love these names"—professing the possibility of a love born out of the conditions of kinlessness. By the poem's end, this love surges into exhortations of comradeship: "Comrades remember our names. / we fought too" (20). Identifying the constitutive queerness of comradeship, Jodi Dean (2019: 64, 65) writes, "Comrade relations are relations of a new type, relations that disrupt the confines of the family, heteropatriarchy, and binary gender," opening onto "a future characterized by . . . a love and respect between equals so great that it can't be contained in human relations" defined by the social dominations of racial capitalism. For McGrath, homeless bare genealogy becomes the fertile ground for comradeship. Comradeship as an emergent, generative mode of homeless kinship materializes at the end of Caldwell's "Slow Death," when the narrator, after being brutalized by a cop who arrives belatedly and heartlessly to the scene of Dave's death, is carried away to safety by a fellow homeless man. As the narrator regains consciousness, he sees "the policeman's nightstick protruding from his [rescuer's] coat pocket" (Caldwell 1933: 29). With the story ending here, the technology of state violence transforms into a symbol of subproletarian collective consciousness, of kin-making forged in both homeless subjection and resistance to state-sanctioned premature death. Comradeship remakes how we see the world, offering us visions of present material conditions burgeoning into relations of interdependence, love, and justice.

One noteworthy Depression-era poem that triangulates homeless kinship with queerness and comradeship is Philip Rahv's "Homeless but Not Motherless" (1934). Across five vignettes, Rahv's poem underscores how kinlessness opens onto forms of kinship beyond heteropatriarchy, following a homeless man as he tramps across the country and reunites with his homeless mother, who could be a biofamilial mother or, according to hobo argot, an older male lover.[12] The poem opens with a rejection of heteropatriarchal kinship, offering an image of diluted blood as a symbol of both queerness and comradeship:

> As the blood mingles with the pure liquid—
> the air of a fresh spring
> with the slogan ALL WAR FUNDS TO THE UNEMPLOYED
> the earth renews itself to me. (Rahv 1934: 17).

While evoking the bloodshed and kinlessness of "bum's blood" in Caldwell's story, Rahv's image of diluted blood runs parallel to an image of comradeship as encapsulated by a communist slogan often written on protest placards and chanted at unemployment marches.[13] Once the property relations of the bloodline are weakened and repudiated, comradeship emerges as a mode of creating kinship otherwise, of homeless kin-making on the paradomestic peripheries of private property. Throughout the poem, Rahv juxtaposes this invocation of blood against images of heteropatriarchal kinship, which the poem's speaker desires but then comes to reject as he chooses to forge kinship with his homeless mother. As the poem's first vignette concludes, the narrator, who is freight-hopping alone, imagines the possibility of alleviating his immiseration by way of heterosexual romance, visioning a cinematic scene at a "windswept crossing" where he meets a young woman who "will carry [him] off beyond the mountains" (17). Entering the second vignette, the narrator's heterosexual desire remains as he speaks of "local boys" parking their cars underneath the "swoonlight" of the backroads, although his reunion with his homeless mother soon supplants this desire, eschewing heteropatriarchal kinship for the queer kinship of the mother's boy:

> On a speeding train I sighted my mother
> dozing wrapped in her shabby coat . . .
> her image a live coal in the
> skull. (17)

By the third vignette, the speaker's heterosexual desire evolves into a critical understanding of heteropatriarchal property relations of gendered-economic domination as he sees a wealthy man and young woman scorn his mother ("homeless and gray as dust") as the couple pass her on the street and enter "a jewelry shop . . . to forge the metaphysic of dividends" (18). In the fourth and fifth vignettes, the speaker's companionship with his mother constitutes kin-making as care and social reproduction while also evolving into a modality of political belonging where the poem's opening radical demand finds its embodiment in the queer comradeship of homeless mother and son. As the poem concludes, the mother and son return to tramping "the wide road" where "business men drive by in fast procession"; however, the duo decides to turn away from the road and turn "their backs on the shiny limousines," culminating in their triumphal declaration:

> It is time to leave off the beaten path
> the old path . . .
> not downward and backward she laughs like a cannon shot
> but forward and upward I roar. (19)

For Rahv, this pivot toward the space on the side of the road is not escapist, nor is it solely a queer refusal of the road's velocity and violence, its nationalist myths of progress, individualism, and mobility. The space on the side of the road is a disgendered space, simultaneously excluded from but subjected to the ravaging velocities of capitalist production and accumulation. Yet, as Kathleen Stewart (1996: 34) writes, the space on the side of the road is as much a geography as it is an epistemology and affective orientation, a space ravaged by production that nevertheless produces new knowledge and feelings of what kinship, interdependence, and love can be. The counterknowledge we learn and counteraffects we feel from "Homeless but Not Motherless" are that the radical demands for economic justice and redistribution—"ALL WAR FUNDS TO THE UNEMPLOYED"—equally necessitate a radical redistribution of kinship. While the era's commentors panicked over the homeless man as a symbol of gender disorder and the undoing of patriarchal masculinity, this poem welcomes this undoing, finding in the much reviled, queer figure of the mother's boy an openness of radical possibilities, belongings, and pleasures. I might even venture so far as to contend that the mama's boy in Rahv's poem is the paradigmatic embodiment and praxis of the comrade, of an incorrigible devotion to shared struggle, and of the queer communist horizons of kinship that can transect and split open, "like a cannon shot," racial capitalist heteropatriarchy.

Postproperty Horizons

Marx and Engels ([1848] 2008: 59) notably called for the abolition of the family, advocating for a "social" education in its stead. Recently, feminist, queer, and trans scholars have rekindled this political horizon.[14] The most ambitious argument for family abolition comes from M. E. O'Brien (2023: 54), who argues that it "must necessarily be the concurrent overcoming of all the expressions of class society: wage labor, private property, the capitalist state, white supremacy, settler colonialism, and anti-Blackness." Here I want to home in on O'Brien's identification of the abolition of private property. The project of family abolition must necessarily entail the abolition of the home, of the commodified, privatized housing that daily narrows our horizons of collective belonging. If the heteropatriarchal bourgeois family constitutes the institution through which capital fully expropriates the value produced by the labor of social reproduction, this institution is literally housed, reproduced, and protected by the physical architecture of the home. As A. R. Veness (1992: 447–49) outlines in an essay on the transformations in housing types across the nineteenth and twentieth centuries, developments in racial capitalism during the industrial era demanded changes in housing architecture that effectively limited what counted as a home, permanently consigning much of the precariously employed and wageless subproletariat to severe housing insecurity and deprivation. "Home was redefined," writes Veness, "to separate and insulate it from the chaotic outside" (447), which included not only the political and public spheres, the market, and the workplace but also those whose kin relations did not match those of the white bourgeois family, namely Black, immigrant, and poor families whose low wages ensured they would never achieve the idealized home as hermetic sanctum. Likewise, forms of collective lodging were condemned and divested from, and "only those configurations of home that were domesticated and functionally subservient to" the interests of capital were approved and sanctioned as housing (449). Family abolition demands a wholesale reimagination of how we design and build residential infrastructure to facilitate the making and flourishing of kinship beyond the bloodline and heteropatriarchy.

In this article's archive of Depression-era literary texts of homeless life and kin-making, we are afforded glances into what postproperty, nonalienated social life and kinship could look like. We experience such a glimpse most potently in *The Girl*'s concluding scene, when Le Sueur's protagonist gives birth to a daughter among a community of women squatting in an abandoned warehouse under siege by the police. Moments before she goes into labor, the young woman suffers the death of her best friend, Clara, a sex worker committed to an asylum where she was tortured with electroshock. In the moments preceding Clara's death, the protagonist holds her friend's ravaged body in her arms as if Clara were her baby: "Clara clung to me and I just rocked her" (Le Sueur [1978] 2022: 186). In the aftermath of Clara's death, the women organize a hunger march where they chant, "Who killed Clara?" (195). Following the protest, as the police descend on the warehouse, the girl gives birth and, as she holds the child in her arms, the infant "turn[s] golden as Clara" (196), prompting the girl to name the baby after her comrade: "Light, I said, Claro Clara" (197). What strikes me most about this scene is how Le Sueur figures the girl's kinship with Clara as a form of reproductive labor that not only engenders the child to whom the girl births but also performs an act of collective love as justice for both deceased ancestors and living kin. In using both the masculine and feminine morphologies to name the baby, the scene's homeless disgender becomes queer kin-making as the girl memorializes Clara in the child's name and identifies the child as Clara's progeny. The girl becomes Clara's mother while Clara becomes the baby's flesh and blood, the baby's progenitor and ancestor. On the periphery of private property, excluded from the home and its architecture of heteropatriarchal kinship, reparative and liberatory kinships emanate from the immiserations of homeless disgender.

Kinship without the home—which is to say kinship without economies of austerity, dispossession, and premature death—is the postproperty future that Le Sueur offers us at her novel's end. Targeted for sterilization and child theft, the girl's pregnancy and childbirth are conditions of disgendered flesh that become the affective-material surplus of social life, the dreams and practices of freedom that open to possibilities of kin-making and loving otherwise.

To conclude, I turn my attention, still on Le Sueur (1977: 1–2), to a statement she made regarding the relationship between her writing and her political praxis:

> [These stories] are the words of women who are now dead, or lost, incarcerated in prisons or asylums, who forgot their names from shock treatments or lobotomies, who went insane from racism or rape. . . . You cannot find or claim them, or recognize them to even say their names. They are outside the economy, the statistics. You cannot even claim the bodies. . . . I saw in the newspaper the picture of an unclaimed body of a woman found raped and dead in the river brush. I went and claimed her.

Comradeship is the intractable devotion to the nameless living and the unnamed dead. Comradeship is the ineradicable struggle for an impossible reclamation and repair. In striving for this impossibility, comradeship is the manifestation of a queer love and dreaming for a radically just future.

Notes

1. See O'Connell (2005) and Hawke, Davis, and Erlenbusch (2007).
2. See Kawash (1998), Mitchell (2003), and Arnold (2004).
3. See Salamon (2010).
4. See Feldman (2004) and Willse (2015).
5. See Bertram (2015).
6. As Willse (2015: 11) writes, "Homelessness is the modern incarnation" of the "historical antecedents of conquest and slavery": just as enslavement created the conditions of possibility for capitalism's expropriation of surplus value, mass homelessness does the same for industrial and finance capitalism, creating and extracting value through the domination and precaritization of certain populations. On the functions of expropriation in racial capitalism, see Fraser (2016).

7. See DePastino (2003).
8. On the ubiquity and fears of male same-sexuality in hobohemia, see DePastino (2003: 85–91).
9. See Vale (2007) and Ryan (2015).
10. On the turn from biologically to culturally deterministic accounts of poverty in Depression-era sociology, see O'Connor (2001).
11. See Kline (2001) on the increased sterilization of poor women under the New Deal welfare state. On the eugenic racialization of hyperfertility, see Stern (2005).
12. See Anderson (1923: 302–3).
13. See Wagenknecht (1931: 341).
14. See Griffiths and Gleeson (2015) and Lewis (2022).

References

Anderson, Nels. 1923. "The Juvenile and the Tramp." *Journal of Criminal Law and Criminology* 14, no. 2: 290–312.

Arnold, Kathleen. 2004. *Homelessness, Citizenship, and Identity: The Uncanniness of Late Modernity.* Albany: State University of New York Press.

Bachelard, Gaston. (1958) 1994. *The Poetics of Space.* Translated by Maria Jolas. Boston: Beacon.

Bahr, Howard, and Theodore Caplow. 1973. *Old Men Drunk and Sober.* New York: New York University Press.

Bentley, Nancy. 2009. "The Fourth Dimension: Kinlessness and African American Narrative." *Critical Inquiry* 35: 270–92.

Bertram, Eva. 2015. *The Workfare State: Public Assistance Politics from the New Deal to the New Democrats.* Philadelphia: University of Pennsylvania Press.

Cacho, Lisa. 2012. *Social Death: Racialized Rightlessness and the Criminalization of the Unprotected.* New York: New York University Press.

Caldwell, Erskine. 1933. "Slow Death." *New Masses* 8, no. 6: 28–29.

Crouse, Joan. 1986. *The Homeless Transient in the Great Depression: New York State, 1929–1941.* Albany: State University of New York Press.

Dean, Jodi. 2019. *Comrade: An Essay on Political Belonging.* London: Verso.

DePastino, Todd. 2003. *Citizen Hobo: How a Century of Homelessness Shaped America.* Chicago: University of Chicago Press.

Fanon, Frantz. 2008. *Black Skin, White Masks.* Translated by Richard Philcox. New York: Grove Press.

Feldman, Leonard. 2004. *Citizens without Shelter: Homelessness, Democracy, and Political Exclusion.* Ithaca, NY: Cornell University Press.

Fraser, Nancy. 2016. "Expropriation and Exploitation in Racialized Capitalism: A Reply to Michael Dawson." *Critical Historical Studies* 3, no. 1: 163–78.

Garon, Paul, and Beth Garon. 2014. *Woman with Guitar: Memphis Minnie's Blues.* Revised and expanded edition. San Francisco: City Lights.

Gilmore, Ruth Wilson. 2022. "Race and Globalization." In *Abolition Geography: Essays towards Liberation*, edited by Brenna Bhandar and Alberto Toscano, 107–31. London: Verso.

Golden, Stephanie. 1992. *The Women Outside: Meanings and Myths of Homelessness.* Berkeley: University of California Press.

Griffiths, Kate Doyle, and Jules Joanne Gleeson. 2015. "Kinderkommunismus: A Feminist Analysis of the 21st Century Family and a Communist Proposal for Its Abolition." New Institute for Social Research. https://isr.press/Griffiths_Gleeson_Kinderkommunismus/index.html.

Harris, Lee O. 1878. *The Man Who Tramps.* Indianapolis: Douglass and Carlon.

Hawke, Whitney, Max Davis, and Bob Erlenbusch. 2007. *Dying without Dignity: Homeless Deaths in Los Angeles County: 2000–2007.* Los Angeles: Los Angeles Coalition to End Hunger & Homelessness.

Kawash, Samira. 1998. "The Homeless Body." *Public Culture* 10, no. 2: 319–39.

Kline, Wendy. 2001. *Building a Better Race: Gender, Sexuality, and Eugenics from the Turn of the Century to the Baby Boom.* Berkeley: University of California Press.

Ladd-Taylor, Molly. 2017. *Fixing the Poor: Eugenic Sterilization and Child Welfare in the Twentieth Century.* Baltimore: Johns Hopkins University Press

Le Sueur, Meridel. 1977. *Women on the Breadlines.* Cambridge, MA: West End Books.

Le Sueur, Meridel. (1978) 2022. *The Girl.* Minneapolis: Midwest Villages and Voices.

Lewis, Sophie. 2022. *Abolish the Family: A Manifesto for Care and Liberation.* London: Verso.

Marx, Karl, and Friedrich Engels. (1848) 2008. *The Communist Manifesto.* London: Pluto.

Maxwell, Cliff. 1929. "Lady Vagabonds." *Scribner's Magazine* 85, no. 3: 288–92.

McGrath, Thomas. 1940. *First Manifesto.* Baton Rouge, LA: Alan Swallow.

Melamed, Jodi. 2015. "Racial Capitalism." *Critical Ethnic Studies* 1, no. 1: 76–85.

Minehan, Thomas. 1934. "Girls of the Road." *Independent Woman*, no. 13: 316–17, 335.

Mitchell, Don. 1997. "The Annihilation of Space by Law: The Roots and Implications of Anti-Homeless Laws in the United States." *Antipode* 29, no 3: 303–35.

Mitchell, Don. 2003. *The Right to the City: Social Justice and the Fight for Public Space.* New York: Guilford.

Newhouse, Edward. 1934. *You Can't Sleep Here.* New York: Macaulay.

O'Brien, M. E. 2023. *Family Abolition: Capitalism and the Communizing of Care.* London: Pluto.

O'Connell, James. 2005. *Premature Mortality in Homeless Populations: A Review of the Literature.* Nashville, TN: National Healthcare for the Homeless Council.

O'Connor, Alice. 2001. *Poverty Knowledge: Social Science, Social Policy, and the Poor in Twentieth-Century US History.* Princeton, NJ: Princeton University Press.

Olivet, Jeff. 2023. *The Federal Strategic Plan to Prevent and End Homelessness*. Testimony before the Senate Housing, Transportation, and Community Development Subcommittee of the Banking, Housing, and Urban Affairs Committee, March 3.

Rahv, Philip. 1934. "Homeless but Not Motherless." *Partisan Review* 1, no. 2: 17–19.

Reckless, Walter. 1934. "Why Women Become Hoboes." *American Mercury* 31, no. 122: 175–80.

Ryan, Erica. 2015. *Red War on the Family: Sex, Gender, and Americanism in the First Red Scare*. Philadelphia: Temple University Press.

Salamon, Gayle. 2010. "Here Are the Dogs: Poverty in Theory." *Differences: A Journal of Feminist Cultural Studies* 21, no. 1: 169–77.

Slocum, William. 1949. "Skid Row U.S.A." *Collier's*, August 27, 26-27, 60-64.

Spillers, Hortense. 1987. "Mama's Baby, Papa's Maybe: An American Grammar Book." *Diacritics* 17, no. 2: 64–81.

St. Clair, Cody. 2022. "The Scene of Eviction: Reification and Resistance in Depression-Era Narratives of Dispossession." *American Literature* 94, no. 3: 497–525.

Stern, Alexandra. 2005. *Eugenic Nation: Faults and Frontiers of Better Breeding in Modern America*. Berkeley: University of California Press.

Stewart, Kathleen. 1996. *A Space on the Side of the Road: Cultural Politics in an "Other" America*. Princeton, NJ: Princeton University Press.

Vale, Lawrence. 2007. "The Ideological Origins of Affordable Homeownership Efforts." In *Chasing the American Dream: New Perspectives on Affordable Homeownership*, edited by William M. Rohe and Harry L. Watson, 12–40. Ithaca, NY: Cornell University Press.

Veness, A. R. 1992. "Home and Homelessness in the United States: Changing Ideals and Realities." *Society and Space* 10, no. 4: 445–68.

Vorse, Mary Heaton. 1933. "How Scottsboro Happened." *The New Republic* 74, no. 962: 356–58.

Wacquant, Loïc. 2009. *Punishing the Poor: The Neoliberal Government of Social Insecurity*. Durham, NC: Duke University Press.

Wagenknecht, Alfred. 1931. "The Struggle against Unemployment in the USA." *International Press Correspondence* 11, no. 7: 340–41.

Wayland, Francis. 1877. *On Out-Door Relief and Tramps*. New Haven, CT: Hoggins and Robinson.

Willse, Craig. 2015. *The Value of Homelessness: Managing Surplus Life in the United States*. Minneapolis: University of Minnesota Press.

Wray, Matt. 2006. *Not Quite White: White Trash and the Boundaries of Whiteness*. Durham, NC: Duke University Press.

COMMUNAL INTIMACIES

Bringing the Domestic into the Public

René Esparza

$\mathcal{W}$hat are for many Americans the common, though still criminal, acts of vagrancy, loitering, and trespass are for many poor, queer people of color the simple act of making a homespace in which they care for themselves and those they love. Privacy, Aída Hurtado (1989: 849) points out, hardly exists for the latter "except that which they manage to create and protect in an otherwise hostile environment." Given residential segregation, mass incarceration, and welfare reform, queer people of color must reshape and repurpose public and commercial space to collectively affirm their erotic desires and care for each other through what I describe as "communal intimacies." This article examines how the spatial-kinship practices of queer people of color, via their representation in two artistic works, reconstruct the public and private divide at the heart of spatial taxonomies in the West to erect queer architectures of the domestic.

Existing at the intersections of "economic precarity, racialized surveillance, and sexual respectability politics" (Plaster 2023: 32), queer people, particularly those who are working class and of color, grapple with a profound crisis of structural carelessness. Neoliberalism amplifies this chronic absence of care, allowing failures in caregiving to appear commonplace and acceptable across all levels as inevitable side effects of the pursuit of market-driven reforms and policies (Care Collective 2020: 10). Instead of investing in social provisions that enhance collective well-being, states opt for surveillance and criminalization against what Clare Sears (2014: 10–12) labels "problem bodies." These are the corporeal embodiments whose racially gendered presence in public space triggers suspicion and mobilizes the state's urban policing arsenal. In this environment of neglect, Said-iya Hartman (2017) reminds us, "care is the antidote to violence." These undesired forms of street life—sex workers, unhoused people, people who use drugs, people who have sex in public—find themselves stripped of what geographers label "the

GLQ 30:4

DOI 10.1215/10642684-11331138

© 2024 by Duke University Press

right to the city": the principle that everyone, regardless of their social or economic status, deserves to shape and participate in the development, management, and use of their city. Under neoliberalism, this right remains a privilege reserved for stakeholders who maintain a claim to private property (Harvey 2012: 4). Those not among these stakeholders become, by default, "problem bodies."

The fact that "problem bodies" are undesired does not mean they disappear from urban space primed for revitalization. Rather, in defiance of the racism and injustice that marginalizes them, they remain, hanging on tenaciously through not only individual moxie and ingenuity but more notably via the practices of love, solidarity, and mutual caretaking that I label *communal intimacies*. Communal intimacies represent forms of sociality that decouple care from the domestic, create a pathway for the transfer of libidinal pleasures, and act as a foundation for envisioning and enacting a world of belonging and transformation. In contrast to neoliberal ideology that empowers gentrification, communal intimacies offset the neoliberal curtailment of the social safety net, the reliance on carceral solutions to social problems, and the displacement that gentrification and heteropatriarchal investments among some families of color entail. They serve as world-making pathways to what Lauren Berlant and Michael Warner (1998: 558) identify as "queer counterpublics," sociocultural spaces where queer people come together to share experiences, express their identities, and foster a sense of belonging while contesting exclusionary bourgeois norms. A counterpublic provides a platform for the elaboration of new cultural and social realms where problem bodies can experience "forms of intimate association, vocabularies of affect, styles of embodiment, erotic practices, and relations of care and pedagogy" (Warner 2005: 57).

Queer counterpublics hold significance for queer people of color in light of the inherent contradictions within the American concept of "home." The maintenance of this space has historically relied on social divisions, such as the racial and gender-based division of domestic labor and the colonial extraction of labor in American colonies, that have rhetorically and materially defined domesticity by its exclusion of people of color (Lowe 2015). But if heterosexual people of color can try, however futilely, to aspire to respectable (white) notions of domesticity, *queer* people of color, often even further expelled by their families, cannot do so and instead turn to an alternative production of domestic relations (Reddy 1998: 359). Chandan Reddy (1998: 366), in his reading of the 1990 documentary *Paris Is Burning*, argues that the transformative potential of ballroom "houses" lies not in their members perpetuating an idealized alternative household but rather in members creating spaces where counterknowledges can emerge that envision and establish social relations distinct from the forms imposed by white heteropatriarchal domesticity. Marlon M. Bailey (2013: 99) offers an example in his concept of "housework," the nonmarket values of care, service, competition, and critique that assuage the debilitating consequences of HIV/AIDS in the daily lives of ballroom members. In Bailey's ethnography of Detroit's ballroom scene, Black LGBTQ people reconfigure kinship by viewing family as a social practice or a form of kin labor that accommodates diverse gender and sexual roles, as well as platonic parenting. Building upon "housework" and its challenge as to who can or should provide the care neoliberalism dictates that only the traditional "family" provides, communal intimacies venture a step further and challenge *where* care can happen, arguing that "home" is a place created by care, not a space purchased by the wages of heteronormativity (and homonormativity) and transacted by the state.

If, as communal intimacies propose, care can potentially happen anywhere, what of the forces that seek to limit the access of "problem bodies" to space? Put bluntly: what about gentrification? Martin Manalansan (2005: 141) has blasted gentrification in New York City as a "violent remapping" targeting queer people of color, but although it may have partially remapped where queer people of color act out their lives, it could not stop them. The Black and Latinx queer characters at the center of the following two cultural texts—John Leguizamo's performance of the "Manny the Fanny" character from his 1991 show *Mambo Mouth*, and Sean Baker's 2015 film *Tangerine*—find themselves barred, like most "problem bodies," from what Gayle Rubin (2006) describes as the "charmed circle": the socially and culturally accepted set of sexual practices and identities considered normal, natural, and morally acceptable within a given society.

It is noteworthy that these texts traverse historical and geographical boundaries because that allows us to document representations of queer sociality overshadowed by homonormative narratives of pride and progress. When *Tangerine* was released in 2015, material conditions for some queer people of color remained as bleak as they had been when Leguizamo performed his show in 1991. Moreover, the geographical diversity across New York City and Los Angeles in these texts underscores the pervasiveness of gentrification in urban centers across the United States, highlighting its different forms and levels. It also sheds light on the potential for collective ties across spatial and identitarian lines. If we think about queerness as relational to power in the Cathy J. Cohen (1997) sense, then we can see how queerness—the "outer limits" in Rubin's case—is also a spatial location relative to private property ownership and the care that is privatized therein.

In addition to offering a critical assessment of gentrification's insidious consequences, these texts show how representation itself can point to alternative community formations. Aesthetics as expressed through print and visual culture play a role in shaping and mediating these alternative community formations. Tyler Bradway and Elizabeth Freeman (2022: 4) introduce "kin-aesthetics" as a methodology within queer kinship theory to understand "how processes of *figuration*, whether they take place as social practice or in imaginative texts, de-form and re-form the categories and genres by which we experience our relationships." Through an exploration of representational strategies, kin-aesthetics reconfigure the social by offering a glimpse into the emergence of new relational forms.

While neoliberalism functions as a territorializing spatial practice by violently demarcating public from private through privatization, gentrification, and securitization, the caregiving practices depicted in these queer characters' lives work to deterritorialize public and private spheres, disrupting the traditional link between care and the domestic. Consequently, the communal intimacies portrayed in these texts offer countermaps—what Juana María Rodríguez (2003: 39) calls "cartographies of insurgency"—to navigate the terrains of racist impoverishment, heteropatriarchal investment, and revanchist urbanism.

Home Is Where the Care Is

With so few economic opportunities provided to queer people of color within expanding, gentrifying neoliberal spaces, sex work emerges as a recurring common theme in the two cultural texts. In the 1991 HBO comedy special *Mambo Mouth*, based on John Leguizamo's award-winning off-Broadway show, Leguizamo hybridizes comedic and dramatic styles to speak about race, class, gender, and sexuality, focusing on how these dynamics impact Latinx people. Leguizamo, of Colombian and Puerto Rican descent, draws from his upbringing in New York City in the 1970s and 1980s, a time when the city became bankrupt and subsequently witnessed the epidemics of AIDS, drugs, and crime (Garcia and Cole 1991). Through five one-man performances, he confronts Latinx stereotypes, including the egotistical Latin lover, an undocumented Mexican detainee, a "reformed" Latinx man pitching the benefits of assimilation, and finally Manny the Fanny (Chirico 2002). A feisty, self-assured, finger-snapping woman, Manny is a transgender Latinx sex worker who takes the stage—a set with graffiti-decorated street bills plastered on brick walls—voguing to the 1987 Pebbles song of female empowerment, "Girlfriend." She has long orange hair and shiny lipstick to match (fig. 1). She wears a skintight hot-pink minidress, black patent-leather pumps, door-knocker earrings, and large, jangly bracelets, and in her black evening bag, she carries a giant knife.

Although Leguizamo presents himself as a cisgender, heterosexual man, he has, according to scholars, if not embraced queer representations then at least

Figure 1. "Manny the Fanny," John Leguizamo's *Mambo Mouth*, HBO, 1991.

been comfortable with them. Mainstream cultural depictions of Latinx masculinity often center around machismo, an exaggerated sense of manliness characterized by dominance, aggression, and emotional suppression. According to Gloria
Anzaldúa (1987: 105), machismo among Latinx men is more of "an adaptation to
oppression and poverty and low self-esteem," the product of "hierarchical male
dominance." Fueled by uncertainty about providing for and protecting his family,
the macho oppresses and even brutalizes women and sexual minorities to offset his
shame. In this context, Leguizamo's deconstruction of machismo becomes particularly meaningful. By challenging the traditional expectations linked to masculinity
among Latinx men, he actively rejects the oppressive aspects that Anzaldúa identifies. Even the most ardently heterosexual character in his performance suggests
a defiance of heteronormative ideals. According to Daniel Enrique Pérez (2009:
40), the *Mambo Mouth* character of Agamemnon—a "traditional" Latin lover with
an unpredictable sexual appetite—implies ambiguity in terms of sexual choices,
and the character's inability to maintain a relationship with one woman suggests
queerness. In 1991, even *suggesting* a queer identity was already provocative, and
explicitly depicting a Latinx transgender woman was virtually unheard of in popular media.

Throughout his career, Leguizamo has taken on such female characters,
from Manny the Fanny in *Mambo Mouth* to drag queen Chi-Chi Rodriguez in

the 1995 film *To Wong Foo, Thanks for Everything! Julie Newmar*. Rather than reducing these characters to mere caricatures, Leguizamo crafts them as fully fleshed-out individuals with their own struggles and aspirations. For instance, in *To Wong Foo*, Leguizamo deliberately addresses internalized racism by tracing Chi-Chi's evolving makeup to match her skin tone, a sign she has come to accept her Latinxness (Rodriguez 2019). His artistic endeavors can be interpreted as a form of social commentary, challenging detrimental stereotypes and advocating for a more inclusive perspective of gender nonnormative people within Latinx communities. Reflecting on the twenty-fifth anniversary of *To Wong Foo*, Leguizamo shared in an interview that over the years, he has received "lots of fan mail from LGBTQ teens telling me how my character helped them come out to their parents." However, he acknowledges the changing landscape, and he emphasizes the importance of providing opportunities for transgender actors to portray such roles in the 2020s: "Not everybody is allowed to play everything, so until we get to that place, it is important for trans actors to get a chance to act" (Kacala 2020).

Manny's scene in *Mambo Mouth* begins when she, who has just been ejected from a restaurant, shouts at the owners: "You people come here, you gentrify the neighborhood, you kick us out, and then you won't let us use the bathroom? You can kiss my amber ass" (Leguizamo 2008: 222). She yells to nearby cops that there is "a case of discrimination going on over here," but when they ignore her, she taunts them with pig noises. Even so, her actions can be interpreted as playful, even coquettish. Her coyness, however, is a rickety barricade from which she lobs critiques of policing and her scorn for it. After telling the cops not to give her that "butch look" and to save it for "the cow at home," Manny quickly retracts with an innocent "Oops—was that me?" Manny toys with them, saying: "This girl's got a big mouth, but she knows how to use it!" She knows the police surveil the area for quality-of-life violations now that restaurants have encroached on the area, and she accepts law enforcement as part of the scenery, but nonetheless she expresses her opprobrium through a gendered flirtatiousness, a strategy available to her as a transgender Latinx sex worker. Under "broken windows policing," a strategy focusing on minor offenses and visible signs of disorder to prevent more serious crimes, police target sex workers (Gray Fischer 2022), but transgender women experience the added burden of being surveilled for being gender nonnormative, a phenomenon that activists and advocates often call "walking while trans" (Panfil 2021: 73).

Manny's behavior could be dismissed by those operating and shaping neoliberal spaces as flippant and even immature, but she better reflects the figure of the "banshee" girl or the *chusma*. *Chusmería* represents a form of unruly behavior enacted by subaltern subjects that subverts conventions of bourgeois comportment within the majoritarian public sphere. Brash and loud, the *chusmería* aesthetic straddles the deliberately tacky, and their sexuality appears excessive and flagrant (Muñoz 1999: 182). In contrast to the neoliberal mandate of purifying the majoritarian public sphere of what Deborah Vargas (2014: 715) calls *"suciedad,"* or dirt, the subaltern behaviors of *chusmas* defy it, effectively announcing both their disapproval of the attempt and celebrating the inability of authorities to "clean up" and remove "filth" like them. Like the accumulation of dirt, *suciedad* indexes the surplus populations that real estate interests deem disposable, those "problem bodies" whose presence threatens the idealized domestic and consumer bliss of a gentrified landscape.

Manny lives in the earliest years of New York Mayor Rudolph Giuliani's quality-of-life campaign, during which police forces not only patrolled wealthier neighborhoods but also sought to eliminate "filth" like her from areas primed for revitalization (Warner 1999: 157–61). The very fact that she needs to piss—and will probably do so on the street—telegraphs that Manny is part of the *suciedad.* Yet her playfulness and the fact that she never breaks any law outright—or at least not in front of the police—allow her to push back and keep a stake in the community that was once hers. By contesting her forced removal, Manny carves out a space for herself to exist and in which to create communal intimacies.

Communal intimacies disrupt conventional notions of care and caretaking not only because they unfold on public streets but also because the needs and desires of those most vulnerable are not normative, and those addressing these needs have limited abilities. If Manny had surrendered to dictates—implied or explicit—to move along until she was undetectable, she would not have been available to her girlfriend Rosanna as she passed along with her face covered. Eager to share details of her previous night's date with a *"papi,"* Manny halts Rosanna, urging her to reveal her face, only to recoil in shock at the bruises. The audience learns that Angel, Manny's brother, beat Rosanna. Manny angrily offers to "hurt him" for Rosanna and "cut his motherfucking *pipi* off" (Leguizamo 2008: 225). In the exchange that follows, Manny advises Rosanna how to exact revenge against someone who has wronged her. Although violently vengeful, the tale bares the broad contours of communal intimacies. In a context where queer people of color lack legal recourse to remedy the wrongs done to them, tutoring a loved one in the kind and level of acceptable violence to protect oneself constitutes an act of care.

Moved by Rosanna's suffering, Manny recounts how she too had once been a *"pendeja"* who handed over "all [her] money, pawned all [her] possessions, and gave up a once-promising career as a cosmetologist" only to find that her "dark prince" spent it on other "bimbettes." Enraged and aware that she had no power within the contours of the law to exact justice, "Sleeping Beauty awoke!" Manny declares. She chose revenge, and one night, as she waited for her lover, she hid in the closet with an iron in one hand and a tube of Krazy Glue in the other. Once the "Judas *hijo de puta*" arrived, she "popped out and conked him on the head with the iron." She "undid his zipper, took out his big ol' *pinga*, and put Krazy Glue up and down, and slapped it to his thigh." She then "dragged the body out and locked the door." Her now-former lover screamed that he would kill her, but Manny ignored him. She reminded Rosanna that "life is too short to let people crush your world" (225–27). Manny accepts that, for a variety of reasons, Rosanna is unlikely to leave Angel now, but she can see in her friend the potential to do so, and she predicts that a day may come when Rosanna herself is hiding in the closet with an iron in one hand and Krazy Glue in the other. "But until that day," Manny advises, "don't live on dreams. Because there are no Prince Charmings coming to save you. Just a lot of frogs" (227).

Manny's on-the-street caretaking of Rosanna, offering both an immediate solution (to hurt her abuser and sever his penis) and a future plan (to exact revenge when she is ready), might appear unrecognizable as a form of care from a privileged standpoint, which pathologizes women who enact violence, particularly if they reap satisfaction from it, as Ruby C. Tapia (2022) reminds us. Such a viewpoint typically assumes that Rosanna has alternatives, among them police intervention and access to women's shelters. However, for some women, particularly those who are poor, Black, and/or Latinx, legal options may be nonexistent. Without institutional support, Rosanna likely felt trapped, lacking financial means or a safe place to go, and even fearing for her life. In this context, Manny's offers and teachings of violence represent queer acts of caretaking, forming communal intimacies.

Manny's confession and advice encourage Rosanna to imagine shifting power dynamics and rejoice in her own empowering, violent revenge fantasy. Although this exchange deviates from conventional notions of care, it meets Rosanna's needs by reminding her she has power—a form of caregiving that Manny, as a vulnerable transgender sex worker threatened with displacement, is uniquely positioned to provide. When women like Manny and Rosanna engage in violence, not as a mimicry of masculinity but as a tangible manifestation of breaking free from violent histories, it represents a radical opening toward new models of care (Tapia 2022).

By bringing private rituals into the public realm, these communal intimacies expose "the artifice of the public/private dichotomy" (Valentine 1996:

154). Manny treats the run-down street corner inhabited by working girls not as a spoiled space, a lot whose only value is its potential redevelopment. Instead, she treats that urban topography as a regenerative hub of communal care. Out of a very anti-queer propertied regime, Manny extrapolates a queer counterpublic where caretaking extends beyond the confines of the private sphere.

Navigating to the Multiple Places of Home

In 1991, during the release of *Mambo Mouth*, LGBTQ Americans were grappling with widespread rates of HIV/AIDS and coming off a decade of social cutbacks and repressive legislation. When routine political channels like lobbying, letter writing, and routine marches proved ineffective in prompting federal action, oppositional AIDS activist groups took to the streets, employing civil disobedience and raucous demonstrations to raise awareness and influence policy changes. By 1992, however, the direct-action AIDS movement began to decline, in part due to a shifting landscape enabled by legal and social openings for *some* LGBTQ people (Gould 2009: 303). With the possibility of social acceptance, there was much to lose and very little to gain by continuing to act out. After the 1996 introduction of protease inhibitors to treat HIV, AIDS went from being a death sentence to a chronic but manageable condition for those with access to pharmaceuticals, prompting the likes of Andrew Sullivan (1996) to suggest AIDS was over. For Sarah Schulman (2012: 49, 71), however, this moment, when the direct-action politics of ACT UP gave way to a politics of assimilation, marked the beginning of "gentrified thought" in the mainstream LGBTQ rights movement, a moment that coincided with the shrinking in economies—and spaces—of mutual care.

The shift toward homonormativity in LGBTQ politics marked a departure from the progressive and radical left politics of the 1960s and 1970s. This movement, focused on transforming personal life by challenging prevailing norms of public and private, evolved into a neoliberal approach emphasizing a "stripped-down, non-redistributive form of 'equality'" that prioritized domestic privacy, the free market, and patriotism (Duggan 2003: xii, 45). Examining the Supreme Court's 2003 ruling in *Lawrence v. Texas*, David L. Eng (2010: 45) argues that the ruling extended the right to privacy to gay men and lesbians "willing to comply with [the state's] normative dictates of bourgeois intimacy, and able to afford the comforts of bourgeois domesticity." By conferring legalized privacy onto some forms of intimacy over others, *Lawrence* reinscribed "a traditional divide between the public and private" (43). Departing from previous discourses linking homosexuality to vice, deviance, and criminality, homonormative narratives, like those used in *Lawrence*, present homosexuality as socially acceptable; but to do so, they must disregard race and the vast economic inequalities that hinder progress for poor queer people of color. In her critique of Dan Savage's 2010 "It Gets Better" campaign, Jasbir Puar (2010: 151) argues that Savage's declaration operates within this homonormative framework as a directive to assimilate into urban, neoliberal gay communities. But as Tavia Nyong'o (2010) emphasizes, "Lots of folks, particularly the gender nonconforming and/or trans, never 'grow out' of the kinds of social reprisals for being physically different." For this reason, subjects like Manny cannot be inspirationally hailed by white gay male liberals. Their stories challenge the teleology of homonormativity by illustrating the impossibility of closure in narratives of racialized and gendered trauma. These stories also undermine the homonormative tendency to delineate public and private as distinct spheres, a theme echoed in Sean Baker's 2015 critically acclaimed indie film *Tangerine*.

"Merry Christmas Eve, bitch," are the opening words in *Tangerine*, which follows Sin-Dee Rella (Kitana Kiki Rodriguez) and Alexandra (Mya Taylor), two transgender sex workers of color in south Los Angeles, during a whirlwind Christmas Eve. Baker, known for humanizing marginalized groups in his films, continues this theme by casting transgender actresses in their debut feature film. While conducting research for the film, Baker—a cisgender, heterosexual white man—met Taylor at the LA LGBT Center. Taylor then introduced him to her friend Rodriguez, who worked as an educator at an HIV/AIDS research center. Together, Taylor and Rodriguez helped Baker with the development of the story, incorporating their own experiences and their knowledge of the local transgender community into the script (Watercutter 2015). Chiefly, they impressed upon Baker the centrality of transience among transgender women of color, a theme Baker made central to the plot via movement. While Taylor and Rodriguez's collaboration might have legitimized the film as a "trans product," challenging the practice of casting cisgender men and undermining narratives of gender dysphoria common in cinematic representations of transgender women, the women did not receive story or screenwriting credits (Macintosh 2023: 226). For this reason, Paige Macintosh (229) warns that, despite the increasing inclusion of transgender roles in films, such inclusion can serve as a facade of progressiveness for film industry elites while denying cultural and financial benefits to transgender performers like Taylor and Rodriguez.

If Manny has only a single corner to enact her care, Sin-Dee and Alexandra have all of Los Angeles. This is by necessity, for queer people of color have to navigate restrictions on their mobility amid the neoliberal restructuring of urban space. Under neoliberal property regimes, an owner uncontestably lays claim to

Figure 2. Sin-Dee Rella (Kitana Kiki Rodriguez) and Alexandra (Mya Taylor), *Tangerine*, Magnolia Pictures, 2015.

the home, but those excluded from the private housing market—like Sin-Dee and Alexandra—must navigate their way to spaces where they can invent their version of caretaking. In addition, given their contestable right to any one space, they must constantly reestablish their claim to it. Given the physical machinery of gentrification that pushes them along, they must move and return, migrating to different locations as opportunities allow. This behavior echoes Theodore Greene's (2014: 100) concept of "vicarious citizenship," or the enactment of rights based on symbolic ties to a neighborhood rather than physical residence. This notion highlights how marginalized individuals, often targeted for exclusion through pricing or policing, employ socioterritorial practices to reshape ideas of community belonging and redefine the boundaries between public and private. Sin-Dee and Alexandra's public display of care unfolds as a transformative spectacle, turning pockets of the bustling Los Angeles streets into a personalized sanctuary of their own making.

The film opens on the morning of Christmas Eve at Donut Time, a twenty-four-hour bakery in east Hollywood that serves as the duo's makeshift living room, where quotidian yet important emotional interactions play out (fig. 2). (In real life, Donut Time had long served as a refuge for transgender sex workers earning a living on the nearby streets.) Sin-Dee, recently released from prison for drug possession (after taking the fall for her boyfriend/pimp), spends her last $2 on a celebratory red-and-green sprinkled donut she shares with Alexandra, the only friend there to welcome her. Even though the two friends are quite different—Alexandra is tall, elegant, and contemplative, while Sin-Dee smaller, quicker, and mercurial—

they fiercely protect each other. They sit opposite one another, Sin-Dee sporting a Tina Turner–style blonde wig, a leopard-print top, and white hot pants, and Alexandra a long, silky curtain of raven hair but more upkept street fashions. The two sit in a booth as, behind them, through smudged windows, people navigate a bustling sidewalk and traffic ekes through a congested intersection. As the camera pans, the streets seamlessly meld into these initial frames, establishing a visual continuum that signifies the women as integral extensions of the urban landscape.

The celebration does not last long, however, as Alexandra reveals that Chester (James Ransone), Sin-Dee's boyfriend/pimp—a scrawny, tattooed, white gangster-wannabe—has been unfaithful with one of his new girls, whom Alexandra describes as a white "fish," a biological woman by the name of Dinah (Mickey O'Hagan). Incensed, Sin-Dee storms off on a vengeful mission to track down and confront Chester and her competition. Broke, she ventures out on foot, and with Eurohouse beats punctuating her every stomp, Sin-Dee takes the audience on a frenetic tour through some of the grittiest neighborhoods of Los Angeles, a stark contrast to the tourist clichés of Hollywood and the glitz and glamour of Beverly Hills. The cityscape amounts to its own character in the film, but whereas the film has other Angelenos trapped in the traffic of urban sprawl, Sin-Dee bypasses the standstill—breezing past the occasional "Do Not Enter" sign—via public transportation and on foot.

In one of the film's more raucous scenes, Sin-Dee barges into a filthy motel-room brothel packed with sex workers and their clients. As the johns, in various stages of undress, look on aghast, Sin-Dee drags a shoeless and shrieking Dinah by her wispy blonde hair onto a public bus, sneaking through the back door. Seemingly violent and adversarial, the dynamic between Sin-Dee and Dinah actually helps reveal how communal intimacies can form in the most unexpected places among unexpected people and can reflect the desires and longings of those in need. At an impromptu stop at a nightclub to see Alexandra sing, Sin-Dee and Dinah sneak into the bathroom to smoke meth. There, Sin-Dee applies a little rouge to Dinah's pale cheeks and teaches her how to apply lipstick. The two women see and recognize in each other a shared pursuit of a high. The application of makeup—a desire for beauty despite the toll meth might take—signals a moment of tenderness between two romantic rivals and serves as evidence of the unspoken bonds between two working girls in the sprawling informal sex industry of Los Angeles.

While viewers might perceive this scene as detrimental to the characters, it actually embodies a form of care. A comparable scenario featuring middle-class white women sharing wine in an upscale home or exchanging prescription pills could easily be seen as a gendered form of nurturing inherent in women's friendships. However, due to the demonization of street drugs and the devaluation of sex workers, these acts of communal intimacy, occurring in a public bathroom, challenge audiences' notions of "caregiving." Meth, in this context, serves as a means of self-medication, numbing individuals to their pain, while makeup becomes an indispensable tool in these women's profession, playing a crucial role in how they present themselves as desirable and, in Sin-Dee's case, "real."

After Alexandra's nightclub performance, the duo of Sin-Dee and Alexandra take a captive Dinah back to Donut Time, where Sin-Dee finally confronts her boyfriend/pimp, Chester. In a bid to redirect Sin-Dee's anger, Chester reveals that while Sin-Dee was imprisoned he slept with Alexandra. Betrayed, Sin-Dee flees Donut Time and hits the streets in search of a client, perhaps for a quick fix of a street narcotic. A car of boisterous men lures Sin-Dee in with the promise of sex work, but instead they hurl a bucket of urine on her and mockingly wish her a "Merry Christmas, you tranny faggot!" Alexandra rushes to her aid, taking her by the hand to a nearby laundromat. There, she helps Sin-Dee undress, removes her soiled wig, and places everything in a washer before helping Sin-Dee wash off in a sink. Stripped of her wig and breast inserts, exposed and vulnerable, Sin-Dee curls into herself, but Alexandra removes her own wig and hands it over to Sin-Dee to wear while they silently wait for the wash cycle. The film's oversaturated colors, previously casting an otherworldly, shimmering, sepia glow, now shift to muted, desaturated tones, reflecting the harsh reality of violence against transgender people.

The film's opening and closing scenes highlight the significance of communal intimacies between Sin-Dee and Alexandra. It starts with them sharing a donut, an item of sustenance, because they cannot each afford to have a donut of their own. The closing scene, set near the initial location, depicts the friends—despite one feeling betrayed—sharing a wig, a symbolic shield meant to protect an aggrieved Sin-Dee from the undeniable violence that afflicts transgender women of color. For poor, transgender women of color engaged in sex work, the wig helps construct racialized genders and sexualities (Bost 2019: 36; Bailey 2013: 58). Customers typically gravitate toward sex workers who depict "realness"—that is, those who pass as women. In a public laundromat, accessible to anyone, Alexandra exposes herself—coming across as "not real"—both as a gesture of solidarity with the affliction of poverty and violence transgender women of color share and, on a more personal level, as a signal to Sin-Dee, who protects herself via fierce defiance, that vulnerability is not fatal. The care between the two women transforms the laundromat—a space where the domestic chore of doing laundry becomes a shared experience—into a homespace in the concrete jungle. A moment of wounded recognition, the gesture alludes to a better tomorrow or what José Esteban Muñoz (2009: 91) calls a "queer futurity" in which quotidian gestures point toward a more just and humanitarian future, or, as he writes, "not an end but an opening or horizon."

Whether they take place in a laundromat, donut shop, or bar bathroom, communal intimacies are fragile by nature. Unlike the structural support provided to heteronormative forms of intimacy vis-à-vis marriage and family law, domestic arrangements, and zoning ordinances, queer people of color must rely on transient expressions of care within urban spaces, making communal intimacies vulnerable to gentrification-fueled displacement. In a case of life imitating art, Donut Time—Sin-Dee and Alexandra's makeshift living room—closed a year after *Tangerine*'s release, giving way to a celebrity-endorsed vegan and gluten-free donut shop marketed to millennials willing to pay a premium (Elliott 2017). This displacement illustrates how spaces not deemed intimate become susceptible to gentrification—buildings razed, lots leveled, and lives displaced. By recognizing that care transcends physical boundaries, and those needing and willing to provide it will do so wherever it is needed, the public domain can transform into a haven of domesticity, challenging us to grapple with the notion that caretaking and kinship practices, traditionally confined to private homes, can flourish within the vibrant embrace of communal spaces.

From Spectator to Invited Guest

The importance of exploring communal intimacies through art lies not only in its ability to bring to the public lives that are excluded and intentionally erased, but also in art's ability to draw in the audience and invite them, however imperfectly, to experience and share the dynamics—scenes and scenarios in which they might never have otherwise participated—that constitute communal intimacy. In essence, the performances invite audiences into the counterpublics these cultural texts create, transforming audiences into recipients of the same communal intimacies that characters actualize on screen and on the stage.

In *Mambo Mouth*, Leguizamo invites the audience in by conjuring up invisible interlocutors who convince the audience he is speaking to someone off stage or even to the audience. This technique creates an intimacy between Leguizamo and the audience that attunes the latter to the struggles of the characters on stage. Leguizamo's use of Spanish and cultural references for a mixed-race (or even mostly white) audience signal to all that they are in on it too and no different from anyone else to whom Manny would otherwise speak. They are so much a part of her world that she does not even translate Spanish slang for non-Spanish speakers; she just plows ahead, confident that everyone understands. She bestows upon the audience the status of "getting it"—or at least the possibility of getting it. In this sense, Manny's use of Spanish represents her confidence that no matter how different or diverse the actual audience may be, they can enter Manny's world and appreciate its communal intimacies. Manny is so confident in her audience that she openly flirts, blowing kisses to the men with genuine glee and none of the calculated, defensive coyishness she deploys with the police. In the televised production, Leguizamo even draws in the home viewers, ending the segment with a close-up of Manny staring into the camera and crooning: "Ay, mira, precioso, mind if I say wow!" (Leguizamo 2008: 228). In Leguizamo's mind, anyone, anywhere—so long as they are present and willing to listen—can witness and sympathize with Manny's communal intimacies.

In *Tangerine*, the filmmakers employed unconventional techniques that connected the film's technical production to its larger themes of communal intimacies (Malone 2020). Sean Baker and his co-cinematographer shot the entire film on iPhone 5s and, using special anamorphic lenses, stretched the aspect ratio out to Super 35 format, resulting in an extensive depth of field that captured all the background elements with sharp precision. This technique departs from the norm of shallow focus, in which one part of an image remains in focus while the rest is out of focus; with everything in focus, everything is part of the action. This technique immerses viewers, forcing them to contend with the surrounding poverty and violence that circumscribe the lives of transgender women of color. Unencumbered by heavy equipment, onerous permits, and a large film crew, Baker approached the script with spontaneity and immediacy, organically capturing Sin-Dee as she traversed Los Angeles. A quick succession of camera shots—combined with casting local transgender women—creates an aura of authenticity that tricks the audience into wondering who is an actor and who is a mere spectator. Speaking about the film's techniques, Baker noted, "It really feels like we're in with these girls, we're living these moments with them, we're intimate, and we're participating in the chaos of their lives" (Baldridge 2015). By lessening the space between characters and the audience—situating the viewer on the ground alongside Sin-Dee and Alexandra—the film establishes a palpable sense of physical closeness, even intimacy.

In the two mediums above, artists present characters carrying out communal intimacies, engaging in relationship-driven actions and sentiments that engender alternative spatial layouts and emotional ecosystems that are different from those limned by private property and its heteronormative (and homonormative) ontologies of privacy. This concept reminds us that public and semipublic spaces can be and routinely are co-opted by the racialized poor (and especially by marginalized queer people of color) to meet essential human emotional and physical needs: a New York City curb transforms into a living room couch, and a laundromat on Sunset Boulevard serves as a bathroom. The concept of communal intimacies aligns with Muñoz's (2020: 6) "critical utopianism," encouraging a reimagining of the built environment to envision "another time and place: a 'not-yet' where queer youths of color actually get to grow up" (Muñoz 2009: 96). Although both works attest to how place and affection are intertwined and crucial to survival, they likewise remind us that, for queer people of color, these places are few and nearly always ephemeral. Ongoing gentrification pushes "problem bodies" to ever more marginal spaces with the hope that they will simply disappear. In that sense, by merely living and remaining, loving others and themselves, those entwined within communal intimacies act out a powerful form of protest and carve out homespaces that defy displacement and challenge the very notion that certain bodies and communities should be devoid of care.

References

Anzaldúa, Gloria. 1987. *Borderlands/La Frontera: The New Mestiza*. San Francisco, CA: Aunt Lute Books.

Bailey, Marlon M. 2013. *Butch Queens up in Pumps: Gender, Performance, and Ballroom Culture in Detroit*. Ann Arbor: University of Michigan Press.

Baker, Sean, dir. 2015. *Tangerine*. Duplass Brothers Productions.

Baldridge, Aimee. 2015. "Sundance Favorite Tangerine Is a Feature Film Shot on iPhones." *Photo District News*, July 2. https://www.pdnonline.com/features /techniques/video/Sundance-Favorite-Tangerine-is-a-Feature-Film-Shot-on-iPhones -14018.shtml.

Berlant, Lauren, and Michael Warner. 1998. "Sex in Public." *Critical Inquiry* 24, no. 2: 547–66.

Bost, Darius. 2019. *Evidence of Being: The Black Gay Cultural Renaissance and the Politics of Violence*. Chicago: University of Chicago Press.

Bradway, Tyler, and Elizabeth Freeman. 2022. *Queer Kinship: Race, Sex, Belonging, Form*. Durham, NC: Duke University Press.

Care Collective. 2020. *The Care Manifesto: The Politics of Interdependence*. New York: Verso Books.

Chirico, Miriam M. 2002. "Laughter and Ethnicity in John Leguizamo's One-Man Worlds." *Latin American Theatre Review* 36, no. 1: 29–50.

Cohen, Cathy J. 1997. "Punks, Bulldaggers, and Welfare Queens: The Radical Potential of Queer Politics?" *GLQ* 3, no. 4: 437–65.

Duggan, Lisa. 2003. *The Twilight of Equality? Neoliberalism, Cultural Politics, and the Attack on Democracy.* Boston: Beacon Press.

Elliott, Farley. 2017. "Actor Danny Trejo Slashes into Hollywood with Coffee and Donut Shop." *Eater Los Angeles*, January 30. https://la.eater.com/2017/1/30/14440506/danny-trejo-trejos-coffee-donuts-donut-time-hollywood.

Eng, David L. 2010. *The Feeling of Kinship: Queer Liberalism and the Racialization of Intimacy.* Durham, NC: Duke University Press.

Garcia, G., and P. E. Cole. 1991. "Mocking the Ethnic Beast." *Time*, October 28. https://content.time.com/time/subscriber/article/0,33009,974142,00.html.

Gould, Deborah. 2009. *Moving Politics: ACT UP's Fight against AIDS.* Chicago: University of Chicago Press.

Gray Fischer, Anne. 2022. *The Streets Belong to Us: Sex, Race, and Police Power from Segregation to Gentrification.* Chapel Hill: University of North Carolina Press.

Greene, Theodore. 2014. "Gay Neighborhoods and the Rights of the Vicarious Citizen." *City and Community* 13, no. 2: 99–118.

Hartman, Saidiya. 2017. *In the Wake: A Salon in Honor of Christina Sharpe.* BCRW Videos. https://vimeo.com/203012536.

Harvey, David. 2012. *Rebel Cities: From the Right to the City to the Urban Revolution.* New York: Verso.

Hurtado, Aída. 1989. "Relating to Privilege: Seduction and Rejection in the Subordination of White Women and Women of Color." *Signs* 14, no. 4: 833–55.

Kacala, Alexander. 2020. "John Leguizamo on 'To Wong Foo' Legacy 25 Years after Cult Film's Debut." *NBCNews.com*, September 7. https://www.nbcnews.com/feature/nbc-out/john-leguizamo-wong-foo-legacy-25-years-after-cult-film-n1239471.

Leguizamo, John. 2008. *The Works of John Leguizamo.* New York: Harper.

Lowe, Lisa. 2015. *The Intimacies of Four Continents.* Durham, NC: Duke University Press.

Macintosh, Paige. 2023. "Melancholy, Respectability, and Credibility in Sean Baker's *Tangerine*." *New Review of Film and Television Studies* 21, no. 2: 211–35.

Malone, Meagan A. 2020. "Celebrating Transness: *Tangerine* and the iPhone." *European Journal of English Studies* 24, no. 1: 65–75.

Manalansan, Martin F., IV. 2005. "Race, Violence, and Neoliberal Spatial Politics in the Global City." *Social Text* 23, nos. 3–4: 141–55.

Muñoz, José Esteban. 1999. *Disidentifications: Queers of Color and the Performance of Politics.* Minneapolis: University of Minnesota Press.

Muñoz, José Esteban. 2009. *Cruising Utopia: The Then and There of Queer Futurity*. New York: New York University Press.

Muñoz, José Esteban. 2020. *The Sense of Brown*. Edited by Joshua Chambers-Letson and Tavia Nyong'o. Durham, NC: Duke University Press.

Nyong'o, Tavia. 2010. "School Daze." *Bully Bloggers*, September 30. https://bullybloggers.wordpress.com/2010/09/30/school-daze/.

Panfil, Vanessa R. 2021. "Gayborhoods as Criminogenic Space." In *The Gayborhood: From Sexual Liberation to Cosmopolitan Spectacle*, edited by Christopher T. Conner and Daniel Okamura, 67–83. Lanham, MD: Lexington Books.

Pérez, Daniel Enrique. 2009. *Rethinking Chicana/o and Latina/o Popular Culture*. New York: Palgrave Macmillan.

Plaster, Joseph. 2023. *Kids on the Street: Queer Kinship and Religion in San Francisco's Tenderloin*. Durham, NC: Duke University Press.

Puar, Jasbir. 2010. "In the Wake of It Gets Better." *The Guardian*, November 16. https://www.theguardian.com/commentisfree/cifamerica/2010/nov/16/wake-it-gets-better-campaign.

Reddy, Chandan. 1998. "Home, Houses, and Nonidentity: Paris Is Burning." In *Burning Down the House: Recycling Domesticity*, edited by Rosemary Marangoly George, 355–79. New York: Routledge.

Rodríguez, Juana María. 2003. *Queer Latinidad: Identity Practices, Discursive Spaces*. New York: New York University Press.

Rodríguez, Matthew. 2019. "How John Leguizamo Became *To Wong Foo*'s Chi Chi Rodriguez." *Out*, May 28. https://www.out.com/film/2019/5/28/how-john-leguizamo-became-wong-foos-chi-chi-rodriguez.

Rubin, Gayle. 2006. "Thinking Sex: Notes for a Radical Theory of the Politics of Sexuality." In *Culture, Society, and Sexuality*, edited by Peter Aggleton and Richard Parker, 143–78. New York: Routledge.

Schulman, Sarah. 2012. *The Gentrification of the Mind: Witness to a Lost Imagination*. Berkeley: University of California Press.

Sears, Clare. 2014. *Arresting Dress: Cross-Dressing, Law, and Fascination in Nineteenth-Century San Francisco*. Durham, NC: Duke University Press.

Sullivan, Andrew. 1996. "When Plagues End." *The New York Times Magazine*, November 10. https://www.nytimes.com/1996/11/10/magazine/when-plagues-end.html.

Tapia, Ruby C. 2022. "'Never Been a Scared Bitch': On the Play of the Fight and 'Bruised' Notions of Gender, Violence, and Necessity." *Los Angeles Review of Books*, May 19. https://avidly.lareviewofbooks.org/2022/05/19/never-been-a-scared-bitch/.

Valentine, Gill. 1996. "(Re)negotiating the 'Heterosexual Street': Lesbian Productions of Space." In *Body Space: Destabilizing Geographies of Gender and Sexuality*, edited by Nancy Duncan, 146–55. New York: Routledge.

Vargas, Deborah R. 2014. "Ruminations on *Lo Sucio* as a Latino Queer Analytic." *American Quarterly* 66, no. 3: 715–26.

Warner, Michael. 1999. *The Trouble with Normal: Sex, Politics, and the Ethics of Queer Life*. Cambridge, MA: Harvard University Press.

Warner, Michael. 2005. *Publics and Counterpublics*. New York: Zone Books.

Watercutter, Angela. 2015. "*Tangerine* Is Amazing—But Not Because of How They Shot It." *Wired*, July 7. https://www.wired.com/2015/07/tangerine-iphone/.

THE LIGHT OUTSIDE PROPERTY

Text by Virginia Thomas
Photographs by Laila Annmarie Stevens

*T*wo lovers recline on a sofa, looking tenderly at one another instead of facing the camera. The room they are in is softly lit by natural light coming in through the window, creating an interplay between what is made available to see and what is present but unseen, remaining in the dark. The sunlight catches the contours of the two lovers' faces and their metal jewelry. It alights on the curl of one of the figure's hands as it lightly caresses the other figure's head. The darkness of their clothing and the sofa, however, takes up most of the frame. The space of shadow eases distinctions between their two bodies so what normally goes unseen can emerge. Darkness, instead of light, produces a space in the photograph for their emotions to mingle and resound beyond the visually constructed boundaries of the body. Here it is not necessarily these two people as individuals that the photographer makes visible as much as it is the loving intimacy they have built together. This photograph is one in a series called "A House Is Not a Home" by photographer Laila Annmarie Stevens.

As is evident in the sense of ease these two have with the photographer, the series stemmed from Stevens's desire to photograph their friends—mostly queer, nonbinary, and trans youth of color in their hometown of New York City—in places where they feel most at home for a class ethnographic project. The project began organically with the photographer's friends, and later it evolved to include others who had learned about the project through mutual friends or Stevens's posting about the project on the Lex app and who wanted to participate. Rather than being set inside houses or apartments, however, most of the photographs were taken outside in natural light. If they are taken inside, Stevens uses only sunlight—that which comes from the outside in—to light participants. Stevens titled the series "A House Is Not a Home" to challenge the commonly held idea that a home can

GLQ 30:4
DOI 10.1215/10642684-11331010
© 2024 by Duke University Press

only exist inside the walls of a privately owned structure. In these images, which Stevens refers to as "photographic safe spaces," queer youth have creative control over how they wish to be portrayed in the spaces they feel most at home.

In another photo, a participant in the series stands outside a beauty supply store. Their long orange nails contrast with their green, pleated, loose-fitting jeans. Their Fendi baguette-esque bag, lip gloss, layers of golden rings, necklaces, earrings, and tube top harken back to the 1990s. Varying representations of femininity echo behind them: large posters with advertisements of beauty products featuring models of color and a row of feminine mannequins peer out from the store window, checkered by reflections from the street. Kendra, the person in the photo, writes, "I chose a beauty supply store to represent what 'home' feels like to me. . . . In general, beauty supply stores have been a consistent safe space for me to go to where I feel secure in my identity as a black queer woman. I feel as though home is a feeling, one that presents itself wherever you feel most secure." The camera is positioned at a lower height, giving Kendra an empowered stance above the viewer, and she meets our gaze with a look of softness and self-assuredness.

Kendra's words gesture toward the reality that the house where one lives has been and continues to be a frequent site of antagonism and unbelonging for LGBTQ+ youth. Indeed, as many public health and sociological studies have shown, LGBTQ+ youth are disproportionately overrepresented among youth who are houseless. While scholars often cite being "kicked out" as the reason for youth leaving their homes, even more often they leave their homes in an attempt to remove themselves from physical, mental, verbal, or other forms of abuse by their biological family. In "A House Is Not a Home," Stevens chose to take photographs of youth who *did* have housing at the time of being photographed. Instead of focusing on youth once they become houseless, Stevens is interested in those who don't get counted in these studies; they are among the many uncounted who do not feel at home in the housing they have access to. Serving as a counterarchive to the traditional family photograph that situates children as heteronormative extensions of their parents, Stevens explores how queer and trans youth define home in their own terms.

Stevens used a Mamiya RB67 film camera to capture the images in "A House Is Not a Home." This model of film camera first emerged in the 1800s, and by the 1990s, it had evolved into the model that Stevens used for this series. Using this camera queers linear time in that images taken almost thirty years later evoke the aesthetics and conditions of the '90s, a period of a growing influx of queer youth into New York City who were fleeing biological families who either rejected or harmed them. When they arrived, these youth formed new models of family and

Andrea Gonzales // she/they // 20 years old // Staten Island

this space, Union Square, has been my home for years now. i feel at peace in this environment, whether its the chess players on the southern steps or the cyphers that happen here every friday night. i feel surrounded by love and by people ye who are authentically themselves i find the most creative, most talented people in this park, inspiring me to persue my own forms of creativity and my own passions. this place has embraced me with open arms, whether its a long day at school or work, i feel alive here. i also have so many happy memories with my loved ones here, birthday parties, picnics, just sitting down and listening to the sounds of NYC + being grounded in this moment. this park reminds me to be grateful for the present and every moment.

i definetly think theres a difference between a house and a home. a house is a physical space, often confining you somewhere, and doesn't gaurentee safety, or love or acceptance. but a home is a place that works towards making you feel whole, it constantly grows and shifts to your needs, its filled with memories that are rooted in love. a home builds itself around you and centers you, and that means your whole self. not a single part of you is omitted from your home.

meanings of home. Despite the decades that have passed since then, Stevens creates an arch of shared experience to bridge the experiences and memories of one genera-tion to another. To Stevens, New York still feels like a haven for queer youth. Despite the vast and increasing wealth gap and extreme gentrification and displacement that characterizes present-day New York, the queer, trans, and nonbinary youth that arrived in the '80s and '90s shaped the networks of care—the resources and centers—that give many nonbinary, queer, and trans youth of today a sense of belonging. In these photographs Stevens taps into an intergenerational history of queer and trans home-building in the city that extends beyond private property.

As one participant put it:

> I definitely think there's a difference between a house and a home. A house is a physical space, often confining you somewhere, and doesn't guarantee safety, or love or acceptance. But a home is a place that works toward mak-ing you feel whole. It constantly grows and shifts to your needs, it's filled with memories that are rooted in love. A home builds itself around you and centers you, and that means your whole self, not a single part of you, is omitted from your home.

Both in their writing but also as image makers, Stevens and the series's partici-pants theorize a fluid, deeply loving, and adaptable version of home that does not depend on the walls of private property to exist. In fact, it exceeds and troubles not only the walls of a house, apartment, or room, but also the constraints a culture so thoroughly shaped by private property and its heteronormative mandates has placed on who deserves love. Here, they shape experimental meanings of home and the love, care, and intimacy that "home" implies.

"A House Is Not a Home" is also a study in the colors and tones of skin under natural light. Like the light-sensitive paper of a photograph, melanated skin responds and attunes with sunlight; in this series, Stevens foregrounds that visual relationship to invite viewers to consider this intimacy between the sun and those who have more melanin as significant. The sun also has the power to transgress barriers that mark boundaries between inside and outside. In these photographs of queer, nonbinary, and trans youth of color, these two seemingly disparate themat-ics come together: those whose skin resonates most with the sun are also troubling norms that white patriarchal property culture has deemed to be natural, especially those who are allowed to experience "home."

As with the photograph of the person standing in the park, most of the pho-tographs in the series were taken outdoors in what photographers often refer to as "natural light." This carries both technical and epistemological weight. Visual and textual discourses concerning "nature" and the "natural" have a robust history of capturing queer, nonbinary, and trans folks—especially those of color—as deviant and unnatural. Using solely natural light to frame these youth challenges this history. Rather than turning to logics of inclusion to stage this challenge, as photographs of queer couples with their biological offspring tend to do (i.e., "We're families, too!"), Stevens's use of sunlight engages this discourse from another angle by creating a visual tension. The tension that Stevens plays with throughout the series exists in their use of sunlight to frame participants while reducing highlights (also called "flattening") in the images during the editing process. Sunlight is known for its ability to dramatize human figures, and photographers often use sunlight to make their subjects stand out from the background, which tends to generate a sublime distinguishing effect that pits the human against their surroundings. Stevens works exclusively with natural light, yet during the editing process, they flatten the images, which reduces the drama and sublime aesthetic and instead disperses the light over the entirety of the scene. Here, queer youth and their surroundings exist on the same plane. Nature is not assumed to be a stable, unchanging universal used to validate or uphold the participants' existence. In "A House Is Not a Home," backgrounds, people, settings, and sunlight collaborate and play off of one another, cocreating each other. Here, queer youth simply exist with ease in the places they call home, in harmony with the elements around them.

While most of these images are of youth outside, they still invite complexity regarding queer youth's proximity to and situatedness within houses. The last image in this series chosen for this gallery is one actually taken inside the house where none of the youth participants lives with their family. The composition falls neatly into the rule of thirds: in the bottom third, the youth is sitting on the couch, their face framed by tendrils of an artificial bouquet. Sunlight seeps into the room through blinds in the middle third, with the outline of a lampshade centered above the youth's head. The upper third shows a print of a painting portraying the story of Jesus healing a blind man. Metaphors around light, sight, unseeing, the natural, the supernatural, and the artificial reverberate around this photograph. In a conversation about this photograph, Stevens told me that this participant lives with her parents, who are very religious and have not accepted her queer identity. Yet, she chooses to live with them and care for them, and she maintains a Christian religious practice herself. The image asks us to linger in seemingly opposing forces: the confinement of the home signified by the barlike presence of the blinds' shadows on the wall, and the sunlight nonetheless entering between the blinds and alighting upon her face. If we cannot always find home inside a house, we cannot

I chose a beauty supply store to represent what "home" feels like to me. Specifically, I chose Young's Beauty Supply on Broadway in Brooklyn, because it's my regular spot. In general, beauty supply stores have been a consistent safe space for me to go to where I feel secure in my identity as a black queer woman. ~~I~~ I feel as though home is a feeling, one that ~~comes with~~ presents itself wherever you feel most secure. Housing insecurity is a huge issue in the lgbtq+ community, and often times we find ourselves in unsafe housing situations simply so that we have a house to live in for the time being. Safe spaces for our community are so important, so that we have somewhere to go to feel at home when our physical homes do not provide that feeling.

— Kendra Shiloh

Amanda Chang
& Aaliyah Garcia // 20 yrs old // she/they // Queens Village
East Harlem

We think of Alley Pond Park as our home.
Amanda and I met almost 8 months ago, and at the end of
each month, we celebrate our time together with a
date. For our 6 months together, we chose to have a
picnic at Alley Pond Park. We ate sandwiches, sat
in the sun, we talked. ~~and laughed together~~ It was very
cheesy, ~~but it was very sweet~~. Our picnic, however, had
~~come to a quick~~ to end as quickly as it started
because it began pouring rain; like thunder and
all. The two of us ran to the parking lot to wait
for our Uber, ~~and still~~ laughing the entire time.
It was like something out of The Notebook, but
gayer. We sat on a bench, hiding under our
picnic blanket, ~~to avoid cold and wet~~, taking pictures, laughing.
It was honestly one of the most fun dates we had
ever been on. Every time we come back to this
park, I think of that moment; How she feels
like home to me. She protects me from the rain,
she makes me smile, she keeps me warm. Amanda
is my home, and Alley Pond ~~place~~ reminds me of that.
~~Maybe~~ So I call this park our home, too.

always find it outside either. Rather, Stevens provides a visual meditation on a version of home this participant has defined through her choices, one that exists in the porous space of the spiritual, the emotional, and the relational—one that they ask us to bear witness to.

All photographs in the gallery were taken by Laila Annmarie Stevens as part of their 2019–2022 documentary project "A House is Not a Home." The scanned notebook pages were written by the participants pictured on the opposing page.

A QUEER IDEA OF HOME

Introduction

Lauren Jae Gutterman, Martin F. Manalansan IV, and Stephen Vider

For anthropologist Mary Douglas, the home is a normative structure. To make a home is to try to control space over time—to introduce daily routines and rhythms to provide the feeling of order and coordination. In her essay "The Idea of a Home: A Kind of Space," Douglas (1991) gives the example of mealtimes, which demand "synchrony": everyone is expected to eat at the same relative pace, and there are no second helpings until the slowest eater has cleaned their plate. For Douglas, that demand for synchrony is also at the heart of the home's tyrannical operations. Yet home might as easily be defined by the queerness that haunts its edges—how easily its order is overturned. The strictness of the home's norms makes their disruption all the more certain.

For this forum, we asked five scholars from across various disciplines, subfields, and stages of their careers, "How does the space of home figure in your work? How does thinking about the queering of domesticity help us to understand home better?" The five short essays here reflect on the home's various normalizing pressures and how home may be queered. Home is, or can be, for these authors, a site of state violence and homonormative surveillance as well as the grounds for queer erotic expression, crip care, and Black freedom making. Home is at once the potential locus of the revolution and a depoliticized retreat from collective struggle. Taken together, these essays provide no easy answers, but they bring us closer to the home's queer contradictions. They challenge us to think more deeply about the promises and the traps the home holds out for those queered in some or many ways by cis- or homonormativity, racism or displacement, poverty or ableism. If the home offers a vantage point beyond the traumas of our present, these essays sug-

GLQ 30:4
DOI 10.1215/10642684-11432687
© 2024 by Duke University Press

gest, it will be only insofar as we can resist its disciplining tendencies and strive for solidarity with one another.

Reference

Douglas, Mary. 1991. "The Idea of a Home: A Kind of Space." *Social Research* 58, no. 1: 287–307.

MAKING BLACK QUEER HOME

Shoniqua Roach

*W*hen I sat down to start my book *Black Dwelling: Home-Making and Erotic Freedom* in the summer of 2020, in the wake of massive personal shifts—having just moved across the country for a new position, bought a home in a predominantly white Boston suburb, and rooted into newly "gay" married life—a pandemic hit, the state locked down, Black Lives Matter was mattering (again), and my white neighbors were glaring at me and my family every time we stepped outside for a breath of fresh air. There were more Trump than BLM signs decorating neighborhood lawns, so we did not have to do much guesswork about the community's political standpoints. And it was terrifyingly easy to imagine how those standpoints might translate into forms of extralegal anti-Black, anti-queer, and anti-trans terror. So when I began to outfit my home with security cameras to countersurveil my neighbors, I had no illusions about Black queer home space as a site of unmitigated sanctuary, though I yearned for that.

I enter into this conversation on domesticity from a queer Black feminist place, one that acknowledges the violence of colonial and cisheteronormative constructions of home as well as the power, pleasure, and possibility of home for minoritized subjects and community formations. I recognize the affordances and constraints of queer identity politics: if I do not name myself for myself, I risk subjection to external definitions, projections, and standards that could never wholly define me (Lorde 1984). I am also fundamentally invested in a Black queer feminist politic that holds space for the Blackness of queerness, or the "Punks, Bulldaggers, and Welfare Queens" (Cohen 1997) who enflesh and embody the nonheteronormativity of Black being and becoming. These punks, bulldaggers, and welfare queens—and their queer homemaking practices—inhabit the center of *Black Dwelling.*

GLQ 30:4
DOI 10.1215/10642684-11331074
© 2024 by Duke University Press

Black Dwelling asks what happens when Black women claim and cultivate home in the United States, a space that has historically denied, and continues to deny, Black women—trans and nontrans—access to privacy and safety.
This deceptively simple question emerged from deep, sustained engagement with
(queer) Black feminist critical and creative thought: Sylvia Wynter's (2003) metic-
ulous geographies of the human; Hortense Spillers's (1987) theoretical excavations
of "the black woman"; Omise'eke Natasha Tinsley's (2008) sensuous writing on
the *mati* work in the slave ship's hold; Angela Davis's (1971) respatialization of the
slave quarters as a countergeography of Black freedom-making; Saidiya Hartman's
(2019) tender portrait of the wayward lives of Black migrant girls and women in US
urban centers; Audre Lorde's (1982) biomythographical pursuit of (Black) lesbian
community in New York City from the late 1950s onward; Alice Walker's (1983)
search for her mother's garden in the US South; bell hooks's (2015) construction of
homeplace as a site of Black feminist resistance; Letisha West's Black living room
lessons in imperial San Diego, California (Roach 2022); and so on.

From Wynter to West, Black feminism and Black women's lived experiences complicate easy understandings of the question of what it means for Black
(queer) women to claim and cultivate home in the United States. The question of
Black women's homemaking necessarily starts with the question: what (or who) is a
Black woman? An "ungendered" (female) social subject whose symbolic and material body constructs the boundaries of what it means to be human (and therefore
a citizen, a member of gendered civil society, a laborer, and so on) (Spillers 1987)
and whose vestibular position in relation to human (and national) culture(s) renders
her the "belly of the world" (Hartman 2016: 166). Black female flesh catalyzed a
new world. And this so-called new world was predicated, in part, on centuries of
Black dispossession and dislocation from any semblance of home—geopolitical
territory, land, nation, culture, community, family, household, self. We find ourselves in queer places when we try to make sense of what these histories might
mean for a Black sense of place (Spillers 1987: 68). Do we imagine home as geopolitical territory, and if so, might that be somewhere along the Gold Coast, where
millions of African people-*cum*-captives were snatched and stolen? Would we have
to lose our mothers to get (back) there (Hartman 2007)? Is Black queer home the
now theoretically revered slave ship? Is it the Black (queer) Atlantic? The sand?
The slave quarters? The "post"-colony?

If normative conceptions of home are defined as "a dwelling place; a person's house or abode; the fixed residence of a family or household; the seat of
domestic life and interests" then Black (queer) home is defined, at least in part,
by dispossession and dislocation from place, self, and normative understandings

of kinship and community.[1] Historically and symbolically, then, the Black home is and remains a queer home. Saidiya Hartman (1997: 160) observes how, in the wake of slavery, the Black domestic became "the ultimate scene of surveillance" wherein state agents policed what they perceived as the queerness of Black being and householding. In *Wayward Lives*, Hartman (2019: 251) centers the ways in which early twentieth-century state authorities marked Black domestic spaces as promiscuous, illegal, and criminal, enabling "great latitude in the surveillance and arrest of black women and tenement residents." The same Black women and tenement residents who were arrested in Harlem probably "quit the south" (Hine 1989: 914)—and the "domestic carceral regimes" (Haley 2016: 55) that defined and delineated Black women's experiences of dwelling and labor (exploitation), only to find themselves on the Bronx slave market. Fifteen years after Ella Baker and Marvel Jackson Cooke documented the relegation of Black women laborers to violent, exploitative white New York City households, the United States Department of Labor commissioned and published a report, "The Negro Family: The Case for National Action," that would scapegoat Black women and their "nonheteronormative" domestic arrangements for the "Black community's" alleged failure to "achieve" social, political, and economic parity with whites, codifying the Black household as a paradigmatic object of state violence, surveillance, and scrutiny (Ferguson 2004).

In 2017, the Institute for Women's Policy Research partnered with the National Domestic Workers alliance to publish the first comprehensive report on "The Status of Black Women in the United States" (DuMonthier, Childers, and Milli 2017). Given the aforementioned history that shapes present-day conditions, it was perhaps unsurprising to encounter statistics demonstrating the mass houselessness crisis affecting Black women throughout the diaspora (a social issue that is now part of public consciousness due to the organizing efforts of Black collectives such as Moms4Housing in the Bay Area) and the overrepresentation of Black women in the (domestic) service economy. The report predicted the "negative public health implications" for (housing-insecure) Black women public-service-sector workers, who are forced to have "frequent contact with the public" without access to basic protections like safe, affordable housing, comprehensive health coverage, and access to sick days.

If we go—or rather, stay—with the hold, we find, in Spillers's words (1987: 72), a critical "counter-narrative" to notions of American domesticity, defined by the "fundamental effacement and remission of African family and proper names." Black domesticity is queer domesticity in relation to colonial-*cum*-state power, yes. But, as I have learned from Black queer dwelling and *Black Dwelling*, there are (and have always been) polymorphous traditions of Black queer domesticity, of making Black queer home. These traditions encompass feeling with and feeling for each other in the hold (Tinsley 2008); negotiating the sumptuous silence around queer Black life on porches in the Caribbean (Silvera 1992); grappling with the polymorphous meanings of quareness and racialized sexuality on our grandmothers' southern porches (Johnson 2000); reclaiming our gardens as sites of beauty, creativity, and Black maternal power (Walker 1983); preparing hot cups of tea in our kitchens as precursors to (hopefully even hotter) lesbian sex (Musser 2015); and designing beautiful Black living rooms that challenge state-sponsored narratives about the value of Black women and our homemaking efforts (Roach 2022). In my work, Black *queer* domesticity offers a way of holding not only the long and ongoing Black (geo)political struggles to (re)claim space and homemake in the context of white heteronormative supremacist imperial terror and violence; it is also a quotidian freedom practice through which we unmake imperial geographies by intentionally cultivating Black queer home in ways that rehearse, imagine, and enact free worlds that have yet to be embodied, inhabited, and made.

Notes

1.　*Oxford English Dictionary*, s.v. "home, n.1 & adj.," I.2.a, accessed January 12, 2024, https://doi.org/10.1093/OED/9487569112.

References

Cohen, Cathy J. 1997. "Punks, Bulldaggers, and Welfare Queens: The Radical Potential of Queer Politics?" *GLQ* 3, no. 4: 437–65.

Davis, Angela. 1971. "Reflections on the Black Woman's Role in the Community of Slaves." *Black Scholar* 3, no. 4: 3–15.

DuMonthier, Asha, Chandra Childers, and Jessica Milli. 2017. "The Status of Black Women in the United States." Washington, DC: Institute for Women's Policy Research.

Ferguson, Roderick A. *Aberrations in Black: Toward a Queer of Color Critique*. Minneapolis: University of Minnesota Press, 2004.

Haley, Sarah. 2016. *No Mercy Here: Gender, Punishment, and the Making of Jim Crow Modernity*. Chapel Hill: University of North Carolina Press.

Hartman, Saidiya V. 1997. *Scenes of Subjection: Terror, Slavery, and Self-Making in Nineteenth-Century America*. New York: Oxford University Press.

Hartman, Saidiya V. 2007. *Lose Your Mother : A Journey along the Atlantic Slave Route*. New York: Farrar, Straus and Giroux.

Hartman, Saidiya V. 2016. "The Belly of the World: A Note on Black Women's Labors." *Souls* 18, no. 1: 166–73.

Hartman, Saidiya V. 2019. *Wayward Lives, Beautiful Experiments: Intimate Histories of Social Upheaval*. New York: W.W. Norton.

Hine, Darlene Clark. 1989. "Rape and the Inner Lives of Black Women in the Middle West." *Signs* 14, no. 4: 912–20.

hooks, bell. 2015. *Yearning: Race, Gender, and Cultural Politics*. 2nd ed. New York: Routledge.

Johnson, E. Patrick. 2000. "From Black Quare Studies or Almost Everything I Know about Queer Studies I Learned from My Grandmother." *Callaloo* 23, no. 1: 120–21.

Lorde, Audre. 1982. *Zami, a New Spelling of My Name*. Trumansburg, NY: Crossing Press.

Lorde, Audre. 1984. *Sister Outsider: Essays and Speeches*. Trumansburg, NY: Crossing Press.

Musser, Amber Jamilla. 2015. "Lesbians, Tea, and the Vernacular of Fluids." *Women and Performance* 25, no. 1: 23–40. https://doi.org/10.1080/0740770X.2014.994841.

Roach, Shoniqua. 2022. "The Black Living Room." *American Quarterly* 74, no. 3: 791–811. https://doi.org/10.1353/aq.2022.0056.

Silvera, Makeda. 1992. "Man Royals and Sodomites: Some Thoughts on the Invisibility of Afro-Caribbean Lesbians." *Feminist Studies* 18, no. 3: 521–32. https://doi.org/10.2307/3178080.

Spillers, Hortense. 1987. "Mama's Baby, Papa's Maybe: An American Grammar Book." *Diacritics* 17, no. 2: 65–81.

Tinsley, Omise'eke Natasha. 2008. "Black Atlantic, Queer Atlantic: Queer Imaginings of the Middle Passage." *GLQ* 14, nos. 2–3: 191–215.

Walker, Alice. 1983. *In Search of Our Mothers' Gardens: Womanist Prose*. San Diego: Harcourt Brace Jovanovich.

Wynter, Sylvia. 2003. "Unsettling the Coloniality of Being/Power/Truth/Freedom: Towards the Human, after Man, Its Overrepresentation—An Argument." *CR: The New Centennial Review* 3, no. 3: 257–337.

LETTING THE DOMESTIC FAIL

Notes on Race, Class, and Transvestites

Jules Gill-Peterson

*T*he home looms large in queer and trans studies, albeit paradoxically. It invites the charge of depoliticized retreat from the public sphere, but it also signifies as a marker of authenticity—the domicile of the self. The trans domestic, specifically, is a condition of possibility for thinking queer sexuality and gender writ large. The cover of Michael Warner's foundational book *Publics and Counterpublics* (2002) is a slightly grainy 1962 photograph of five transvestites in someone's home, all holding cameras. Three figures on the front cover, perfect portraits of midcentury white femininity, point their shutters at Lili, a Japanese woman in a turquoise mod dress, who returns their gaze with her own camera. A fifth white woman points her camera directly at the photographer, locking one eye with the viewer. The picture comes from a scrapbook of photos taken at Casa Susanna, a transvestite resort in upstate New York that hosted regular get-togethers in the 1950s and 1960s. The queering of domesticity depends in this text, as it has in so much queer theory, on interpreting trans femininity.

For Warner, the photo ignites the signal question of his book: what constitutes a public? The home answers counterintuitively. The women of Casa Susanna "might seem not to be public at all," writes Warner. "They might seem merely to imitate familiar mass media genres" by dressing up and posing for one another behind closed doors. "If so," however, "it is at least interesting that the ambition of publicity matters so much to them. Why should it?" (2002: 12–13). The question is not rhetorical, though it is difficult to answer definitively. "The suburban, domestic scene in which we find them," he continues, "is being put to an unusual use. It is a space of collective improvisation, transformative in a way that depends on its connection to several publics—inducing a dominant and alien mass public." In short, "the private setting protects them from an environment of stigma, but clearly their aspiration is to

GLQ 30:4
DOI 10.1215/10642684-11331050

do a different kind of publicness" (13). The women of Casa Susanna are not mournfully domesticating a femininity they cannot risk enjoying in public. Rather, the circulation of domesticity through photographs configures the home to mediate an "indefinite" sorority of like-minded strangers, which Warner calls a counterpublic. The transvestites are conscious that they lack the sanction of, and thus they express a desire to alter, the mass public in which they cannot participate openly.

Warner's is a seductive reading, although by relying on a single magazine article, it gets several details wrong. Most importantly, he terms the pictured women "drag queens" when they and their host, Susanna Valenti, a featured columnist in Virginia Prince's magazine *Transvestia*, hailed from the distinct and wealthy social class of transvestites. The flattening of trans femininity in queer theory and gay male cultural imaginaries is not a special fault of Warner's. Both *Casa Susanna* (Hurst and Swope 2014), a coffee-table book of photographs, and a PBS documentary of the same title (American Experience 2023) about the resort repeat the error, calling its patrons "transgender women" in the contemporary declassed sense, which these 1960s transvestites would have also rejected. Warner (2002: 14) is right that "the queens of Casa Susanna are revising what it means to be public," but queer theory's impulse to declare they are making a *better* world by virtue of world-making misrepresents them by ignoring their class interests.

The pages of *Transvestia* in which Valenti and other regulars at Casa Susanna wrote demonstrate that their privacy, though it constituted a counterpublic, nevertheless ratified a bourgeois distinction between public and private. Casa Susanna–type transvestites predominantly dressed only part time, on evenings and weekends, and some exclusively at the resort. How happy that made them varied, but the practice permitted them to retain the powerful station of married white men in 1960s America. Valenti (1962: 69), who ran the resort as a business, described "most of the members of the group" as "fairly well educated people (many college graduates, professional people: lawyers, doctors, etc.)." Their domesticity was arranged so that they did not risk their public jobs, their legal rights as white men, and especially their marriages to women, many of whom accompanied them upstate. Although the desire to dress in public was a perennial source of angst and debate, these midcentury transvestites distinguished their aspirations (Prince 1962: 72–75) from contemporaneous gay and transsexual publics, especially those seeking political transformations of the public sphere.

In short, Casa Susanna's transvestites fail the political test of "queering domesticity." They cultivated a form of publicness from the privacy of their homes by affirming their wealth, whiteness, and heterosexuality. That cultivation, moreover, relied on its antagonistic relationship to the trans feminine publicity associated with poor street queens and sex workers, especially Black transvestites. A contemporary film, *Behind Every Good Man* (Ursin 1967), dramatizes the difference. The eight-minute short follows an unnamed Black transvestite for a day in Los Angeles. She first appears, unsurprisingly, in public, walking down the street. Her voiceover narrates, "I'd like to live a respectable life, that's for sure . . . I'd like to settle down," but her words are played for irony. Close-up shots depict an incredulous white-male public overreacting to her presence. Managing their latent threats with demure playfulness, she chats up a young man, flirting with him until they make plans for a date. The film then cuts to her apartment, lingering on the spectacle of her getting dressed for the evening, alone. Waiting beside a candlelit table for her date, it becomes clear that he isn't going to show. She blows out the candles, sits alone in the dark, and the film fades to black.

Pairing Casa Susanna with *Behind Every Good Man*, I'd suggest that it's important to let the white trans domestic fail our queer idealizations. Otherwise, we cannot appreciate how the Black trans domestic was constituted *as* failure—an iteration of the impossibility often ascribed to midcentury Black trans femininity, as C. Riley Snorton (2017: 157) has shown. As I see it, the home is not a willing participant for theorizing whatever meaning we might wish to retrieve out of the genuinely strange privacy that attends forms of queer and trans living. It is, rather, a fault line composed of class and race, one that routinely punctures the aspirational unity of queer and trans as the ideational anchors of our fields.

Jules Gill-Peterson is an associate professor of history at Johns Hopkins University. She is the author of *Histories of the Transgender Child* (2018) and *A Short History of Trans Misogyny* (2024).

References

American Experience. 2023. *Casa Susanna*. Aired June 27, on PBS.

Hurst, Michael, and Robert Swope, eds. 2014. *Casa Susanna*. New York: Simon and Schuster.

Prince, Virginia. 1962. "Virgin Views." *Transvestia*, no. 18: 72–75.

Snorton, C. Riley. 2017. *Black on Both Sides: A Racial History of Trans Identity*. Minneapolis: University of Minnesota Press.

Ursin, Nikolai. 1967. *Behind Every Good Man*. UCLA Legacy Project for LGBT Moving Image Preservation.

Valenti, Susanna. 1962. "Susanna Says." *Transvestia*, no. 14: 69–70.

Warner, Michael. 2002. *Publics and Counterpublics*. New York: Zone Books.

THE (CRIP) REVOLUTION BEGINS AT HOME

Jina B. Kim

The introduction to the 1981 anthology *This Bridge Called My Back*, coauthored by Chicana lesbian feminists Cherríe Moraga and Gloria Anzaldúa (2015: xlvii), concludes with an act of inception: "The revolution begins at home." Home, for Moraga and Anzaldúa, not only names a physical structure or a place of attachment, but also a practice of collaborative survival, of bridge-building, and of "not settling for less than freedom even in the most private aspect of our lives" (Moraga 2015: xli). And as I chewed on this roundtable's prompt, placing it alongside my own work on disability politics and US welfare reform, I began to further situate this dream of home within the material crises of housing and state care intensified by the Reagan administration, which had begun its deadly reorganization of state infrastructure at the time of Moraga and Anzaldúa's writing. Ten years after Ronald Reagan's first presidential election, sociologist Loïc Wacquant (2009: 159) notes that the respective budgets for public housing and prisons "had nearly reversed," citing a $19 billion increase for penal maintenance and a $17 billion subtraction for housing. Such a reversal, Wacquant (2009: 160) writes, rendered "the construction of prisons . . . *the country's main public housing program*." What does it mean, then, for these queer Chicana feminists to imagine home as the genesis of revolution during a time of accelerating resource deprivation, when stable, decent, and affordable housing was becoming less and less accessible?

Disabled writers and activists in both the rights and justice movements have taken up the paradox of home as both revolutionary promise and locus of material contradiction. Deinstitutionalization, which began in the 1950s and gained prominence in the 1970s, sought to move people with developmental and mental disabilities out of institutions, such as long-term psychiatric facilities or state-run hospitals.[1] Dominant narratives of disability rights highlight the foundational role of the Independent Living Movement in the empowerment of people with

GLQ 30:4
DOI 10.1215/10642684-11331090
© 2024 by Duke University Press

disabilities, which includes the right to live in our communities with the necessary supports.[2] Further, as the Disability Justice Culture Club put it in 2019, "disabled wisdom knows home is a holy place" (Piepzna-Samarasinha 2022: 263), and as disability justice writer-activist Leah Lakshmi Piepzna-Samarasinha (2022: 266) explained, "the right to have a place of your own where you can be as messy and uncombed and sad and weird-bodied as you want . . . is partly why so many of our disabled struggles have centered on home."

Still: home, when placed in the context of disability, often invokes disabled misery and isolation; in the able-bodied imagination, we are homebound, bed-bound, wheelchair-bound. If queer people have been long positioned as "home's outsiders," as Stephen Vider (2021: 11) so aptly put it, then disabled people have inversely been positioned as home's insiders—but to a pathological degree. Yet, despite being bound to home, home has become less and less bound to disabled people, who have been especially hard hit by the escalating US housing crisis (CHRT 2002). The Faircloth Amendment of 1998, which ended the use of federal funds toward the construction of new public housing, contributed to "a nation-wide shortage of accessible and affordable housing for those who were eligible—affecting affordable independent living options for those with disabilities" (Rogers, Impink, and Ziegler 2023). Further, prolonged housing insecurity, as Craig Willse (2015: 2) has argued, is a profoundly disabling condition. After all, a house, Willse writes, is not only a material structure, but also a "technology for the organization and distribution of health, illness, and death."

In my own research, I examine how disabled, feminist, and/or queer of color writers navigate these disabling infrastructural crises—such as the dis-mantling of affordable and accessible housing—while simultaneously dream-ing of more and better arrangements of support. Home, for writers like Piepzna-Samarasinha, becomes the impetus to reimagine movement organizing altogether, as well as the imaginative parameters of what disabled living spaces entail. Rather than going the typical nonprofit route, Piepzna-Samarasinha (2022: 269) asks, what if we arranged movement-building around "creating more disabled homes" and "continuing to dream on and experiment with what disabled homes could be?" Like Anzaldúa and Moraga, Piepzna-Samarasinha believes that the (crip) revolu-tion begins at home. And while the home and the bed have long been imagined as symbols of disabled immobility, my work demonstrates how these literary practices of infrastructural dreaming work to reframe the notion of freedom itself—as con-tingent upon, rather than distinct from, systems of collective support.

I register the shape and force of these literary interventions through an analytic I call a crip of color critique, which demonstrates how disability politics and aesthetics can interrupt dominant narratives about who deserves care (and what that care looks like). And it is through the crip of color framework that I will now briefly examine the possibilities afforded by queering (and cripping) domesticity. Broadly speaking, cripping domesticity continues the very queer work of defamiliarizing dominant scripts for intimacy, care, and kinship. It also demonstrates the very crip practice of understanding care labor as not only socially reproductive, but also creative and transformative—the work central to building the world we want to inhabit.

Cripping domesticity, then, both registers and denaturalizes the repressive calculus of support, dependency, and care upheld by the single-family home. This dominant structure and ideology dictate which needs are acceptable and who is expected to tend to them. That is, when organized around the wifely labor of caring for a (white, middle-class) husband and children, the home becomes an object of sentimental attachment. However, when inhabited by personal care attendants supporting disabled people, the home is refashioned as a place of pity and immiseration. Disabled culture workers and activists, such as Alice Wong, Stacey Park Milbern, and Kennedy Healy, have refused this set of associations through their narrative and community-building projects that center crip homemaking. In pieces such as "Care during COVID: A Photo Essay on Interdependence" (Molkentin and Healy 2022) and Alice Wong's (2022) recent autobiography *Year of the Tiger: An Activist's Life*, these culture workers frame often-stigmatized relations of care (e.g., with a personal care assistant, a member of your care web, or a parent after the point of reaching adulthood) as pleasurable and life-giving rather than inherently sad, sterile, or even shameful.

Cripping domesticity would further involve reimagining the form and function of the home's built environment, outfitting it with couches, access equipment, and all the things that make one's crip life enjoyable. It would highlight housing access as a key disability issue, and it would interrupt pro-austerity belief systems around who deserves a home (Berne et al. 2018). Finally, it would mean understanding home work *as* change-making work, expanding our movement imagination beyond the public sphere of protests and marches to the "bed activism" theorized and practiced by crip luminaries like Johanna Hedva (2016), Akemi Nishida (2022), and Leah Lakshmi Piepzna-Samarasinha (2018). As these culture workers show us, the (crip) revolution does not only begin at home; it lives there too.

Notes

1. For more on the history and reasoning behind deinstitutionalization, see Goffman (1961) and Ben-Moshe (2020).
2. For more on the Independent Living Movement, see Shapiro (1994), Heumann (2021), and Hayman (2019).

References

Ben-Moshe, Liat. 2020. *Decarcerating Disability: Deinstitutionalization and Prison Aboli-tion*. Minneapolis: University of Minnesota Press.

Berne, Patricia, Aurora Levins Morales, David Langstaff, and Sins Invalid. 2018. "Ten Principles of Disability Justice." *WSQ* 46, nos. 1–2: 227–30. https://doi.org/10.1353 /wsq.2018.0003.

CHRT (Center for Health and Research Transformation). 2002. "Housing Crisis Is Magni-fied for People with Physical Disabilities." December 12. https://chrt.org/publication /housing-crisis-magnified/.

Goffman, Erving. 1961. *Asylums: Essays on the Social Situation of Mental Patients and Other Inmates*. New York: Anchor Books.

Hayman, Bridget. 2019. "Independent Living History." *Access Living*, May 31. https:// www.accessliving.org/newsroom/blog/independent-living-history/.

Hedva, Johanna. 2016. "Sick Woman Theory." *Mask Magazine*, January 19. https://www .maskmagazine.com/not-again/struggle/sick-woman-theory/ (site discontinued).

Heumann, Judith. 2021. *Being Heumann: An Unrepentant Memoir of a Disability Rights Activist*. Boston: Beacon Press.

Molkentin, Marley, and Kennedy Healy. 2022. "Care during COVID: Photo Essay on Interdependence." Disability Visibility Project, February 8. https://disabilityvisibility project.com/2022/02/08/care-during-covid-photo-essay-on-interdependence/.

Moraga, Cherríe. 2015. "La Jornada: Preface, 1981." In *This Bridge Called My Back: Writings by Radical Women of Color*, edited by Cherríe Moraga and Gloria Anzaldúa, 4th ed., xxxv–xli. New York: SUNY Press.

Moraga, Cherríe, and Gloria Anzaldúa. 2015. "Introduction, 1981." In *This Bridge Called My Back: Writings by Radical Women of Color*, edited by Cherríe Moraga and Gloria Anzaldúa, 4th ed., xliii–xlvii. New York: SUNY Press.

Nishida, Akemi. 2022. *Just Care: Messy Entanglements of Disability, Dependency, and Desire*. Philadelphia: Temple University Press.

Piepzna-Samarasinha, Leah Lakshmi. 2018. *Care Work: Dreaming Disability Justice*. Vancouver, BC: Arsenal Pulp Press.

Piepzna-Samarasinha, Leah Lakshmi. 2022. *The Future Is Disabled: Prophecies, Love Notes, and Mourning Songs*. Vancouver, BC: Arsenal Pulp Press.

Rogers, Sawyer, Rosalyn Impink, and Alison Ziegler. 2023. "Community Living for People with Disabilities in Public Housing: Evaluating the Frank Melville Supportive Housing Investment Act of 2010." *Journal of Public and International Affairs*, May 26. https://jpia.princeton.edu/news/community-living-people-disabilities-public-housing-evaluating-frank-melville-supportive.

Shapiro, Joseph P. 1994. *No Pity: People with Disabilities Forging a New Civil Rights Movement*. New York: Times Books.

Vider, Stephen. 2021. *The Queerness of Home: Gender, Sexuality, and the Politics of Domesticity after World War II*. Chicago: University of Chicago Press.

Wacquant, Loïc. 2009. *Punishing the Poor: The Neoliberal Government of Social Insecurity*. Durham, NC: Duke University Press.

Willse, Craig. 2015. *The Value of Homelessness: Managing Surplus Life in the United States*. Minneapolis: University of Minnesota Press.

Wong, Alice. 2022. *Year of the Tiger: An Activist's Life*. New York: Vintage.

QUEER HOMES IN DIASPORA

Gayatri Gopinath

Questions of home, dwelling, and domesticity have fueled my work ever since I wrote my first book, *Impossible Desires: Queer Diasporas and South Asian Public Cultures* (2005), almost twenty years ago. I understand "home" in that book across different spatial scales: as household/domestic space, as racialized community space, and as national space. In all three instances, I am interested in how queer desires, embodiments, and subjectivities are held as ex-centric to the space of "home" and are seen as perennially outside and antithetical to its fictions of purity, sanctity, and cultural authenticity. The concept of queer diaspora, as I theorize it in *Impossible Desires*, makes a central intervention into the "home" as imagined within dominant nationalist and diasporic discourses. The queer diasporic texts that concern me in *Impossible Desires* carefully delineate the patriarchal strictures of familial, communal, and nationalist home spaces and the violences they exact on nonconforming desires, embodiments, and subjectivities. Yet rather than simply imagining home as a space to leave behind in order to escape into a more liberatory elsewhere, these texts remake the space of home from within. As I write: "For queer racialized migrant subjects, 'staying put' becomes a way of remaining within the oppressive structures of the home . . . while imaginatively working to dislodge its heteronormative logic. . . . Home is a vexed location where queer subjects whose very desires and subjectivities are formed by its logic simultaneously labor to transform it." I continue: "These queer diasporic texts evoke 'home' spaces that are permanently and already ruptured, rent by colliding discourses around class, sexuality, and ethnic identity. They lay claim to both the space of 'home' and the nation by making both the site of desire and pleasure in a nostalgic diasporic imaginary. The heteronormative home, in these texts, unwittingly generates homoeroticism" (Gopinath 2005: 14).

GLQ 30:4
DOI 10.1215/10642684-11331154
© 2024 by Duke University Press

By excavating the ways in which queerness emerges in the interstices of heteronormative structures, the queer diasporic texts that are the focus of *Impossible Desires* powerfully repudiate colonial and developmentalist discourses that posit the space of the home in the global South as a homogenous site of oppression, as opposed to the apparent freedom and liberation offered by the global North. The notion of queer diaspora and queer diasporic aesthetic practices make the double move of undoing this progress narrative while always remaining cognizant of the very real material and psychic violences of home spaces in multiple national locations. Queer diasporic practices render intelligible those forms of queer relationality, eroticism, and embodiment that inhere within these home spaces of apparent "unfreedom." I therefore suggest the need for a "queer diasporic reading practice" that makes these forms of queerness intelligible and that can "see" what queerness looks like across different diasporic and national registers (26). In my reading of the 1996 film *Fire*, for instance, which depicts two sisters-in-law who are also lovers in a middle-class household in Delhi, their performance of hyperbolic femininity for each other becomes a marker of queer desire rather than of their availability to heterosexuality. Without this queer diasporic reading practice, I argue, forms of queerness as they emerge within the home may simply be misread as an adherence to normativity when seen through a hetero- or homonormative lens.

My more recent work continues this interest in what queerness looks and feels like within the home in all its valences. In *Unruly Visions: The Aesthetic Practices of Queer Diaspora* (2018), I open with a meditation on a particular series of photographs from contemporary Lebanese artist Akram Zaatari. Zaatari excavates and places back into circulation the studio photographs of Hashem El-Madani, a photographer from Zaatari's hometown of Saida in southern Lebanon, taken some fifty years earlier. One series of portraits from El-Madani's collection that Zaatari reproduces is that of a gender-nonconforming figure named simply as "Abed, a tailor," who is pictured posing with stereotypically feminine gestures with friends (perhaps lovers) and family members with ease, confidence, and intimacy. I open *Unruly Visions* with this image of "Abed, a tailor," since Zaatari's project of resurrecting and resignifying El-Madani's images continues my own interest in how to read queerness across time and space, in different "home" spaces. Zaatari's re-presentation of "Abed, a tailor"—the portraits' seeming depiction of a gender-nonconforming individual ensconced within a social world—suggests how queerness was simply part of the texture and weave of everyday life in mid-twentieth century south Lebanon, rather than being exceptional and aberrant.

As in the texts I consider in *Impossible Desires*, Zaatari situates queer embodiment, intimacy, and relationality squarely within the space of the home rather than outside of it. In so doing, Zaatari enacts what I term a "queer regional imaginary," where I add the region in its subnational sense as another spatial scale through which to understand the "home" (Gopinath 2018: 5). In his re-presentation of the portraits of "Abed, a tailor," Zaatari excavates a regional photographic archive in south Lebanon to bring its queer valences to the fore. He evokes the alternative gender and sexual arrangements that may exist in the imagined space of the region but that get occluded within nationalist historiography. My reading of Zaatari therefore suggests that the story of the region, as an alternative space of home, is not the story of the nation: there can be something queer about the region that puts it out of step with the temporality of the nation. It is in that temporal and spatial slippage where queerness—in the sense of alternative forms of gendered embodiment, relationality, desire, and intimacy—can emerge. Zaatari's work poses the question that animates both *Impossible Desires* and *Unruly Visions*: how does one dwell in the context of displacement? The aesthetic practices of queer diaspora that have concerned me throughout my career poignantly suggest the imaginative possibilities of precisely those forms of dwelling, of making home, in the context of precarity and disorientation, uncertainty and suspension.

Reference

Gopinath, Gayatri. 2005. *Impossible Desires: Queer Diasporas and South Asian Public Cultures*. Durham, NC: Duke University Press.
Gopinath, Gayatri. 2018. *Unruly Visions: The Aesthetic Practices of Queer Diaspora*. Durham, NC: Duke University Press.

THE DISCIPLINE OF FAMILY

Queering the History of Reproductive Labor

Sara Matthiesen

*F*or a book about reproductive labor, surprisingly little of the history charted in my book *Reproduction Reconceived* takes place in the home (Matthiesen 2021). That was in some ways the point. I had wanted to explore how increasing inequality and precarity at the end of the twentieth century forced different people's family making into various societal margins. In the process, I found that maintaining family under violent systems like mass incarceration or for-profit health care produced new, historically specific forms of reproductive exploitation *outside of the home.* Inspired by both Sarah Haley's (2016: 160) notion of the "domestic carceral sphere" produced by Jim Crow capitalism and social reproduction theory that looks to the many institutions that reproduce the working class, I deliberately sought to stretch the 1970s Marxist feminist insight that the most important shop floor was the home, not the factory.[1] What forms did the reproductive labor extracted from families forged amid Medicaid restructuring, underfunded public hospitals, greater reliance on faith-based charities for aid, mass incarceration, and the HIV/AIDS epidemic take? I wanted to understand how violent systems disrupted the deep association between "family" and "home," forcing the labor of maintaining familial ties into various sites of neglect *beyond* the home, while denying that most of the subjects in my book counted as "family" at all.

It is not a coincidence that the major exception to this approach was the lesbian/queer family making that begins the history charted in *Reproduction Reconceived*. Lesbians who became pregnant through artificial insemination beginning in the 1970s explicitly identified home, family, and reproduction as necessary sites of political transformation. I wanted to know: what labors were required to radically remake notions of family and home, especially when the

GLQ 30:4
DOI 10.1215/10642684-11331042
© 2024 by Duke University Press

criminalization of homosexuality rendered gay men and lesbians unfit for parent-hood in the eyes of the law at the same time that economic insecurity and the backlash against civil rights made caring for children more difficult? I will con-fess that my scholarly curiosity was also driven by my own queer, feminist desire to seize the means of reproduction/reproductive health from the medical estab-lishment. How was a radical experiment in deliberately making families without "Father"—one that sidestepped physician gatekeeping by creating networks of community-sourced sperm—so quickly replaced by fertility clinics that turned lesbians' social infertility into a medical problem in need of treatment, as well as an opportunity for profit?[2]

Exposing the artifice of the dominant norm through a focus on its abnor-mal, deviant counterpart is perhaps the oldest trick in queer studies, but in this case queering the family revealed that heterosexual procreation was but one requirement for normalcy—and privacy. As lesbians helped one another achieve pregnancy through artificial insemination, they advocated welfare as a way to make ends meet, especially during the first months of their infants' life. Those who relied on this strategy found that their request for aid prompted the state to go looking for the player so central to the privatization of dependency: Father. As I chart in the book, in some cases, this resulted in sperm donors being granted access to a child despite the birth mother's wishes to the contrary. Had lesbians managed to cover the tab of queer family making themselves, *especially* when that venture deliberately removed the male breadwinner from the equation, they might have afforded themselves more privacy and thus more control over the terms of their child's upbringing. Instead, by achieving pregnancy without paternity and then seeking aid from the state, lesbian mothers threw a wrench in the gear that is the family within racial capitalism.[3]

The necessary repair? There were of course the court-ordered interven-tions that brought specific individuals' familial arrangements back into line. But I also gestured to a broader, more transformative disciplining made possible by the legal structure of the family itself (and helped along by a good dose of fear that the state would take away lesbians' children). To ensure absolute rights to one's child, more well-resourced lesbian mothers traded in community sperm runners for fer-tility clinics because sourcing sperm through these professional channels nullified donors' parental rights. They also catered to a predominantly white, middle-class clientele, thus reinforcing with a queer twist the bargain between the state and the nuclear family: privacy in exchange for normative self-reliance. Queers who, by choice or necessity, figured out how to get pregnant and have kids through less legally tidy means received no such guarantee.

In other words, the history of lesbian self-insemination and late twentieth-century reforms to parentage law helps explain in part how well-resourced, predominantly white lesbians were allowed to queer the family, just so long as that queering happened along the axis of same-sex sexuality only. Concerned with elevating "families on the margins" in my book, I have since wondered if I inadvertently produced an updated binary of the very sort Cathy Cohen (1997) warned against: those picket-fence, homonormative families versus all nonnormative queers.[4] And so for this roundtable on queering domesticity, I want to be clear about the disciplining effect of being subsumed into the norm. There is the resource and labor extraction fundamental to the privatization of dependency, which is surely bad enough. But that is only the most obvious toll of this intensive process. The feeling that you are the only thing keeping your dependents safe and cared for is surely a special kind of dread.[5] This stress and anxiety frequently turns individuals inward, away from a broader community that could be a bulwark against both psychological distress and material need.

This inward orientation also makes it much harder to cultivate the type of solidarity that Cohen advocated for. After all, the nuclear family is also meant to reproduce normative, disciplined subjects; to interrupt this process would entail refusing not only the fragile protection of privacy, but also remaining true to one's own sense of self even if it means betraying one's family.[6] The fact that "chosen family" constitutes so many queer and trans peoples' lifelines illustrates how this betrayal is often met with expulsion.[7] But there are more ways than one to be a traitor. It has been devastating if clarifying to reflect on what "queering home" can teach us while bearing witness to an ongoing genocide that is being denied in both the halls of power and many a home, queer and straight alike, in the United States. No doubt many of those chanting "Free, Free Palestine!" are learning that refusing to turn inward, away from the suffering that is all of ours to bear, is a costly queer politics when it comes to their place within the family. May this growing refusal mean that "home" can one day mean true, unconditional safety for everyone, which is every living being's birthright.

Notes

My gratitude to the editors for the opportunity to reflect on the theme "queering the domestic" and to Emily L. Thuma for her sharp and kind edits.

1. On social reproduction theory, see Bhattacharya (2017). On key 1970s-era Marxist feminist theorizations of reproductive labor, see Federici (1975) and Fortunati (1981). Another key text from this era that highlighted the racial myopia of the "wages for

housework" campaign and criticized the demand on strategic grounds is Angela Davis's (1983) *Women, Race, and Class.*

2. For a sociological study that explores the biomedicalization of lesbian family making, see Mamo (2007).

3. My analysis of this archive was largely inspired by Cathy Cohen's (1997: 447) landmark article "Punks, Bulldaggers, and Welfare Queens," in which she theorizes an intersectional queer politics comprising subjects whose "nonnormative procreative patterns and family structures" placed them outside of dominant power structures.

4. Cohen (1997: 438) was concerned by and aimed to intervene in a binary she described as "heterosexual and everything 'queer'" that characterized some queer activist groups' political analysis during the 1990s.

5. Add to the list of threats the state itself if your care is labeled as neglect or abuse, and the dread gives way to the nightmare of having your child taken from you. Poor, Black mothers' care and parents trying to care for trans children in states with antitrans laws are most likely to be distorted in this way. This serves to reinforce the race, class, and gender lines around "family" while encouraging its normative subjects to consider such punishment reassurance that they will be spared (all the while dulling their capacity to see that an injury to one is an injury to all). Cohen's (1997: 457) provocation that "maybe most of us" are beyond the protective reach of heteronormative power is instructive here.

6. Recent feminist work on the abolition of the family has been critical to my assessment of the disciplining effects of inclusion in the norm. See especially King (2018), Weeks (2023), Lewis (2022), and O'Brien (2023).

7. For a forthright reflection on the necessity, complexity, and joy inherent in such arrangements, see Malatino (2020: 1–3).

References

Bhattacharya, Tithi, ed. 2017. *Social Reproduction Theory: Remapping Class, Recentering Oppression.* London: Pluto Press.

Cohen, Cathy. 1997. "Punks, Bulldaggers, and Welfare Queens: The Radical Potential of Queer Politics?" *GLQ* 3, no. 4: 437–65.

Davis, Angela. 1983. *Women, Race, and Class.* New York: Vintage Books.

Federici, Silvia. 1975. *Wages against Housework.* Bristol, UK: Power of Women Collective and Falling Wall Press.

Fortunati, Leopoldina. 1981. *The Arcane of Reproduction: Housework, Prostitution, Labor, and Capital.* Translated by Hilary Creek. Brooklyn, NY: Autonomedia.

Haley, Sarah. 2016. *No Mercy Here: Gender, Punishment, and the Making of Jim Crow Modernity.* Chapel Hill: University of North Carolina Press.

King, Tiffany Lethabo. 2018. "Black 'Feminisms' and Pessimism: Abolishing Moynihan's Negro Family." *Theory and Event* 21, no. 1: 68–87.

Lewis, Sophie. 2022. *Abolish the Family: A Manifesto for Care and Liberation.* New York: Verso.

Malatino, Hil. 2020. *Trans Care.* Minneapolis: University of Minnesota Press.

Mamo, Laura. 2007. *Queering Reproduction: Achieving Pregnancy in the Age of Techno-science* Durham, NC: Duke University Press.

Matthiesen, Sara. 2021. *Reproduction Reconceived: Family Making and the Limits of Choice after Roe v. Wade.* Berkeley: University of California Press.

O'Brien, M. E. 2023. *Family Abolition: Capitalism and the Communizing of Care.* London: Pluto Press.

Weeks, Kathi. 2023. "Abolition of the Family: The Most Infamous Feminist Proposal." *Feminist Theory* 24, no. 3: 433–53.

THE DIFFERENCE QUEER AESTHETICS MAKE

Hentyle Yapp

Since *GLQ* was launched in 1993, the journal has included a dossier on film and video, most recently known as the Moving Image Review, that has provided pivotal theoretical and pedagogical pieces that engage queer-oriented films and related topics. This section is shifting to Queer Aesthetics to expand the framework by which to understand and situate queer practices across a broad range of media. This isn't simply indicative of a shift away from a singular medium into the expansion of multiple practices, although that certainly indexes part of this move. This section is also meant to highlight the centrality and import of the analytic of the aesthetic for queer theory, particularly as it relates to key questions surrounding representation, media forms, liberalism, and the academy. I discuss below how this shift to Queer Aesthetics indexes changes in media practices that are indicative of technological advances as well as questions of power as they relate to representation and discourse. Put differently, this new section is meant to capture what the aesthetic broadly indexes in terms of cultural practices and the questions available to queer critique.

This new section will focus on the aesthetic as an organizing rubric for understanding historical and contemporary queer practices. These practices can range from immediately legible media approaches like visual art, film, literature, sound, performance, and new genres, among others, to less legible practices like activist actions or social and political movements that can benefit from being understood through material and aesthetic forms. The range of practices that will be considered in this new dossier is purposely broad, as we are interested in expanding and stretching what might be considered queer, aesthetic, and political. To put it explicitly, queer aesthetics is not meant to segregate the aesthetic from other realms like politics; rather, we hope this section can offer space to expand what the aesthetic can be, as it is not simply another word for "culture" but is

GLQ 30:4
DOI 10.1215/10642684-11331026
© 2024 by Duke University Press

rather deeply imbricated across social power, political economy, and structures. And although this section is certainly invested in queerness, we are focused less on furthering its representation. Queer aesthetics as a framework is meant to place pressure on and question representation as a default discourse, to push toward exploring what else queer aesthetics do in the world, and to think about what representation might enable at the structural level rather than remaining within liberal individualist presuppositions around equity, diversity, and inclusion.

Further, queer aesthetics is meant to capture a few currents working across multiple fields. First, we hope to articulate the desire to produce a purposefully unruly and undisciplined approach that is not wedded to specific field debates, although this frame will certainly be shaped by them. Second, queer aesthetics is meant to push toward a political project that simply does not linger in the aesthetic for aesthetic's sake. Instead, there has been a key concern to think through aesthetics and form as they relate to social structures and histories of violence and dispossession. Below, I trace a genealogy of the discourse around queer aesthetics in order to note some of the main concerns that have historically animated the material discussed in this new section and that will continue to do so. Afterward, I'll turn to the work of Sir Isaac Julien to further illustrate the need to shift from the moving image to queer aesthetics, particularly as his work relates to changes in media form alongside shifts in liberal governance; tensions across the representation of the subject and subjectless critique; and the need to work differently within academic discourse.

Queer Form and Aesthetics: A Genealogy

The citational trail around queer aesthetics is tethered closely to the idea of form. Jennifer Doyle and David Getsy's conversation, initiated in 2010 and published in *Art Journal* in 2013, has become an anchor for tracing a genealogy of queer form and aesthetics. These thinkers work against the limits of art history as a field, particularly as it has been strongly inflected by the likes of Clement Greenberg and Michael Fried. As such, Doyle and Getsy work through the limits of existing discourse around formalism, which often segregates form from politics, whereby queerness is relegated to identity and politics while formalism and form have their own sanctioned and sanctified space. This leads to a discourse that disaggregates queerness from the aesthetic, rendering minoritarian discourse, more broadly, to always be "about" the political or indexical to a particular identity and experience. Kandice Chuh (2021) astutely names this as a condition called "aboutness" that plagues minoritarian discourse, whereby work done by minoritarian artists comes to be discussed in limited ways that become simply about their respective group rather than about broader ideas. To push against this limiting divide of aesthetics from politics/identity, Doyle and Getsy (2013: 65) work through what queer form and aesthetics might do:

> That representation of queer scholarship as "only" about identity (as if what that meant were somehow simple or obvious) erases this feminist and queer attention to certain kinds of labor and attention, ways of working with things—that physicality, that kind of maintenance, sculptural housework. It disavows the erotic, as a language or set of affects animating and inhabiting this kind of work, but also as a mode of knowing (or even being known by) the object.

To rethink how form has been historically considered of and about the provenance of whiteness and men, the turn to queer aesthetics and form is not meant to simply depoliticize queerness but rather to produce a more dynamic method for thinking queerness and aesthetics together. In particular, scholars have worked toward theorizing queerness and social difference, more broadly, as ontological rather than additive to our universal and organizing terms (Ferreira Da Silva 2007; Weheliye 2014; Wynter 2003). As such, queer aesthetics is not meant to bring queerness closer to or simply queer the aesthetic but rather to name how aesthetics need to be rethought and reimagined through histories of power in which queerness is one key component alongside other axes of difference.

Building on this work, queer of color critique has been important in further developing an apparatus and method for the aesthetic, or things deemed minor and less important than the political. By refusing to disaggregate culture from the social, Roderick Ferguson (2003) and Chandan Reddy (2011) produced the groundwork to imagine a more nuanced approach for queer aesthetics. Picking up on this call, Amber Musser, Kadji Amin, and Roy Pérez (2017: 232) refuse the simplistic separation of form from social difference, whereby "form focuses attention on how violence—homophobia, racism, gentrification, capitalism, and colonialism, for instance—has structured conditions of possibility in material and epistemological ways. Violence is both what must be rejected and what must be worked through."

This body of scholarship has led to the aesthetic becoming a key locus to rethink epistemological and ontological structures, deploying the idea of form and aesthetics well beyond the provenance of culture (Bradley 2023; Jackson 2020; Wynter 1992). One key component of this reworking has existed in the works of

Kandice Chuh (2019) and David Lloyd (2018), where they each differently focus on the idea of common sense based on the work of Jacques Rancière. Their approaches diverge with regard to sense: Chuh relies on common sense, along with the work of Sylvia Wynter, as a key component of working with the aesthetic, whereas Lloyd critiques Rancière's notion of common sense for its relationship to a liberal logic of representation. Regardless, they collectively locate sense as a central concern, for which form and aesthetics have become integral components. Most importantly, the larger affective turn was and continues to be a key area that informs the apparatus to think with and through queer aesthetics and sense (Alvarado 2018; Chen 2012; Huang 2022; Kapadia 2019). This direction in queer aesthetics can be traced to the work of José Muñoz, whose earlier work on Richard Fung focused on a Marxist sensibility that Muñoz highlights as "sensuous contemplation" (2000). He further builds upon this work to think through modes of racialized relationality, what he calls a sense of brown, to centralize queer aesthetics as working well beyond the realm of culture (2020). This apparatus has been furthered through the work of Amber Musser (2018, 2024) and Tavia Nyong'o (2018), whose approaches centralize sensation and fabulation for queer aesthetics.

Collectively, these theorists signal the ways in which the disciplinary home for the aesthetic has shifted from art history, visual studies, philosophy, and literature and has commingled with performance and media studies, among other fields. This expansion of fields invested in both queerness and the aesthetic allows us to understand the framework of Queer Aesthetics to be about not only expanding media forms, but also broadening the types of theoretical investments and questions we are enabled to ask. In particular, as stated in the first issue of *GLQ*, the idea of a moving image review was meant to explore the "synchronicity between lesbian and gay culture in the 1990s and the mediums of film and video" (Rich 1993: 83). As B. Ruby Rich reminds us, the journal's initial focus on the space of representation was critical. Film, photography, and video became the primary loci in which the culture wars played out, with conservatives defunding works by the likes of Marlon Riggs and Robert Mapplethorpe. In 1997, Muñoz provided a Film and Video Review titled "Dead White: Notes on the Whiteness of the New Queer Cinema" that focused on the limited representational politics surrounding what has been called New Queer Cinema through his review of films by Todd Haynes, Christopher Ashley, and Todd Verow. Muñoz notably draws from a 1988 special issue of *Screen*, coedited by Julien and Kobena Mercer, cheekily titled "The Last Special Issue on Race." Beyond highlighting the sheer amount of intertextuality embedded across these thinkers, I want to note how Muñoz builds upon this work and refuses to remain within a critique of whiteness, alongside the limits of representation for cinema. Instead, he unpacks how whiteness enables and is used "in the service of creating antiwhite-supremacist critiques" (Muñoz 1998: 138). As Richard Rodriguez (2019: 66) further elucidates through Muñoz, we might then use queer aesthetics to "expose whiteness's incessant ambition to pass as common sense."

I bring these figures from across the pages of the Moving Image Review into my framing to help us understand the shift in the types of questions and concerns we can engage with Queer Aesthetics. I hope to hold onto these earlier concerns while expanding theoretical investigations that rethink what counts as queerness, aesthetics, and politics, or what an expansion away from representation might do for us. Muñoz's 1997 call to consider the function of whiteness, rather than solely being a critique of the whiteness of New Queer Cinema, resonates with his 2009 provocations around what we do with queerness and aesthetics. For him, queer aesthetics allow us to move away from accepting what merely is toward imagining what could be (Muñoz 2009). When we take Muñoz's idea that "queerness is not yet here," queerness becomes less of an identity and more of a gesture toward living otherwise. In other words, the aesthetics of queerness begin from questions of representation but extend into what surrounds and exceeds a subject. In this way, the questions we might consider under the rubric of Queer Aesthetics hold onto this spirit to expand the purview of a subject's excesses and, in turn, the scope of what becomes legible in our critical inquiry.

The development of queer form and aesthetics from the publication of Doyle and Getsy's 2013 conversation to the creation of this new section in 2024 only spans about a decade. This rapid discursive production of queer aesthetics and form developed across disciplinary divides and discipline-specific debates. Further, as I'll discuss below, it also developed amid rapid shifts in how queer and trans lives have existed, from inclusion via marriage rights to complex disavowal within the confines of late liberalism, particularly for the trans community. Certainly, many thinkers around these questions draw from an even longer genealogy of queer aesthetics across history and space. I thus provide this admittedly brief and incomplete genealogy in order to illustrate the speed with which something like queer aesthetics has emerged and how it might assist in rethinking the broader and admittedly undisciplined field of queer and trans studies and theory.

As such, the shift from the Moving Image Review to Queer Aesthetics is meant to capture the evolving landscape of aesthetic practices as well as the need for a renewed use for theorizing connections across aesthetics, politics, and political economy. These connections lead us to rethink practices of media as they relate to liberal representation, the idea of what counts as political and social "change," and academic discourse. In the remainder of this essay, I'll work through these components and illustrate these changes as they relate to the work of Julien. Born in 1960 in London, Julien has become a canonized artist who indexes many of the changes above. First, after working heavily in moving images, his art practice has expanded well into performance and installation art. Second, his work further indexes changes across political and academic landscapes. I will briefly touch upon key moments in his work, while Darius Bost contributes to this dossier by offering a closer look at Julien's classic film *Looking for Langston* through the frame of queer aesthetics.

From *Bowers* (1986) to *Obergefell* (2015) and then to *Masterpiece Cakeshop* (2018); A History of Media and Law; or, A History of Late Liberalism

Moving Image Review has been an important section to trace changes in representational practices. The medium of film has been pivotal to working with and against popular depictions of sex, sexuality, and gender. Film has dominated both how we present ourselves and how we understand representation as an apparatus. Moving Image, as a framework, has captured this idea, along with film's relationship to its predecessor, photography. Starting with the first photographs, known as daguerreotypes, in 1839, image capture has been pivotal to memorialize moments of individual and collective splendor, alongside the policing of communities and the proliferation of dehumanizing images of the other. In other words, images have been central to not only daily public life but also practices related to academic disciplines like anthropology, history, the law, sexology, medicine, and criminology, to name a few.

At the end of the nineteenth century, many experiments went toward the development of cinema, with the Lumière brothers conducting the most famous examples through their expansion from single images to moving images in which to capture both splendor and the dehumanization of specific populations. Certainly, these practices went toward scientific experimentation but also were expanded to have commercial use, shaping consumer practices ranging across cameras, recorders, phones, and other devices. This production has come to be regulated, spurring debates around intellectual property, consumer rights, and privacy. But what these changes in media practices also highlight are not just how we come to be surveilled and policed (Browne 2015) but also what we use to establish proof and evidence (Moore 2022). In other words, media is also indicative of how people come to exist within state and legal regimes.

From this basic premise, we might then historicize the idea of moving images within changes across liberalism, alongside that of queer aesthetics. We can locate the founding of the Moving Image Review in the early 1990s as part of a larger push for representation to work against the long history that has criminalized and policed trans and queer bodies. Representation certainly matters in light of the overlapping histories surrounding photographic capture in anthropology, sexology, law, and criminology at the end of the nineteenth century and well into the twentieth. Representation makes sense as a call to work against liberal and neoliberal practices that seek to erase gender and sexuality and, more broadly, minoritarian difference from the political landscape and cultural imaginary. As we know from the likes of Lisa Duggan (2004), among others, these social categories of difference are deeply imbricated within political economy and culture at large. If we understand moving images as part of a larger toolkit to be used in producing counterrepresentations, this certainly makes sense across most of the twentieth century. Media from photography and film were used to push against and humanize queer and other minoritized populations, which ultimately attempted to challenge and call out the myth of liberal inclusion. The proliferation of moving images has certainly provided the means to work against negative representations that have nonetheless expanded despite the promise of liberal ideals around equality and freedom.

It is no surprise, then, that representation becomes a key discourse in which to understand media practices alongside the law. Representation becomes the logic in which to imagine culture as the means to counter the legalized, state-sanctioned forms of violence that target specific groups. Representation itself is not inherently wrong; it is a practice meant to work against state and legal regimes and cultures that have historically situated the other as abject, inhuman, uncivilized, and criminal. Images can become proof against dominant liberal representations by the state and police power. The simplest example involves citizens filming police misbehavior in order to work against the record and the problematic common sense that presumes the criminality of those racialized, primarily Black, Latinx, and working-class populations. The stakes of representation matter.

However, with the rise of late liberalism, I want to suggest that this dominant discourse of representation is insufficient to fully grapple with changes in media practices—the apparatuses we now use to represent ourselves. Within this context, Julien is a key figure for the idea of moving images alongside queer aesthetics. For the former, his 1989 experimental film, *Looking for Langston*, is heralded as a classic of queer and Black film. A key component of the film's content surrounds practices of representation that expand how we understand the Harlem

Renaissance and the Black Arts Movement beyond a politics of respectability, and it centers Black queer life in important ways. Julien's work around representation operates as a way to reimagine how gender and sexuality, in their relations to racialization, need to be rethought and re-presented in ways that counter the dehumanizing images that arise from a variety of disciplines, even with their liberal leanings. Liberalism promises equality and freedom, yet in 1986 during the AIDS crisis, the case *Bowers v. Hardwick* reproduced the cultural fear of queer bodies as contamination, with the US Supreme Court holding that there was no constitutional protection for sodomy, meaning questions of how to police its practice should be left to states (resonant with the status of abortion rights today). These anti-sodomy laws in the United States find kinship with British common law similarly barring sodomy, with these laws being expanded with Britain's colonial projects throughout the seventeenth and well into the eighteenth, nineteenth, and twentieth centuries. Some of these laws continue in Commonwealth nations. Considering that Julien works within this particular context of British colonialism, it is important to understand how his work in moving images during the 1980s operates as a project against negative representation. However, it is also important to note that Julien's engagement with representation runs alongside a formal experimentation that expands beyond a single medium. In addition, the film is produced by Sankofa Film and Video Collective, which was cofounded by Julien, Martina Atille, Maureen Blackwood, Nadine Marsh-Edwards, and Robert Crusz. This collective exemplifies a broader push to produce media that could grapple with colonialism in a relational way by critiquing British imperialism from the vantage of the many territories and peoples ravaged in its wake, working with the public representation of populations across the Caribbean, Africa, South and Southeast Asia, Australia, New Zealand, Central and South America, and Africa—what we might call the global majority. Sankofa Film and Video Collective was a crucial experiment in seizing the means of representation to counteract centuries of colonial violence as exhibited by the state, disciplines like anthropology, and cultural production.

Julien's prolific career indexes many things. But I want to highlight how his more recent experimentation that moves from the moving image into multiple screens and installations indexes not only an interdisciplinary practice, but also a way to engage the limits of representation and the import of thinking with queer aesthetics. Julien's most recent works have expanded into multiple large-screen installations. Notably, his 2019 *Lessons of the Hour* draws from daguerreotypes and films to highlight multiple media practices as they relate to the liberal idealization of freedom. The work, involving ten screens, meditates on the life of Frederick Douglass. Notably, Julien films moments of photographic capture and reenacts some of Douglass's most famous speeches. This work, I contend, is notable for what it indicates about the need for queer aesthetics to grapple with this expansion of media practices, as well as what it indicates in terms of changes in liberal governance.

Lawrence v. Texas (2003) reversed the decision in *Bowers* (1986) and led to the opening of marriage rights in *Obergefell v. Hodges* (2015). This rapid shift in the expansion of rights occurred within the span of less than thirty years. Representation has certainly contributed to these legal changes. However, what scholars have continued to show is that this expansion of rights does not mean better representation and equality per se; instead, it produces what David Eng calls queer liberalism (2010) and what Jasbir Puar names homonationalism (2007). These terms remind us how queerness and transness are not simply about specific minoritarian lives. As Eng, Puar, and others have established, these identity formations are also tied to and legible through consumer practices. Was the point of more representation to obtain the right to consume, like all other citizens? Or was there a larger point to these queer activist projects beyond the expansion of becoming proper consuming subjects? And even if queers can consume like all others, the structures that continue to police queer lives both nationally and transnationally have become further entrenched.

This attention to consumption, however, is not meant to simply dismiss the practice. After all, Muñoz's work on disidentifications was pivotal to understanding relationships to capital that were more complex, expanding well beyond Frankfurt School theorizations of aesthetics and the culture industry (1999). This collective work has enabled the queer left critique of rights and has articulated the need for a call beyond gay and lesbian assimilation and for the import of focusing beyond a single-issue politic. Further, this focus on aesthetics and queer consumption emphasizes how the transnational rewrites many tenets and assumptions across the field (Liu 2022; Puar 2017; Savci 2020). Within this context, Julien has been creating work that does not necessarily argue for more representation but instead coincides with this radical queer left critique in ways that signal the need for aesthetics to do something beyond furthering a queer liberalism and its attendant projects of representation, inclusion, and consumption. For example, in *Lessons of the Hour*, Julien uses the form of multiple screens to oversaturate the representational landscape. A viewer becomes overwhelmed and wrapped within the narrative in ways that illustrate the complexity of representation rather than its straightforward mediation of images and ideas. Under Julien's astute use of media forms, representation becomes a problem rather than a simple answer.

This aesthetic effect indicates that inclusion and representation have been helpful in one particular historical context. But within the expansion of queer liberalism and liberalism itself from neoliberalism to late liberalism, we are learning that representation has limits. Following *Obergefell*, the 2018 case *Masterpiece Cakeshop v. Colorado Civil Rights Commission* exemplifies these limits and shifts from neoliberalism to late liberalism. *Masterpiece Cakeshop* is notably not a Fourteenth Amendment case involving the equal protection or due process clauses; instead, the case is centered around the First Amendment involving free speech, particularly with regard to religion. Although queer rights have been expanded to marriage and sexual privacy, this case indicates that even if you increase your representation and rights, the larger structure around speech will not necessarily shift. This means that there are limits on representation at the structural level.

These limits are indicative of changes in liberal practices. From classical liberalism into neoliberalism, we are now living what Elizabeth Povinelli (2011) calls late liberalism and what Roderick Ferguson (2012) calls new liberalism. Both of these concepts capture the idea that minoritarian difference has increased its representation, but there hasn't been substantive structural change to rework how institutions operate. You can have your rights, but you can't eat your cake too. And beyond limiting the bounds of cake making, late liberalism also reveals how the expansion of rights leads to structural limits around speech, particularly with recent laws banning books and drag performances that help us rethink the normative operations of cisness and its relationship to other forms of difference. Queer lives have undergone multiple whiplashes during the late twentieth century, which coincides with changes in liberal practices. From *Bowers* to *Obergefell* and then finally to *Masterpiece Cake*, we have gone from negative representation to positive and back to a more complicated picture that highlights the limits of representation.

Julien's work in 2019 and more recently dealing with the oversaturation of representation formally points to the dominance of new and late liberalism. In particular, the oversaturation of screens and images highlights the expansion of representational practices across media. Yet many of the key issues that a figure like Frederick Douglass faced continue to permeate well into today. Institutions might increase representation, but many underlying issues continue, which is the main idea of late and new liberalism. There are limits to the practice of representation. You can display and do it beautifully across multiple screens, but this display will not be enough to manifest the idealizations of liberalism.

Liberalism often presumes representation to be an unmediated good. However, I offer queer aesthetics as a way to place pressure on the logic of representation itself, which has become an even more ubiquitous idea within late liberalism, particularly with the growth of media like the internet and social media that expand representational access and practices. Representation has dominated how we can think and talk about images and its saturation, with the proliferation of images across social media, the internet, and televisual and cinematic cultures. With such a rapid increase in representation, should we not have achieved more in terms of social change? Rey Chow directs us to the limits of representation and its relationship to critique, particularly in this era of expanding rights and media practices. Chow emphasizes how the rise in moving images increases surveillance while highlighting the limits of critique. She reveals how critique relies on the staging of specific problems, connecting discourse from the likes of Louis Althusser and Laura Mulvey back to Bertolt Brecht. This desire to stage our multiple forms of alienation requires that we use images and media to show and display our alienation so as to induce reflexivity, which has become a tenet of critique. "The entanglement of reflexivity and artistic media" means that critique has been based on an idea that media and artistic practices should reveal something about power, which should then lead to reflection (Chow 2012: 24). For example, for both Althusser and Mulvey, art and film should show us something about capital or the male gaze, which should in turn lead to reflection. Within this formula, the proliferation of art and media should theoretically induce more self-reflection; however, Chow notes how this produces instead a much different situation that doesn't simply wed increased cultural representation to legal or social progress.

Both Julien and Chow emphasize the limits in the expansion of media. More screens do not mean better representation. My proposal for this new section is that queer aesthetics doesn't necessarily remove us from this bind. Queer aesthetics accepts these very limits and rather works within and alongside them. Queer aesthetics, I hope, will not reproduce the logic of queer liberalism and late liberalism. Instead of understanding advances in media practices within a teleology where things like performance or new media are better, newer, and expand our modes of representation, we might instead heed the call of Julien and Chow to rethink the apparatus of representation itself rather than simply abandoning it. Queer aesthetics might help us pause from the appeals of liberalism.

To sum up this perhaps untidy argument: *Bowers* enshrines the long logic against queerness that was entrenched in British common law and furthered throughout colonial exploits. This logic permeated well throughout the twentieth century, as exemplified by the holding in *Bowers*. Media representation has worked as a way to rethink these liberal and neoliberal limitations around minoritarian difference. But after *Obergefell* and then *Masterpiece Cakeshop*, queerness has taken on different logics within the era of late liberal governance. We see queerness and transness accommodated but existing within structural limits. As such, it's important to clarify representation as a logic and how a shift toward aesthetics provides space to rethink its dominance. My focus on the law is meant to emphasize how the larger critique of the norm, arising across disciplines, isn't simply a call to show that it simply exists or to seek an expansion of the norm to accommodate more subjects. Instead, both queer studies and disability studies (what has come to be known as "crip theory") establish the radical critique of the norm. Rather than merely assimilating more individuals into the norm, we must restructure in ways that remove the value hierarchies that do not simply increase representation to include more people in the idea of a norm. Instead, the focus on those outside the norm is meant to reorganize the value systems at hand and reimagine them from the ground up. This is another difference we hope queer aesthetics might make.

Representing the Subject and Subjectless Critique: Figuration and Abstraction

Representation, which I take to be a dominant logic and rhetorical structure, informs how both the law and media function, along with how each work with and against one another depending on the historical moment. Representation is where the law and media, which I take to be the juridical and social, come to be negotiated. To be clear, I do not consider representation to be a terrain or ground upon which the state and the social simply fight for the best or right representation. I find this to be a limited idea that either fetishizes individual and collective agency (through a narrative of aesthetic resistance) or overstates the presence of the state (with the law or culture industry creating ideological dupes out of us). Instead, I turn to queer aesthetics precisely because it expands the logics and available language that inform how we make sense of things with and beyond representation. Queer aesthetics, with its attention to not only the visual but also the affective, aural, sonic, haptic, sensual, erotic, visceral, and oral, stretches the logics and rhetorical approaches we have for thought and critique. However, this expansion of senses and media forms shifts how we perceive and make sense even as it provides new forms of argumentation. In turn, we may work toward developing a critical and theoretical apparatus, like queer aesthetics, that might not default into dominant liberal presuppositions.

I thus follow a range of theorists who have been reworking representation. Many across disciplines from transnational feminism (Grewal and Kaplan 1996; Shohat 1989) to art history (Gaines 1993; Mercer 1990; Min 2018; Thompson 2015) have sought to complicate this term for some time. Collectively, what many have argued is that representation has often been deployed against women and queer and trans individuals, particularly those racialized. The politics of respectability often structure how representation comes to be policed within and outside of one's own groups. Rather than arguing over good/bad, appropriate/inappropriate, or proper/improper representation, we need to think of representation as an apparatus, logic, and structure that polices how populations exist. More recently, scholars have emphasized how visibility is a trap (Gossett, Stanley, and Burton 2017), and they have critically directed us toward working with and through opacity (Glissant 2006; Léon 2017), negativity and inconvenience (Berlant 2022), the unruly (Gopinath 2018), the ornamental (Cheng 2018), unbelonging (Ramos 2023), the reject (Goh 2014), and fungibility/indeterminacy (Snorton 2017) as ways to operate beyond representation as the default positivist answer. Meanwhile, representation provides both an entry point to many critical discourses and an important apparatus for critique. It would be too simplistic to dismiss the practice of representation, but it would be similarly limited to uncritically invest in the idea as an ideal. This space for critique has often been understood through what queer theory has called subjectless critique, which comes into tension with the dominant cultural reliance on the representation of the subject (Chuh 2003; Eng, Halberstam, and Muñoz 2005; Keeling 2007).

Beyond those listed above, this turn to subjectless critique can be traced to earlier transnational feminist discourse, particularly Gayatri Spivak's provocations around the subaltern and the representation of the West. In her canonical essay "Can the Subaltern Speak?" she distinguishes two forms of representation: "How the staging of the world in representation—its scene of writing, its *Darstellung*—dissimulates the choice of and need for 'heroes,' paternal proxies, agents of power—*Vertretung*" (Spivak 1988: 74). This distinction across aesthetic representation and political representation is pivotal, as it highlights both overlaps and differences across these realms. Certainly, the aesthetic representations of the other have been expanded in terms of media practices, as exemplified by Julien's career. However, why have we not similarly aimed to expand the very notion of political representation beyond the dominant liberal idea of democratic representation? Liberalism has singularly defined political representation as limited to the notion of democratic representation, which presumes that all citizens have equal access and agency to enact change. However, we know this to not be true (Hartman 1997). Marxism provides a different genealogy of the subject from the comrade to the horde, and some scholars across disciplines have worked hard to rethink the liberal tradition around the subject and its representation. Aesthetic representation has expanded, yet political representation continues to primarily exist within the idea of "'heroes,' paternal proxies, and agents of power" (Spivak 1988: 74).

With this return to Spivak, I offer that subjectless critique can be recast as an attempt to rethink how the very idea of the liberal agentic subject comes to be represented, not only aesthetically but also politically. We can consider subjectless critique then to be a theory of representing the subject that isn't wedded solely to liberal ideals of a whole subject that has agency to enact change, presumably like all others. Instead, the very project of queer of color critique has been to think about the subject through limited modes of agency and within social structures. This larger project, within the language that Spivak provides, has been about expanding the very idea of political representation beyond liberalism. In this vein, subjectless critique greatly informs queer aesthetics as a frame in that it is simultaneously indebted to identity formation while also working well beyond it. Queer aesthetics similarly aims to use queerness and its entangled categories of difference as ways to theorize and expand how we think about political representation beyond the language of liberalism. For example, in Julien's examination of Douglass, he brings us to the nineteenth century to place pressure on the very notion of representability amid the development of US democracy. As the most photographed US citizen in the nineteenth century, Douglass does not simply reproduce the idea that more aesthetic representation equates to better political representation. Rather, Julien directs us to this farce.

The use of Douglass as a figure and this history take us to broader debates around how to present the subject. Subjectless critique, as discussed above, expands the available language and logics to imagine who and what subjects are and how they act. This subject is both concrete and abstract, which is to say that subjectless critique takes us to the terrain of figuration and abstraction. A literal, figurative, or concrete representation of the subject is, at times, heralded as a more political and urgent approach; meanwhile, the abstracted subject is seen as less political, although many will debate if and how the abstract is necessary for the material, literal, and figurative to exist. This ongoing debate is, in my opinion, unanswerable in the sense that we cannot simply privilege one over the other. Rather, this debate is often structured by an anxiety around how politically representable a subject must and can be in relation to a specific political project. If liberalism predetermines this idea of the representability of the subject (since we are presumably equal and fully agentic), then perhaps figuration, humanization, and the literal initially appear more politically astute. However, the abstracted subject and perhaps subjectless critique provide key entryways to think beyond these dominant liberal logics. Thus, we must account for what is lost by not expanding our understanding of political representation and the attendant subject.

This debate is akin to how capital is understood through abstraction and figuration/literalness. When Marx (2005: 449–50) describes "capital in general," he relies on abstracting the very material manifestations of an everyday, concrete economic system. As Stuart Hall (2021: 89) reminds us, this relationship across abstraction and the concrete is not a clean binary:

> Observing, theorizing, and abstraction are inseparable. Similarly, theory is never totally devoid of reference to the real world. . . . What [Marx] says is that, in the first instance, any set of historical events presents itself to us as a mask of complex, unordered, and contradictory phenomenal forms or events. One has to break into them with the necessary abstractions. One has to cut into the thick texture of social life and historical experience with clearly formulated concepts and abstractions. The end result is what he calls the production of "the concrete in thought." . . . Historical understanding always involves a detour through theory; it involves moving from the empirical to the abstraction and then returning to the concrete.

Unsurprisingly, what Hall and others privilege is the *dialectic* produced through figuration and abstraction, which ultimately provides space to return to the concrete. If we think of the liberal representation of subjects and subjectless critique as central parts of this dialectic, we might come close to the idea of queer aesthetics itself, which is a dialectical engagement across form and content; aesthetics and politics; figuration and abstraction; and subject and subjectlessness. Together, they produce the ground upon which to engage and rethink the concrete, which I take less to be about politically legible representation and more about rethinking the terms of political representation beyond liberalism.

Academic (so to) Speak

I hope it is now clear that queer aesthetics is not meant to be discipline specific and is shifting away from the commitments of a single field. Although this dossier is certainly interested in anchoring in field-specific concerns, our hope is that we can use them in ways that broaden their appeal to work across fields. Further, this dossier is meant to expand beyond aesthetics within the field of philosophy proper, although we certainly welcome meditations on the philosophical traditions that inform queerness and aesthetics. This undisciplined orientation follows the example of artists like Julien who have highlighted the limits of academic discourse, pointing to the insufficiencies in our analytics. For example, Samuel Delaney has been and continues to be a key figure for queer thought whose work often precedes academic trends. His centering of explicit sex occurred well before the important and critical work on this topic, which has had an exciting development (Miller-Young 2015; Nash 2014; Rodriguez 2014). Of course, part of this can be attributed to trends in the academy. But most importantly, much of this has to do with the temporality of academic publishing. Although this dossier provides space to shorten the time within academic journal publication, we find it important that this section not simply be fast reviews or criticisms of cultural events, or even rebuttals to them. Although this is helpful for particular genres of writing, we hope that this dossier can work within the limits of academic writing as a genre. This means that we intend for this dossier to run a bit faster than traditional academic publishing but also be geared toward taking time and hesitating on judgment.

In other words, this new dossier, we hope, will provide the space to think deeply with queer practices that can be imagined and written through ideas of aesthetics and form. As such, on a practical level, we will curate and invite works that can range from the thematic (on negative affects or the impossible in queer aesthetics, for example) to media specific (such as queer film of the 1990s or speculative fiction) or a focus on individual artists (like Julien and others). The range of format is also open, including but not limited to interviews, roundtables, profiles, reviews, and short essays. The hope is that pieces are shorter in length (around 2,500–4,500 words) and meant to be theoretically rigorous and/or pedagogically helpful. I will curate sections in this way, but I also welcome proposals from readers of the journal.

Regardless of the organization of this new dossier section, the hope is that Queer Aesthetics provides space to work at a different temporal speed than both popular criticism and traditional academic publishing. I write this in light of the fact that there are calls across the university and other institutions to make statements about current events. I would like to propose that what feels like the longue durée of academic publishing can be a strength that provides space to reflect and think with conflict rather than solely against it. There are certainly views worth immediately challenging, but there are also those that make our ideas better and less reactive. I find this an asset for academic writing as a *specific* genre and one that I hope Queer Aesthetics can help foster that isn't completely wedded to the full length of academic time nor to the rapid pace of likes, clicks, hot takes, and clapbacks. I hope this section can be an experiment within the genre of academic writing. I look forward to curating this section in ways that build upon the work of my predecessors, who made Moving Image Review an important go-to place to think with culture at large. My hope is that Queer Aesthetics can follow this crucial grounding put in place by those I deeply respect and can expand it to account for the wily and expansive queer aesthetic practices taking place today.

References

Alvarado, Leticia. 2018. *Abject Performances*. Durham, NC: Duke University Press.

Berlant, Lauren. 2022. *On the Inconvenience of Other People*. Durham, NC: Duke University Press.

Bradley, Rizvana. 2023. *Anteaesthetics: Black Aesthesis and the Critique of Form*. Stanford, CA: Stanford University Press.

Browne, Simone. 2015. *Dark Matters*. Durham, NC: Duke University Press.

Chen, Mel. 2012. *Animacies*. Durham, NC: Duke University Press.

Cheng, Anne. 2018. *Ornamentalism*. Oxford: Oxford University Press.

Chow, Rey. 2012. *Entanglements, or Transmedial Thinking about Capture*. Durham, NC: Duke University Press.

Chuh, Kandice. 2003. *Imagine Otherwise*. Durham, NC: Duke University Press.

Chuh, Kandice. 2019. *The Difference Aesthetics Makes*. Durham, NC: Duke University Press.

Chuh, Kandice. 2021. "It's Not about Anything." In *Saturation: Race, Art, and the Circulation of Value*, edited by C. Riley Snorton and Hentyle Yapp, 171–82. Cambridge, MA: MIT Press.

Doyle, Jennifer, and David Getsy. 2013. "Queer Formalisms." *Art Journal* 72, no. 4: 58–71.

Duggan, Lisa. 2004. *Twilight of Equality*. Boston: Beacon Press.

Eng, David. 2010. *The Feeling of Kinship*. Durham, NC: Duke University Press.

Eng, David, Jack Halberstam, and José Muñoz. 2005. "What's Queer about Queer Studies Now?" *Social Text* 23, nos. 3–4: 1–17.

Ferguson, Roderick. 2003. *Aberrations in Black*. Minneapolis: University of Minnesota Press.

Ferguson, Roderick. 2012. *The Reorder of Things*. Minneapolis: University of Minnesota Press.

Ferreira Da Silva, Denise. 2007. *Toward a Global Idea of Race*. Minneapolis: University of Minnesota Press.

Gaines, Charles. 1993. *Theater of Refusal*. Irvine: Irvine Fine Arts Gallery, University of California.

Glissant, Edouard. 2006. *Poetics of Relation*. Translated by Betsy Wing. Ann Arbor: University of Michigan Press.

Goh, Irving. 2014. *The Reject: Community, Politics, and Religion after the Subject*. New York: Fordham University Press.

Gopinath, Gayatri. 2018. *Unruly Visions*. Durham, NC: Duke University Press.

Gossett, Reina, Eric Stanley, and Johanna Burton. 2017. *Trap Door*. Cambridge, MA: MIT Press.

Grewal, Inderpal, and Caren Kaplan. 1996. "*Warrior Marks:* Global Womanism's Neo-Colonial Discourse in a Multicultural Context." *Camera Obscura* 13, no. 3: 4–33.

Hall, Stuart. 2021. *Selected Writings on Marxism*. Durham, NC: Duke University Press.

Hartman, Saidiya. 1997. *Scenes of Subjection*. Oxford: Oxford University Press.

Huang, Vivian. 2022. *Surface Relations*. Durham, NC: Duke University Press.

Jackson, Zakiyyah Iman. 2020. *Becoming Human*. New York: New York University Press.

Kapadia, Ronak. 2019. *Insurgent Aesthetics*. Durham, NC: Duke University Press.

Keeling, Kara. 2007. *The Witch's Flight*. Durham, NC: Duke University Press.

Léon, Christina. 2017. "Forms of Opacity." *ASAP/Journal* 2, no. 2: 369–94.

Liu, Petrus. 2022. *The Specter of Materialism*. Durham, NC: Duke University Press.

Lloyd, David. 2018. *Under Representation*. New York: Fordham University Press.

Marx, Karl. 2005. *Grundrisse*. New York: Penguin Books.

Mercer, Kobena. 1990. "Black Art and the Burden of Representation." *Third Text* 4, no. 10: 61–78.

Miller-Young, Mireille. 2015. *A Taste for Brown Sugar*. Durham, NC: Duke University Press.

Min, Susette. 2018. *Unnameable: The Ends of Asian American Art*. New York: New York University Press.

Moore, Kelli. 2022. *Legal Spectatorship*. Durham, NC: Duke University Press.

Muñoz, José. 1998. "Dead White: Notes on the Whiteness of the New Queer Cinema." *GLQ* 4, no. 1: 127–38.

Muñoz, José. 1999. *Disidentifications*. Minnesota: University of Minnesota Press.

Muñoz, José. 2000. "Revisiting the Autoethnographic Performance: Richard Fung's Theory/Praxis as Queer Performativity." In *Like Mangoes in July*, edited by Helen Lee and Kerri Sakamoto, 46–57. Toronto: Insomniac Press. http://www.richardfung.ca/index.php?/writings/jose-esteban-munoz/.

Muñoz, José. 2009. *Cruising Utopia*. New York: New York University Press.

Muñoz, José. 2020. *The Sense of Brown*. Edited by Joshua Chambers-Letson and Tavia Nyong'o. Durham, NC: Duke University Press.

Musser, Amber. 2018. *Sensual Excess*. New York: New York University Press.

Musser, Amber. 2024. *Between Shadows and Noise*. Durham, NC: Duke University Press.

Musser, Amber, Kadji Amin, and Roy Pérez. 2017. "Queer Form." *ASAP/Journal* 2, no. 2: 227–39.

Nash, Jennifer. 2014. *The Black Body in Ecstasy*. Durham, NC: Duke University Press.

Nyong'o, Tavia. 2018. *Afro-Fabulations*. New York: New York University Press.

Povinelli, Elizabeth. 2011. *Economies of Abandonment*. Durham, NC: Duke University Press.

Puar, Jasbir. 2007. *Terrorist Assemblages*. Durham, NC: Duke University Press.

Puar, Jasbir. 2017. *The Right to Maim*. Durham, NC: Duke University Press.

Ramos, Iván. 2023. *Unbelonging*. New York: New York University Press.

Reddy, Chandan. 2011. *Freedom with Violence*. Durham, NC: Duke University Press.

Rich, B. Ruby. 1993. "Reflections on a Queer Screen." *GLQ* 1, no. 1: 83–91.

Rodríguez, Juana María. 2014. *Sexual Futures, Queer Gestures, and Other Latina Longings*. New York: New York University Press.

Rodriguez, Richard. 2019. "Undead White." *GLQ* 25, no. 1: 63–66.

Savci, Evren. 2020. *Queer in Translation*. Durham, NC: Duke University Press.

Shohat, Ella. 1989. *Israeli Cinema*. Austin: University of Texas Press.

Snorton, C. Riley. 2017. *Black on Both Sides*. Minneapolis: University of Minnesota Press.

Spivak, Gayatri. 1988. "Can the Subaltern Speak?" In *Marxism and the Interpretation of Culture*, edited by Cary Nelson and Lawrence Grossberg, 271–313. Basingstoke, UK: Macmillan Education.

Thompson, Krista. 2015. *Shine*. Durham, NC: Duke University Press.

Weheliye, Alexander. 2014. *Habeas Viscus*. Durham, NC: Duke University Press.

Wynter, Sylvia. 1992. "Rethinking Aesthetics." In *Ex-iles: Essays on Caribbean Cinema*, edited by Mbye B. Cham, 237–79. Trenton, NJ: Africa World Press.

Wynter, Sylvia. 2003. "Unsettling the Coloniality of Being/Power/Truth/Freedom." *New Centennial Review* 3, no. 3: 257–337.

THE BLACK GAY MALE IMAGE UNDER SIEGE

Darius Bost

*I*n his analysis of *Looking for Langston*, queer theorist José Esteban Muñoz (1999: 57), drawing from the work of Caribbean feminist theorist Sylvia Wynter, set the task of film studies in the twenty-first century as "decipherment," compelling film scholars to join Julien in meditating on what the film "does." In that vein, this essay approaches this task by considering what *Looking for Langston* "does" to 1980s Black British political culture, of which visual culture was a significant part. It evaluates some of the "procedures" the film uses to intervene in these politics (Muñoz 1999: 57). In so doing, I join a range of critics who have situated the film within the political crises faced by Black, queer, and Black queer people in the 1980s (Carroll 2018; Gilroy 2013; Keeling 2009). I build on this work with particular attention to the power of the image in that time and place. I will show how Julien's focus on embodied performances of waiting, use of the montage, and constructed scenes of Black queer lifeworlds, past and present, challenge the linear modes of temporality. These modes have confined Black politics to a perpetual state of deferment and the modern notion of vision under which the Black gay male image remains under siege.

My interest in the film's relationship to Black British urban politics and culture derives from Julien's use of the refrain "montage of a dream deferred," which Muñoz (1999: 59) identifies as a key Langston Hughes phrase and challenging image that Julien takes up in the film. Julien takes the phrase and image from Hughes's eponymous long poem, which uses the "riffs, runs, breaks, and distortions" of Black popular music to reflect the deferred "dream of political and social empowerment for blacks" in 1940s Harlem.[1] In that time and place, Black people faced segregation, housing shortages, unemployment, and overpolicing. Dissatisfaction with these conditions fueled the 1943 Harlem Riot, which ensued after a white police officer shot a Black soldier for intervening in an arrest. Like Hughes's

GLQ 30:4

DOI 10.1215/10642684-11331002

© 2024 by Duke University Press

use of Black popular music to represent the conditions of Black life in 1940s Harlem, Julien's film is a meditation on the political crises plaguing Black lesbian and gay Britons in the 1980s. Deciphering the urban uprisings in Britain in the 1980s as a form of refusal of what Julius B. Fleming Jr. (2019: 589) calls "black patience," I illustrate how *Looking for Langston* reflects the lived conditions and deferred political dreams of Britain's urban Black communities, and it unsettles the racial-temporal violence that deferred Black gay liberation struggles due to the political crises already facing Black British communities in the 1980s. I decipher the character Beauty's performance of waiting as an expression of Julien's political desire for the materialization of a Black gay male image—photographic, cinematic, and public—unregulated by modern notions of visuality and temporality.

In what follows, I first provide a brief overview of the issues faced by Black British people in the 1980s. I then focus on three ways the Black gay male image became a contested terrain in this period. I link the film's depiction of a bar raid to the police raid that sparked the 1985 Brixton riot and to a gay bar raid in London in 1986. I suggest that this moment in the film shows how Black lesbian and gay British communities were surveilled and targeted. Next, I focus on stereotypes of Black lesbian and gay people in Black media in the 1980s to show how the Black community's concerns about the linkage between negative media representations and overpolicing did not always extend to the Black lesbian and gay community. I suggest that it is the deferment of Black lesbian and gay struggles against patholo-gizing visual representations amid this broader fight that animates Beauty's performance of waiting. Finally, I home in on a 1986 court ruling that forced journalists to turn over footage from the 1985 Bristol riots to the police. This legal struggle over the use of still photographs and film footage as evidence demonstrates how the image became a disciplinary frame. In this way, Julien's choice to "look for" Hughes in *Looking for Langston*, rather than using a documentary approach based on factual evidence, speaks to a broader struggle over the disciplinary uses of the still and moving image in Black Britain in the 1980s.

The 1980s was a tumultuous time for Black Britons. In an editorial reflection on the trials and triumphs of that decade, *The Voice* (1989) newspaper editors called it "the decade of despair." Margaret Thatcher was elected as prime minister in 1979, and her administration's neoliberal policies devastated urban Black communities. Thatcher continued the regressive immigration policies from previous decades through the 1981 Nationality Act, making it harder for those not born in Britain and those seeking to immigrate from Britain's former colonies to attain citizenship. Unemployment skyrocketed to levels unseen since the 1930s due to cuts in industrial training boards, skill centers, information technology grants, and university funding, among other programs. The administration also cut funding for primary and secondary schools and public housing. The gains made by minority groups in the arts, politics, and community organizing receded due to budget cuts to arts funding bodies and community centers. Although civil rights legislation made it illegal to discriminate in state-based institutions, Black people faced widespread racist discrimination and violence. The Tory party's emphasis on law and order did not protect vulnerable Black (a category that included people of African, Caribbean, and Asian descent) communities. Crime rates soared in inner cities due to poverty and illicit economies. Increased crime rates exacerbated the violent policing of inner-city Black communities, which sparked youth-led rebellions in Black enclaves across the country throughout the 1980s.

The "decade of despair" suffered by Britain's Black community serves as a political backdrop for *Looking for Langston*, which Julien made while he was based in London. As film theorist Kara Keeling (2009: 570) observes, "With the emergency siren sounding at the beginning and the end, *Looking for Langston* indicates that its meditation on the past is a response to present pressing concerns." Much of the attention paid to visual representations of the political turmoil in Britain in the 1980s has focused on the Black Audio Film Collective's experimental documentary *Handsworth Songs*, since it directly addresses the riots in inner-city London and Birmingham. However, *Looking for Langston* can also be viewed as a response to Black British people's deferred "dream of social and political empowerment." Julien (1989) alludes to Black Britain's state of emergency through the character Beauty's line, "I'll wait," the sole direct speech act in the film, and through the depiction of the raid by armed civilians and police officers on the underground queer nightclub.

As Alex walks across the marshy grass and confronts Beauty in a dreamlike sequence, Richard Bruce Nugent's short story "Smoke, Lillies, and Jade" is recited in the background. When the two characters confront one another in the film, Beauty speaks a line from the story—"I'll wait Alex"—without the direct object. This slight differentiation opens the scene to a broader discussion of political deferment referenced in the film. Literary scholar Rachel Jean Carroll (2018: 503) reads the line as adding an investment in futurity regarding Black gay desire and Black sexual politics: "Beauty's promise introduces futurity in a film otherwise preoccupied with the present and the past. Beauty waits at the edge of the film and of politics." While I agree that this scene marks the film as concerned with Black (gay) politics, the film's suspicion of linear temporality and discursive ordering leads me to question how Beauty's speech act relates to broader concerns about time and Black politics.

The phrase "I'll wait" brings to mind literary scholar Fleming's (2019: 589) theorization of "black patience," which he defines as "a racialized system of waiting that has historically produced and vitalized anti-Blackness and white supremacy by compelling Black people to wait and to capitulate to the racialized terms and assumptions of these forced performances of waiting." Fleming's theory is beneficial for deciphering *Looking for Langston* because it demonstrates how Black cultural producers challenged "black patience qua black patience—a performative attempt to unsettle 'the wait' in and through a radical performance of waiting" (590). Fleming provides a way to read the film's retreat into the realm of fantasy, its quietness, monochrome texture, and emphasis on aesthetic beauty as aligned with, rather than contrary to, Black politics.[2] Except for the bar raid at the end of the film and the alarms, the film seems less concerned with the political crisis in Britain than with the silencing of queer identity and cultural expression in Black American culture. However, Kobena Mercer (1993: 249) views Julien's aesthetic strategy of meditation as a link to the political dreams and desires of Black Britons:

> The film is as much a meditation on the psychic reality of the political unconscious—which concerns the imaginary and symbolic conduits of the diaspora, through which black Britons have sought to symbolize our dreams and desires in part through identifications with black America and black Americans—as it is a poetic meditation on the psychic and social relations that circumscribe our lives as black gay men.

Thinking Fleming and Mercer together permits a reading of Julien's "meditation" as a performative unsettling of the "racialized system of waiting" that plagued the lives of Black Britons in the 1980s.

Black Britons' forced performances of waiting grew out of the failures of the Race Relations Acts of the 1960s and 1970s to mitigate anti-Black discrimination and violence—in the forms of racist policing, social and economic neglect, and white supremacist terror—after the rise of the National Front and the right turn in politics in England in the mid- to late 1970s. The urban uprisings of the 1980s can be interpreted as a form of resistance to this "racialized system of waiting" and a refusal "to capitulate to the racialized terms and assumptions of these forced performances of waiting." These uprisings were often the culmination of histories of racist policing, which sometimes resulted in injury or death. The riot in the Brixton neighborhood in south London, where *Looking for Langston* was screened shortly after its release, was sparked by the police raid on the home of Dorothy "Cherry"

Groce. The police shot and permanently injured Groce while trying to execute a warrant on her twenty-one-year-old son, Michael. The raid on an underground club by police officers and armed civilians in the film situates *Looking for Langston* among the aesthetic responses to urban uprisings in Britain in the 1980s. It links the film's generic structure to the temporal logics of "black patience." As a montage that traverses the lines between past and present and skirts the conventions of the documentary form, the film circumvents the modes of temporality that undergird post–Civil Rights narratives of liberal progress.

The Black community's struggle against the negative media representations that fueled overpolicing did not often encompass the lesbian and gay community. If the police raid speaks to Black urban rebellions in Britain in the 1980s, the mob's targeting of an underground club for same-sex-desiring men recalls the history of police raids on gay bars. The 1969 Stonewall Rebellion in the Greenwich Village neighborhood of New York City influenced LGBTQ rights movements across the globe, including the United Kingdom, as seen in the formation of the London Gay Liberation Front in October 1970 and the first Pride March on July 1, 1972. The Stonewall Rebellion did not end LGBTQ people's struggles against policing, however. In 1986, three years before the release of *Looking for Langston*, the police raided the historic gay bar Royal Vauxhall Tavern to seize poppers—chemical substances inhaled to produce a temporary euphoric sensation—which the media had linked to HIV infection (Kelleher 2021). If we suppose the film is about the desire for Black gay identity, then Beauty's vow to wait is also about the multiple marginalizations of Black lesbian and gay people in the 1980s and how their ongoing struggles for liberation were often deferred because of the political crises already facing Black communities.

Black lesbian and gay people were also fighting against section 28 of the Local Government Act, which outlawed among local authorities the promotion of homosexuality and the publication of any materials that would promote homosexuality. The 1988 law followed the moral panic over introducing educational materials about homosexuality and gay parenting to young schoolchildren. The Conservative Party used this controversy in political attacks against the Labour Party, which controlled one of the local education authorities where the materials were being distributed. Black lesbian and gay activists feared that the law would force community spaces like the Haringey Black Lesbian and Gay Centre in London to close, leaving many Black lesbian and gay people in "isolation and despair" (*The Voice* 1989). However, the law drew support from some Black church leaders who wanted to protect "young children from an evil society" (*The Voice* 1987).

The marginalization of Black lesbian and gay identities extended to their struggles against communal violence. Though Black communities were actively contesting the visual representations that made them subject to increased policing, the Black media often stereotyped lesbian and gay people as perpetrators of violence. In the 1980s, the Black newspaper *The Voice* was riddled with front-page stories representing sexual minorities as deviant. Headlines like "Male Model Chopped up Gay Lover" (*The Voice* 1988), "Woman Jailed over Lesbian Love Shooting" (Collins 1989), and "I Was a Kinky MP's Rent Boy" (Harrison 1987) made it to the newspaper's front pages. On the day section 28 was passed, *The Voice* ran the cover story "Evil Gay Sex Boss Jailed" (Stewart 1988). The focus on scandal, criminality, and illicit sex diverted attention away from Black lesbian and gay community members' vulnerability to violence and harm.

Numerous articles demonstrate how race and sexuality converged to make Black lesbian and gay community members targets for victimization. For example, a Black social worker trainee left his job because of campaigns accusing him of having HIV/AIDS, false police reports accusing him of burglary, and calls for him to be shot (Solanki 1989). In another case, when a family petitioned the police to solve the murder of their son, the police suspected that the son's murder was related to his involvement in the gay community. The family denied that their son was gay and viewed this turn in the case as a diversion tactic used by the police to discontinue their investigation into the real motive (Hinds 1987). In another case, a young gay Black man in southeast London went into hiding after a two-year campaign of harassment against him and his family. The Brixton-based Lesbian and Gay Black Group, of which Julien was once a part, launched a campaign for his protection after someone tried to run over the young man's roommate with a car. The group called the attack an escalation of other such attacks in the area (*Caribbean Times* 1989).

Historian Kieran Connell (2012: 130) has discussed how the appearance of the infamous photograph of a "black bomber" taken during the Handsworth Riots on the front page of every national tabloid became emblematic "not only of the riots in Handsworth but also of the perceived nature of the area as a whole." The photograph exemplified for outsiders the consequences of Black settlement in inner cities and stereotyped Black youth as driven by "bloodlust" (133). The Black press's front-page stories of Black lesbian and gay criminality similarly portrayed the community as a whole as deviant. Black media representations of Black lesbians and gays in the 1980s bring me back to the bar raid that punctuates the film. The scene of the bar raid by Black and white armed civilians and police officers makes visible the Black gay British community's targeting on multiple fronts. That the club is besieged brings to the fore the hypervisibility and surveillance of Black lesbian and gay people amid the anti-Black racism, AIDS pandemic, and state-based homophobia of the 1980s. The clubgoers' disappearance emblematizes how their vulnerability to policing was obscured and Julien's political desire for a Black gay image not under siege.

Julien's exploration of the convergence of the image and criminalization is also evidenced by his choice to avoid the trappings of documentary realism in his search for the queer life of Langston Hughes. Instead of a documentary approach that seeks to "arrive at an unequivocal answer embodied in factual evidence," Julien's film unsettles the wait for the "gatekeepers and custodians" of Black history and culture to end their practice of omitting any references to Hughes's ambiguous sexuality (Mercer 1993: 249). The struggle to control the image—particularly its use as factual evidence—was also an issue within the political context of Black rebellions in 1980s Britain. In October 1986, BBC TV and Harlech Television went to court to fight an order by Bristol police to confiscate the photography and film footage taken by local journalists after the riots in the city's St. Paul neighborhood. Journalists opposed the order because of the risk it posed to journalists, given that photojournalist David Hodge had been killed one year earlier in the Brixton riots, and it jeopardized editorial confidentiality (Dean 1986). The court battle was a test case for the police's power to seize evidence under the 1984 Police and Criminal Evidence Act. BBC and Harlech lost the case and were ordered to release the footage for police review (*The Voice* 1986). Although journalistic material, such as documents held in confidence, was protected under the act, the judge ruled that footage of the riot served the public interest. Julien's choice to "look for" Langston Hughes instead of outing him reflects the "present pressing concerns" regarding how the image's claim to truth could be used by the state to discipline and punish.

In its focus on Hughes and the Harlem Renaissance, *Looking for Langston* may not seem to belong among the artistic responses to Black British communities' political crises in the 1980s and their riotous refusals to wait on the state to alleviate their circumstances within the terms of law and order. Yet Julien's focus on embodied performances of waiting and cinematic techniques positions him among this group. Fleming (2019: 589) demonstrates how Black people have used performance to make an "embodied claim to a different time-space horizon." I would include the racial and sexualized performance of waiting enacted by the character Beauty. Beauty's promise to "wait" calls forth a desire for a Black gay male image—photographic, cinematic, and public—to materialize beyond narratives of racial and sexual deviance and for Black gay political issues not to be deferred by an intraracial demand for gay patience. Circumventing the linear modes of temporality that leave Black lesbian and gay politics in a perpetual state of deferment, the film "unsettles" Black gay male performances of waiting for an image that is not always under siege (Fleming 2019: 589).

Notes

1. *Oxford Reference*, s.v. "Overview: Montage of a Dream Deferred," https://www.oxford reference.com/view/10.1093/oi/authority.20110803100206738 (accessed March 11, 2024).
2. Kobena Mercer (1993: 239) describes the film as creating "a dreamlike space of poetic reverie" and one that "self-consciously places itself in the art cinema tradition."

References

Caribbean Times. 1989. "Homophobes Hound Gay Man." August 25–31.

Carroll, Rachel Jean. 2018. "Can You Feel It? Beauty and Queer of Color Politics in *Looking for Langston*." *Criticism* 60, no. 4: 487–509.

Collins, Yvonne. 1989. "Woman Jailed over Lesbian Love Shooting." *The Voice*, November 14, 1.

Connell, Kieran. 2012. "Photographing Handsworth: Photography, Meaning, and Identity in a British Inner City." *Patterns of Prejudice* 46, no. 2: 130.

Dean, Malcolm. 1986. "Media to Fight Police Demands for Riots Films." *The Guardian*, October 14.

Fleming, Julius B., Jr. 2019. "Transforming Geographies of Black Time: How the Free Southern Theater Used the Plantation for Civil Rights Activism." *American Literature* 91, no. 3: 587–617.

Gilroy, Paul. 2013. "Bad to Worse." In *Isaac Julien: Riot*, edited by Isaac Julien and Cynthia Rose, 35-44. New York: Museum of Modern Art.

Harrison, Mark. 1987. "I Was a Kinky MP's Rent Boy." *The Voice*, April 1.

Hinds, Simon. 1987. "Family Deny Dead Son Was Gay." *The Voice*, November 17.

Julien, Isaac, dir. 1989. *Looking for Langston*. London: Sankofa Film and Video.

Keeling, Kara. 2009. "Looking for M—: Queer Temporality, Black Political Possibility, and Poetry from the Future." *GLQ* 15, no. 4: 565–82.

Kelleher, Patrick. 2021. "Revisiting the Outrageous 'Poppers Raid' That Saw Police Arrest 11—including Lily Savage." *Pink News*, October 10. https://www.pinknews .co.uk/2021/10/10/royal-vauxhall-tavern-popppers-hiv-police/.

Mercer, Kobena. 1993. "Dark and Lovely Too, Black Gay Men in Independent Film." In *Queer Looks: Perspective on Gay and Lesbian Film and Video*, edited by Martha Gever, Pratibha Parmar, and John Greyson, 238–256. New York: Routledge.

Muñoz, José Esteban. 1999. *Disidentifications: Queers of Color and the Performance of Politics*. Minneapolis: University of Minnesota Press.

Solanki, Paresh. 1989. "Social Worker Flees Anti-Gay Threats." *The Voice*, September 12.

Stewart, Annie. 1988. "Evil Gay Sex Boss Jailed," *The Voice*, May 24.

The Voice. 1986. "BBC Lose 'Riot' Film Case: Police Get the Bristol Footage." November 29.

The Voice. 1987. "Gays Fight Tory Ban." December 5.

The Voice. 1988. "Male Model Chopped up Gay Lover." January 19.

The Voice. 1989. "Decade of Despair." May 9.

"READ BETWEEN THE LINES"

Theorizing Media and Activism in China

Zhen Cheng

Digital Masquerade: Feminist Rights and Queer Media in China
Jia Tan
New York, NY: New York University Press, 2023. 208 pp.

Setting eyes on contemporary China, Tan Jia's new publication, *Digital Masquerade: Feminist Rights and Queer Media in China*, is an ambitious attempt at theorizing "rights feminism" and queer activism in digital media culture in today's China. This exploration into the contemporary, which utilizes materials gathered from 2012 to 2019 alongside Tan's field research in 2014 and 2019, may present a perspective that is highly curated and subjective. While Tan does not explicitly justify her selection of this particular time frame, she anchors the book's delineation of "contemporary" to a period she identifies as witnessing a "resurgence of rights connotations" in feminist practices and discourses (2). As the foundational concept of this book, Tan introduces and elaborates on "rights feminism," which is a translation of the term *nüquanzhuyi*. The book traces the concept of *nüquan* (women's rights) back to the early twentieth century and showcases how rights feminism has emerged as a new wave in the twenty-first-century Chinese feminist movement.

The five chapters are thematically linked through the concept of "digital masquerade," by which Tan describes the ways in which queer and feminist media users and activists navigate "the technological affordance and regulatory environment," which are simultaneously liberating and constricting (18). Chapter 1 examines the strategic practice of digital masking and masquerade in feminist activism. It delves into the historical development of feminist and queer media activism, highlighting how these movements have shaped the current landscape of new rights feminism. Focusing on the Youth Rights Feminist Action School and the Feminist Five's detention, the first chapter discusses how feminists use media to circumvent censorship, craft narratives, and stage provocative online and media performances. As one of the pillar concepts, masquerade is defined as "to pose for the camera, the journalist, and ultimately the reader of the news or the Internet user" (43) and to "stage controversial bodily performances for the media" (48). Chapter 2 deals with "the rights feminism," a term introduced by Tan to highlight the interconnected focus on a range of rights-based issues within activism, including human rights, equal rights, and women's rights. The chapter explores the pivotal role media plays in shaping *quan* (rights) in new rights feminism and LGBT activism, primarily in NGOs. The chapter traces the rise of new rights feminism and its intricate links to the global human rights framework. It examines the flexible and nuanced deployment of rights across international, domestic, and legal spheres. Specifically, this chapter introduces the concept of performative rights, underscoring the reciprocal influence of rights and media, which, according to Tan, comprises three elements: the disruptive appropriation of rights frameworks, the tactical and situational use of rights, and the media's foundational role in shaping rights discourse.

With Chapters 1 and 2 establishing the bases for the two main conceptual innovations of this book, the rest of the chapters provide diverse case studies. Chapter 3 examines the role of filmmaking in feminist and queer NGOs as a crucial medium for articulating queer experiences. It highlights how initiatives like Queer University's (*ku'er daxue*) film workshops influence video-making and circulation, with films like *Comrade Yue* (2013) defying mainstream narratives by portraying diverse and evolving queer lives. Employing concepts from "accented cinema" and queer Sinophone studies, the chapter showcases how filmmaking serves as a means of investigating identity and fostering community. Chapter 4 shifts attention to the Asia Pacific Queer Film Festival Alliance's (APQFFA) role in circulating queer cinema across Asia and the Pacific, critiquing the Euro-American focus in queer studies through diverse disciplinary lenses, including transpacific, inter-Asia, and indigenous studies. Through analyzing the Tonga documentary film *Lady Eva* (2019) and APQFFA's engagement with queer rights, this chapter examines how these queer media disrupt the "spatiotemporal hierarchies" (28). The most relevant to the concept of digital masquerade in this chapter are the guerilla-like tactics of ShanghaiPRIDE's film festival organization, employing *huodong* (events) as a means to circumvent surveillance. Chapter 5 looks at short films and videos that are funded and circulated by lesbian social networking platforms, namely LESDO and the L. Going beyond mere advertising and entertainment, these short films "inspire female same-sex desire" and generate new sociality, albeit with a focus on urban, middle-class life (29). With these discussions, Tan raises the concept of "platform presentism," a very different take on what we usually think about presentism, to refer to the ways these apps produce contemporary, "light" content that evades censorship and breaks away from previous representations of lesbianism as the mournful past.

Tan's book offers an ambitious and extensive exploration of the dynamic interplay between digital media, feminist rights activism, and queer culture, interrogating the ever-evolving landscape of contemporary queer media. It thoughtfully integrates the practices and experiences of the queer community, especially lesbian, into the narrative of feminist activism, positioning them as central to the movement's evolution. Rich in references, the book serves not only as an extensive bibliography for scholars and readers who work in related fields but also as a crucial archive for activism, preserving the core of feminist and queer efforts that face the threat of erasure due to escalating censorship in China.

However, Tan demonstrates a tendency to base her ideas on sweeping claims. In order to distinguish the new wave of feminist activism from its historical counterparts, Tan posits that "the notion of women's rights came under attack" during Mao's socialism and brackets the nuances of this earlier era (12). Plenty of historical and anthropological studies such as Yan Yunxiang's *Private Life under Socialism: Love, Intimacy, and Family Change in a Chinese Village, 1949-1999* (2003) have offered ample evidence probing bottom-up agency and mobility of women's rights, despite the seemingly "monopolized" official discourse. Readers should be cautioned about these generalizations and not to perceive concepts such as "Mao's period" or "contemporary China" as a fixed landscape.

In terms of scope, the book embraces a broad array of topics, which sometimes may dilute the focus on the specificities. While the inclusion of theoretical hot words such as "neocolonialism" and "indigenous studies" is inspiring, a concentrated and grounded analysis might offer a more incisive look at the nuances of the valuable cases. Moreover, while the book initially presents "masquerade" and "rights" with clarity, these concepts tend to expand to such a degree that they risk becoming overly inclusive, diminishing their critical sharpness. A delicately balanced approach to these complex theories could serve as a more precise guide, helping readers navigate the intricate layers of contemporary activism without the terms becoming too general and all-encompassing.

While Tan's theoretical approach to contemporary queer media culture may not be her most pronounced achievement, the book's significant merit lies in its integration and juxtaposition of a varied collection of primary sources, enriched by her embodied experiences. A particularly captivating section is Tan's vivid account of her experiences participating in a *huodong* at the ShanghaiPRIDE Film Festival. She describes a last-minute venue shift due to political interference, which led her to a small, overcrowded bar with less-than-ideal screening equipment. With the unique autoethnographic touch and the irreplicable firsthand materials, what Tan modestly refers to as "minor, mundane, and ephemeral" details could very well be the most enlightening, engaging, and compelling aspect of this book (149).

Zhen Cheng is a PhD candidate in the Department of Performing and Media Arts at Cornell University.

DOI 10.1215/10642684-11331082

THE QUEER WORK OF ABSTRACTION

Joseph Henry

Dragging Away: Queer Abstraction in Contemporary Art
Lex Morgan Lancaster.
Durham, NC: Duke University Press, 2022. 208 pp.

Between the domains of practice, theory, and the market, queer contemporary artists have for a number of years now fortified their positions on either side of a figuration-abstraction debate. Figurative art, typically in painting, has been affirmed by critics, institutions, and audiences for picturing underrepresented subjects and conveying the intimacy and materiality of queer life. Abstract art, alternatively, has been supported for its tactical avoidance of such literalism and for a more capacious understanding of politics and aesthetics. Lex Morgan Lancaster's *Dragging Away: Queer Abstraction in Contemporary Art* arrives as one of the few scholarly treatments to analyze this latter dynamic in depth. While it contributes a much-needed sustained study, it at times undersells the historical and theoretical complexity of its subject matter.

Lancaster defines their titular concept as the general queering of "older modernist aesthetics" by contemporary artists, mostly figures working in the United States. Ulrike Müller, for examples, attenuates hard-edge geometry in her enamel paintings; Lorna Simpson qualifies the regularity of her gridded photographs with the textures of felt; and Tiona Nekkia McClodden imbues high-design Bauhaus objects with a queer touch of BDSM. Queer abstraction for Lancaster thus need not be produced by queer-identifying artists or resemble something like capital-A Abstract Art. Instead, it performs a broader visual and material "catachresis," "a formal property or technique that exceeds immediate reference or classification through a promiscuous deployment of materials that cross categorical boundaries, allowing a specific medium to perform in ways that depart from its normal function" (15).

As *Dragging Away* acknowledges, this subversion of modernism was already an operative strategy in the work of postwar artists like Harmony Hammond and Jasper Johns. Lancaster's historiographic intervention is then to move beyond an older art history of the closet, as it were, that insisted on occluded sexuality in otherwise non-representational artwork. These earlier arguments read abstract form, per Lancaster's words, "as an implicit bodily reference, reducing abstraction to a signifying content—a phallus here, a breast there" (9), working "only by way of reference" and not addressing "the queering work of abstraction itself" (37). A more astute read of queer abstraction instead looks to artwork that politically challenges the "demand that artists who are marked by difference must 'show up' in ways that are expected" and, in so doing, creates "a site to generate alternative spaces and worlds" (8).

Lancaster returns repeatedly to this catachrestic alterity as the prime accomplishment of their chosen objects. These works "sometimes [render] the mediated space of the canvas or screen as one where something appears but is *not* stabilized or fixed" (11). They "[produce] possibilities for alternate movements and undefined directions, a slipperiness that does not slide into settled singular meaning but can chart new territories for something like belonging or freedom" (40). They "actively [refuse] categorical visibility" and "[make] spaces for something else" (117). Although these claims may generously encourage interpretive porousness, even reparative reading, in their sheer repetition throughout the book they also tend to produce counter-significatory force precisely as a transcendental signified to which all abstraction aspires. If all queer abstraction refuses fixity, such categorical refusal can in turn generate its own normativity. One longs for a more pointed, less withheld analyses of specific case studies in *Dragging Away*.

These theses lose an interventional edge because Lancaster often presents contemporary practice in a binary comparison with an older, less capacitating modernism. Müller's enamel paintings, for example, queer and disrupt the "straight lines and limited primary color palette" (43) of László Moholy-Nagy's so-called *Telephone Pictures* (1923), now held by the Museum of Modern Art in New York. "In Moholy-Nagy's work," Lancaster affirms, "figure-ground relations are not complicated—it appears as if the black, red, and yellow lines are set as figures against the larger white field" (45). That description may be disputable as a matter of interpretation—the *Telephone Pictures* in fact tend to buckle and warp through the undulations of their steel supports—but it more problematically permits a construction of something like a totalizing "crisp Bauhaus aesthetic" (38) mobilized by Lancaster but refuted by the actual craft, montage, performance, film, and indeed queer work also produced by the German school. The readymade, likewise, for Lancaster now disturbs "settled operations" in contemporary hands, no matter the (often libidinal) semiosis in which its original modernist applications already traded (130). Regarding postwar genealogies, we learn too late in the book of the "lesbian feminist artmaking tactics" (119) of the 1970s that seemingly informed what queer abstraction is now. Such underarticulated art history in *Dragging Away* threatens to not only flatten certain narratives but rob contemporary artists of their more dialectical engagement with the past.

A withdrawal from close historicist examination is a deliberate strategy by Lancaster, who instead targets "haptic forms and visceral material operations" to locate "the social and political potential of abstraction" (32). This strategy may have limited the book's overall contribution in advance. An excellent section interprets Lorna Simpson's print ensemble *The Park* (1995), a divided a series of panels depicting an urban greenspace with a felt grid and accompanying text that features distanced observation of the park's cruising activities. Lancaster considers the top-down organization of *The Park*'s composition against the sheer touch of its felt and the sexual object of its investigation. "While the grid would seem to be one of the most formulaic and absolute forms of modernism," the author argues, "producing an endless repetition of lines that demarcate and divide, this particular technology for organizing space can in fact generate intimate spaces of contact that do not collapse the specific into the general" (67). The grid departs from a context of pictorial abstraction to become an affective model of erotic impersonality, where queer life can still play out within and beyond a certain pleasure of regulation. Here, as in an intriguing discussion of the pride flag and its para-collectivity, abstraction is not just something made of queer life but already immanent to it. Abstraction may be an interesting property of art objects, but it thrives in art's subjects, too.

Joseph Henry is the Florence B. Selden Fellow in the Department of Prints and Drawings at the Yale University Art Gallery and a PhD candidate in the art history program at the Graduate Center of the City University of New York.

DOI 10.1215/10642684-11331106

A CRITICAL LOOK AT MALE HETEROFLEXIBILITY IN LATIN/O AMERICA

Richard Mora

Neobugarrón: Heteroflexibility, Neoliberalism, and Latin/o American Sexual Practice
Ramón E. Soto-Crespo
Columbus: The Ohio State University Press, 2023. 210 pp.

Neobugarrón is a timely and thought-provoking contribution to queer studies literature. Soto-Crespo examines the discursive, visual, and literary representations of *bugarrón*, a traditional sexual practice of heteroflexible men who "perform only the 'active,' 'penetrative,' or 'insertive' role" in sex with other men and "maintain their identity as straight men" (46). Over the course of four chapters, as the cultural history of the *bugarrón* sexual practice comes into focus and we are introduced to the neo*bugarrón*—"a key component in the relationship between capital and sexuality in the Caribbean and the Global South"—it is evident that this nonexclusive heterosexuality is deserving of scholarly attention (49).

The opening chapter examines how, during the 1990s, anthropologists and public health officials erased and demonized *bugarrón* practitioners as HIV/AIDS proliferated throughout Latin America. Ethnographic studies of sexual cultures in Central America, Mexico, and in the US-Mexico border region reduced *bugarrón* practitioners to the sex acts they engaged in. More to the point, the anthropological discourse presented these men as closeted homosexuals and referred to them as *bugarrón*, even though they identified as heterosexual and did not use the term *bugarrón* as their sexual identity. Unaccounted for in the ethnographies was the fact that "*bugarrón* sexual practice shows a continuum from homosociality to non-gay sexual desire between men" (156). Nonetheless, medical professionals turned their attention to the *bugarrón*, as defined in the anthropological discourse, and considered them transmitters of HIV between the homosexual and heterosexual communities. Public health officials who employed the concept of men-who-have-sex-with-men (MSM) in their HIV prevention efforts implemented initiatives to surveil *bugarrón* practitioners. In a damning indictment, Soto-Crespo contends that as HIV spread, both sexual anthropologists wanting to make a scholarly impact and medical professionals seeking to secure additional public health funding targeted *bugarrón* practitioners.

The second chapter details how the neoliberal economies of Latin America and the Caribbean have commodified the *bugarrón* sexual practice, disconnecting it from its historical meaning, and giving rise to the image of the *bugarrón* as sex worker. Soto-Crespo refers to this new subject of capital within the sexual tourism markets of the Caribbean as the *neobugarrón*. Social media photos, online ads, and visual art representations of the *neobugarrón* make this sexual subject culturally visible, unlike the traditional *bugarrón* practitioner, and contests the visual representation of gayness. Soto-Crespo convincingly argues that the wide use of the term *bugarrón* to refer to male sex workers is why the emergence of the *neobugarrón* has gone unnoticed.

In the third and fourth chapters, Soto-Crespo examines the representation of the *bugarrón* sexual practice in film and literature, respectively. He analyzes the visibility of *bugarrón* sexual practice in Latino American films produced since the end of the last century that represent male heteroflexibility and gave rise to the cinematic *bugarrón*. To depict *bugarrón* sexual practice, filmmakers modified their techniques. With their visual representation of a nonexclusive heterosexuality that diverges from the heterosexual/homosexual divide, the films expand the representation of male pleasure and "complicate the theoretical frameworks that normally analyze homosexuality, queer, and exclusive heterosexuality" (121). Similarly, Soto-Crespo analyzes a selection of Caribbean and Latin American literary works that rely on *bugarrón* tropes. With his critical readings, he makes the case that these texts, including ones that equate *bugarrón* sexual practice with a closeted gay identity, comprise an initial thread of *bugarrón* representation in literature. Tellingly, English translations of some of the works make clear that the *bugarrón* sexual practice, like the term *bugarrón* itself, is untranslatable.

Neobugarrón, an accessibly written book, is highly recommended for course adoption. The interdisciplinary examination of a sexual practice that has received scant scholarly attention makes it an excellent text for courses in the areas of gender, sexuality, and queer studies, especially those with a focus on Latin America, the Caribbean, and the diaspora. The discussion of both the link between sexuality and neoliberalism and the nonexclusive heterosexual men who do not fit neatly into sexual categories will undoubtedly provoke in-class deliberations as well as significantly inform future scholarship.

Richard Mora is a professor of sociology at Occidental College.

DOI 10.1215/10642684-11331122

RACIALIZATION AND SEXUAL MODERNITY IN THE UNITED KINGDOM

Gee Imaan Semmalar

Deadly and Slick: Sexual Modernity and the Making of Race
Sita Balani
London: Verso, 2023. 224 pp.

Sita Balani's first single-authored monograph, *Deadly and Slick: Sexual Modernity and the Making of Race*, is an exploration of the co-constitution of race and sexuality primarily based on the British Empire and contemporary United Kingdom. The title derives from the description by Cedric J. Robinson (2007: 4) that "race is mercurial—deadly and slick" in the book *Forgeries of Memory and Meaning*. Grounded in the tradition of British cultural studies, the book is divided into eight chapters, arguing that it is the co-imbrication of the development and management of sexual modernity and racialization that gives race its "slickness" and durability. Many scholars like Kimberlé Crenshaw (1991), Anjali Arondekar (2009), Ann Laura Stoler (2010), and Maria Lugones (2007) have argued that gender and race are co-constitutive in their productions and should not be taken as discrete categories of analysis, so this work seems to be a contribution to a well-established field of feminist scholarship. *Deadly and Slick* is well suited for undergraduate curriculums as an introduction to questions of gender, sexual modernity, and racialization.

Balani relies on literary fiction, Netflix series, and secondary historical texts to present a cultural critique of shifting racial-gendered formations, swiftly moving across different sites and time periods. The book begins with sexual modernity as rooted in taxonomies of colonial disciplines such as zoology, botany, and eugenics and the ways in which racialized sexual difference is produced through them. According to her, the collusion of "racial hygiene" and sexual modernity produces the "others" who are the subjects of her book: single mothers on state benefits, "bogus asylum seekers," "homophobic Muslim parents," Muslim "terrorists," and "jihadi brides" in the United Kingdom (38, 60, 81, 152, 111, 129). All of these categories of people who are excluded from or who are perceived as rejecting sexual modernity become the "other" against whom violence and disciplinary practices are poised by the British state. Throughout the book, Balani refers to the construction of these racialized "others" as "folk devils," although there is no explanation for the use of this term (8, 81, 103, 112).

The contemporary commentary on racialized state violence against these othered categories is the most persuasive parts in the book. The ahistorical linearity drawn between violent practices and tropes of racialized sexual modernity in history and their contemporary iterations are not as compelling. For instance, virginity testing of South Asian women who went as brides to the United Kingdom in 1979 is compared to the use of medical testimony in 1888 colonial South Asia; the 1857 trope of the sexually violent Indian man is linked to a 1974 Runnymede Trust paper on Asian men involved in sexual offenses; and the construction of "Asian gangs" in the United Kingdom is described as an "echo of the moral panic over Thuggee" from mid-nineteenth century colonial South Asia. These ahistorical links and parallels pose not just methodological issues but also undercut the central argument of the book about the fluidity of racial formations coproduced by and with sexual modernity.

Drawing heavily from Lugones's (2007: 187) work on the "the modern/colonial gender system," Balani theorizes sexual modernity as having a "light" side and an "underbelly" (8, 15, 58). The former is rooted in the development of capitalist socioeconomic relations that produce systems of kinship, sexual relationships, and gendered norms and concepts like autonomy and freedom. The "underbelly" is posited as the racialized gendered violence that sexual modernity perpetrates on the "others" who are placed outside of it. Despite this conceptual borrowing from Lugones's work, the author does not engage with the vast body of decolonial scholarship, dismissing the modernity/coloniality couplet of "Lugones and other decolonial thinkers" as too "definitive" (8–9). Additionally, Balani attributes early sexual modernity to the late seventeenth century when companionate marriage, complementary gendered roles, and freedom from extended family reigned supreme, with the "racial others" measured by their distance from this kinship structure. She attributes modern sexual modernity to the twentieth century when sexuality is formulated as the right of the "autonomous" individual, with "others" measured in terms of their distance from this "freedom." This framing presents a rigid temporality to the genealogies of sexual modernity, foreclosing the coexistence of many of these elements of sexual modernity in contemporary racialized, gender regimes. Another issue with this conception of sexual modernity is that it becomes the exclusive prerogative of the British/European colonialists. Especially because the book makes many references to colonial South Asia, this has the effect of erasing the multiple modernities asserted by anti-caste movements in the nineteenth century, like the *Kallumaala samaram* (stone necklace protest) in Travancore organized by Mahatma Ayyankali and the Channar Revolts (N.V. 2015; Valsa 2018). While there is a nod to caste endogamy and the co-constitution of caste and gender through Ambedkar's (1917) scholarship in the preface, the author is quick to admit that the book does not address the dynamics of caste or religion in South Asia (xx, xvi).

Particularly due to the incorporation of historical details from colonial South Asia to Balani's critique of contemporary racial orders of sexual modernity in the United Kingdom, the absence of caste analysis becomes problematic. For instance, the Contagious Diseases Act of 1868 is presented as leading to the surveillance and genital examination of "all Indian women" by the British state (46, 166). However, previous scholarship on prostitution and deviant female sexuality points to the differential treatment of women based on caste (Banerjee 1998; Mitra 2020). Importantly, South Asian scholarship on colonial legal reforms related to Sati and female infanticide point to a cautious approach taken by the British administration when dealing with dominant caste women (Mani 1987; Malavika Kasturi 1994). This lack of attention to caste permeates into the critique of contemporary United Kingdom as well. Thus, the author makes the claim that Hindus and Sikhs are placed closer to people racialized as white in their ostensible acceptance of sexual modernity than Muslims (82–83). However, the central question of the caste positions of these Hindus and Sikhs is left unaddressed. Racialization, sexuality, gender, and caste are intimately linked and coproduce each other. Consequently, any book that brackets out one or more of these structures has the potential to present only a partial or skewed analysis.

Gee Semmalar is a legal historian and currently a Max Weber postdoc fellow at the European University Institute, Florence.

References

Ambedkar, Bhimrao R. 1917. "Castes in India: Their Mechanism, Genesis and Development." *Indian Antiquary* 46: 81–95. https://hdl.handle.net/2027/coo .31924079326603.

Arondekar, Anjali R. 2009. *For the Record: On Sexuality and the Colonial Archive in India*. Next Wave. Durham, NC: Duke University Press.

Banerjee, Sumanta. 1998. *Under the Raj: Prostitution in Colonial Bengal*. New York: Monthly Review Press.

Crenshaw, Kimberlé. 1991. "Mapping the Margins: Intersectionality, Identity Politics, and Violence against Women of Color." *Stanford Law Review* 43, no. 6: 1241–99. https:// doi.org/10.2307/1229039.

Lugones, María. 2007. "Heterosexualism and the Colonial / Modern Gender System." *Hypatia* 22, no. 1: 186–209.

Malavika Kasturi. 1994. "Law and Crime in India: British Policy and the Female Infanticide Act of 1870." *Indian Journal of Gender Studies* 1, no. 2: 169–94.

Mani, Lata. 1987. "Contentious Traditions: The Debate on Sati in Colonial India." *Cultural Critique*, no. 7: 119–56. https://doi.org/10.2307/1354153.

Mitra, Durba. 2020. *Indian Sex Life: Sexuality and the Colonial Origins of Modern Social Thought*. Princeton, NJ: Princeton University Press.

N.V., Sheeju. 2015. "The Shanar Revolts, 1822–99: Towards a Figural Cartography of the Pretender." *South Asia Research* 35, no. 3: 298–317. https://doi.org/10.1177 /0262728015598689.

Robinson, Cedric J. 2007. *Forgeries of Memory and Meaning: Blacks and the Regimes of Race in American Theater and Film before World War II*. Chapel Hill: University of North Carolina Press.

Stoler, Ann Laura. 2010. *Carnal Knowledge and Imperial Power: Race and the Intimate in Colonial Rule: With a New Preface*. Berkeley: University of California Press.

Valsa, M. A. 2018. "Dalit Women Empowerment Struggles in Pre-Independent Kerala." *Proceedings of the Indian History Congress*, no. 79: 583–90.

DOI 10.1215/10642684-11331018

LIFE, LIVABILITY, AND THE SELF

Niyati Misra-Shenoy

Changing the Subject: Feminist and Queer Politics in Neoliberal India
Srila Roy
Durham: Duke University Press, 2022. 280 pp.

And one of us did not even dream any dreams. . . . The same Sandhya
who wants to state her opinions very excitedly and stubbornly about
everything became quiet every time the subject of love or sexuality
came up. She even wrote in her diary once: "I feel suffocated every
time there is a conversation on sexuality, intimacies between
women and men or *samlaingikta* [same-sex sexuality]. I just want
them to shut their mouths up. . . . My husband also worries why I am
always avoiding these subjects." . . . The thing she does know with
certainty is that she never dreamed a single dream of love, romance,
or marriage.
–Sangtin Writers and Nagar, *Playing with Fire* (2006: 33–34)

These lines issue from *Playing with Fire*, a groundbreaking indictment of the
"woman empowerment" sector of India's NGO-industrial complex, written collectively by seven female nonprofit outreach workers in rural north India who formed
a feminist consciousness-raising group with the support of a US-based scholar of
women's studies. They are the only lines in the book—an otherwise deeply revealing, unsparing work of grassroots theory and (self) critique that mines every aspect
of the lives and memories of its writers, from birth to death—that, to me, tele-
graph an unmistakably queer affect. Sandhya's sense of suffocation and entrapment is triggered within both hetero- and homosexual frames of intimacy, imping-
ing upon the deep homosocial camaraderie that she has built in conversation with
the diverse women who share her critiques of the nonprofit for which they work
at the lowest reaches. It's a refusal not simply of the exploitative global social
relations into which their feminist labors are embedded, but also of the sexual
futures that feminist and lesbian activisms dream, share, and are shaped by, and

that can seemingly only be made real if they are named and embraced. Sandhya's silence—fragmentary and yet voluble in its resolute nonconjugality, asexuality, and aromanticism—has always driven me to wonder: what triggers this refusal of the subject of sexuality? What triggers the wish that others would shut up—that they would change the subject—along with the courage to admit it, and face being "judged as judgmental" toward not only neoliberal regimes of power, but also the desires of others (Ahmed 2017: 2)?

That eloquent silence leapt to mind immediately when I read Srila Roy's *Changing the Subject*, published sixteen years after *Playing with Fire*. In this book, Roy returns to two of the most fundamental problematics of Indian and global feminisms—namely the rural, subaltern South Asian woman in whose name one speaks, and the costs and risks of internal critique, along with diminishing space and affective agency to entertain such critique—in an attempt to approach them otherwise. Roy is generally successful in her reassessments of both and self-reflective in her treatment of her decade-long sites of research: two nonprofit feminist and queer activist organizations, Sappho for Equality (SFE) and Janam, which focus on queer, trans, and lesbian rights and rural women's empowerment, respectively, and are located in the city of Kolkata, West Bengal, where the first Pride walk in India was held in 1999. Although her approach is primarily ethnographical, Roy's other strength is her ability to contextualize these activist structures, cultures, and affects within both recent and deep history. The India of Sandhya's repressive sexual unease is now a country in which, as of 2018, sodomy has been decriminalized—the culmination of several years of organized activism that departed from the mainstream feminism of what is known as the Indian Women's Movement (IWM) to explicitly focus on sexuality. Roy effectively recaps these developments, showing how the co-optive professionalization of gender rights work, the emergence of local and transnational governance feminisms (Halley et al. 2018), and the rise of self-advocating activism for and by sex workers and those with HIV/AIDs have combined to complicate the original self-constitution of Indian feminism. The IWM, she concludes, has historically been marked by "a split between a feminist self, comprising middle-class metropolitan women, and its object of investigation and reform—poor, rural women at the grass roots, or 'out there.'" This split has repeatedly "helped to establish the cultural authenticity and local legitimacy of an otherwise elite, Western, and alien social movement" (13).

Tackling this avowedly "self-less" feminism head-on, *Changing the Subject* defines governmentality as "a highly generative, mobile, and reversible set of relations and techniques through which a self is both governed and governs itself" (8). Linking this concept of governmentality to her treatment of the legacies of the IWM, Roy relates how, as the political space for queer activism in India expanded and evolved, "lesbian groups, without their own material resources and organizational infrastructure, had to rely on mainstream women's groups in ways that also necessitated certain ideological positions, such as the need to speak in the language of culture and nation that had served to marginalize lesbians in the first place" (51). Lesbians and other gender-minoritized subjects—like the poor rural woman in whose name they, too, campaigned for equal rights—thus fell into what the philosopher Kate Manne, in her analysis of misogyny, has called "asymmetrical moral support roles" in order to partake of mainstream feminisms' cultural capital and financial resources (Manne 2018: xv). "Even as they changed the subject of Indian feminism," Roy argues, "queer feminist activists took recourse to the established political repertoires and cultures"—a recourse that is most obvious in their fetishization of "the *graamer meye*, the subaltern lesbian of rural Bengal, who haunted what metropolitan queer feminists could do and be in a new millennium" (51).

Queer feminist governmentalities thus "reveal a deep and dynamic historic architecture, which while entangled in global neoliberalism, is not reducible to it" (4). Roy's research is less interested in assessing the impacts of these feminist nonprofits' activism on their intended beneficiaries and more focused on how the subjectivities of feminists themselves are shaped by the hauntological accusations of an older model of upper-caste social activism. This model has largely prioritized an uncompromisingly political, collective feminism that is forged in relation to others—transforming nations, rescuing silent victims—and not in relation to transforming the self (Fisher 2012). Thus, even as one of Roy's interlocutors states, "What is energizing about queer activism is that the people who are engaged with it [themselves] have something at stake" (11), those stakes are shown to be disciplined by older ideals of feminism and what the uses and spaces of feminism are for. Even as new generations of activists who have more diverse identifications within hierarchies of caste, class, and gender conformity have proved unruly and resistant in many ways to such disciplining, they too "looked toward the *graamer meye* for moral direction—as a way out of the co-opting potentials of the present" (166). Roy engages extensively with the lived experiences of such activists, who are more or less out of the closet in a city where wider social awareness of queerness in heteronormative spaces is still nascent. Roy defines her subjects' visibility as a kind of strategic revelation and concealment, "less about revealing an inner self than about navigating norms that afford one life and livability, recognition and inclusion" (80). Her overarching finding—"across the divides of class and caste, the urban and the rural, the local and the translocal"—is that "queer activists and development workers engaged not just in new acts, tastes, and relations but also in experiments in becoming different people" (10). Their self-fashioning, whether with or against the grain of social norms, whether embodied, aesthetic, or moral, is a record of the internal politics of feminism.

Perhaps the most broad and contentious thesis of *Changing the Subject* is the following: "Development and activist spaces proved far more productive for individuals to work on, care for, and transform themselves than to empower others" (164). One of the most interesting passages in this book combines this thesis with a plea against defensiveness—"the preferred affect of the feminist academic who feels too much the weight of judgment for her own capacity to judge, to count, and to discount" (169)—and calls for a space to critique with care. Discussing an online forum moderated by SFE to reach non-urban queers, Roy narrates:

> Here is one representative post, which has been translated from Bengali (most of the posts on the page were in English): "I'm single. I have not found someone—and maybe I never will—to love me. I am very depressed. I am very simple. . . . if there is someone who is genuinely interested then contact me. I need *bhalobasha* [love]." The group's response to such posts was always the same: "Sappho for Equality is an activist forum and not a dating site." (65)

Roy condemns this policing of new queer publics, which has made "the bearers of feelings of love and longing—marked by linguistic, locational, and political failure—seem out of place as space invaders" (67). She echoes certain activists who feel that, with online expansion, in-person spaces of feminist care and support are vanishing without an equivalent to replace them:

> For years I had struggled to understand why such a radical and self-reflexive organization needed to hold on to a safe space, one that evoked an archaic model of activism and reductive ideas of sexual identity. But with its loss, I shared in the sadness that one member expressed when she said to me, "Nobody talks about their feelings. How will they? The Sunday meetings were meant for that, and they don't happen anymore." (67)

My own reading of this moment, notwithstanding its validity, is to gently accuse it of nostalgia. The old spaces of feminist consciousness-raising—as the queer silence with which I opened shows—perhaps never truly existed in separation from the "bad feminist habit" of judging and being judged, especially for our equally "bad" feelings. Even in moments of dire necessity, when all we have is trust and each other, we continue to sometimes arrive at an impasse between politics and the personal, with someone or another forever wishing to change the subject. To me this continues to be the radical engine, and the bane, of feminist community.

Niyati Misra-Shenoy is a doctoral candidate in the Department of Middle Eastern, South Asian and African Studies at Columbia University.

References

Ahmed, Sara. 2017. *Living a Feminist Life*. Durham: Duke University Press.

Fisher, Mark. 2012. "What is Hauntology?" *Film Quarterly* 66, no. 1: 16–24.

Halley, Janet, Prabha Kotiswaran, Rachel Rebouché, and Hila Shamir, eds. 2018. *Governance Feminism: An Introduction*. Minneapolis: University of Minnesota Press.

Manne, Kate. 2018. *Down Girl: The Logic of Misogyny*. Oxford: Oxford University Press.

Sangtin Writers and Richa Nagar. 2006. *Playing with Fire: Feminist Thought and Activism through Seven Lives in India*. Minneapolis: University of Minnesota Press.

DOI 10.1215/10642684-11331034

About the Contributors

Rasel Ahmed is assistant professor of theatre, film, and media arts at Ohio State University. Their dialogical film experimentations concern the relationships between displacement, citizenship, border, and loneliness. Ahmed also cofounded Queer Archives of the Bengal Delta, a community-based transnational archive.

Miguel A. Avalos is a doctoral candidate in the Department of Sociology at the University of Illinois at Urbana-Champaign. Their interdisciplinary research uses a spatial and temporal lens to examine transborder commuters' experiences negotiating US immigration enforcement practices in the San Diego-Tijuana border region, specifically focusing on US land ports of entry. Additionally, they explore how transborder commuting queers normative dimensions of everyday life for border residents undertaking this cross-border practice.

Darius Bost is associate professor of Black studies and gender and women's studies at the University of Illinois at Chicago. He is the author of *Evidence of Being: The Black Gay Cultural Renaissance and the Politics of Violence* (2019).

Ariel M. Dela Cruz is a doctoral candidate in the Department of Performing and Media Arts at Cornell University. Their doctoral research examines how Filipinx tomboys engage in and reimagine care work across the Filipinx labor diaspora. They are particularly interested in how tomboys utilize performance to negotiate gendered spaces in global cities. They hold a BSc in neuroscience and psychology and an MA in women and gender studies from the University of Toronto, and their doctoral research is supported by the Social Sciences and Humanities Research Council of Canada Doctoral Fellowship.

René Esparza is assistant professor in the Department of Women, Gender, and Sexuality Studies at Washington University in St. Louis. His research focuses on the racial and sexual politics of urban space, particularly as these dynamics relate to public health. He is the author of the upcoming manuscript *From Vice to Nice: Race, Sex, and the Gentrification of AIDS*. His work has been published in *Radical History Review*, *Journal of the History of Sexuality*, *Journal of African American History*, and *Feminist Formations*, among others. He holds a PhD and an MA in American studies from the University of Minnesota, Twin Cities.

Jules Gill-Peterson is an associate professor of history at Johns Hopkins University. She is the author of *Histories of the Transgender Child* (2018) and *A Short History of Trans Misogyny* (2024).

Gayatri Gopinath is professor in the Department of Social and Cultural Analysis and the Director of the Center for the Study of Gender and Sexuality at New York University. She works at the intersection of transnational feminist and queer studies, postcolonial studies, and diaspora studies and is the author of two monographs: *Impossible Desires: Queer Diasporas and South Asian Public Cultures* (2005) and *Unruly Visions: The Aesthetic Practices of Queer Diaspora* (2018). She has published numerous essays on gender, sexuality, and queer diasporic visual art and culture in anthologies and journals such as *Journal of Middle East Women's Studies*, *GLQ*, and *Social Text*.

Lauren Jae Gutterman is associate professor of American studies and women's, gender, and sexuality studies at the University of Texas at Austin. She is the author of *Her Neighbor's Wife: A History of Lesbian Desire within Marriage* (2019). Her next book project, *Queer Survival: Gender, Sexuality, and the History of Childhood Sexual Abuse*, examines the shifting cultural, political, and intellectual connections between queerness and surviving childhood sexual abuse from the late nineteenth century to the present.

Efadul Huq is assistant professor of environmental science and policy and affiliate faculty in urban studies and for the Program for the Study of Women, Gender, and Sexuality at Smith College. Their work concerns the relationship between space, nature, and informality from a queer and transnational perspective.

Holly Jackson is the Bernard Bailyn Editor of *The New England Quarterly* and the Chair of the Department of American Studies at the University of Massachusetts, Boston. She is the author of two books, most recently *American Radicals: How Nineteenth-Century Protest Shaped the Nation* (2019), and a number of essays in both scholarly and popular venues including *PMLA*, *American Literature*, *New York Times*, and *Washington Post*.

Jina B. Kim is assistant professor of English and the study of women and gender at Smith College. Her book, *Care at the End of the World: Dreaming of Infrastructure in Crip of Color Writing* (Duke University Press, forthcoming) brings a disability lens to bear on feminist and queer of color literature in the aftermath of 1996 US welfare reform. Developing an intersectional disability framework called "crip of color critique," it demonstrates why we need radical disability politics and aesthetics for navigating contemporary crises of care. Her writing has appeared in *Signs*, *Social Text*, *American Quarterly*, *MELUS*, *Disability Studies Quarterly*, and the *Asian American Literary Review*.

Martin F. Manalansan IV is professor of women's, gender, and sexuality studies at Rutgers University, New Brunswick. He has taught at the University of Minnesota, the University of Illinois Urbana-Champaign, New York University, New School University, and the University of the Philippines. He is the author of *Global Divas: Filipino Gay Men in the Diaspora* (2003). His forthcoming book is titled *Queer Dwellings: Mess, Mesh, Measure*. He is president of the Association for Asian American Studies.

Sara Matthiesen is associate professor of history and women's, gender, and sexuality studies at George Washington University. Her first book, *Reproduction Reconceived: Family Making and the Limits of Choice after Roe v. Wade* (2021), shows how incarceration, for-profit and racist healthcare, disease, parentage laws, and poverty were worsened by state neglect in the decades following *Roe*. It received the 2022 Sara A. Whaley Prize from the National Women's Studies Association. She is currently working on a history of the multiracial, feminist activism that opposed state and medical control of abortion throughout the era of choice.

Shoniqua Roach is assistant professor of African and African American studies and women's, gender, and sexuality studies at Brandeis University. Her work appears in *American Quarterly*, *boundary 2*, *differences*, *Feminist Theory*, *Signs*, and *The Black Scholar*, among other venues. Roach's forthcoming book, *Black Dwelling: Home-Making and Erotic Freedom*, offers an intellectual and cultural history of black domestic spaces as tragic sites of state invasion and black feminist enactments of erotic freedom. Roach has been awarded a number of awards and fellowships, including those from the American Council of Learned Societies and the Ford Foundation.

Maggie Schreiner is a doctoral student of history at the Graduate Center, City University of New York. Her research focuses on queer and trans organizing for affordable housing in New York City between the 1960s and the 2010s. She has over a decade of experience working in archives and public history and was previously the Manager of Archives and Special Collections at Brooklyn Historical Society (now the Center for Brooklyn History).

Laila Annmarie Stevens (b. 2001) is a Black Queer photographer and visual artist born and raised in South Jamaica Queens, NY and based in Brooklyn, NY. She received her BFA in photography and related media at the Fashion Institute of Technology. Their work is frequently published in *The New York Times* and featured in *National Geographic, The Nation*, and *The Guardian* among other publications. Stevens is a 2023 Magnum Foundation Fellow, part of Eddie Adams Workshop Class of XXXIV, and a full member of Black Woman Photographers, Diversify Photo, and Scope of Work (SOW).

Cody C. St. Clair is faculty in the Department of Writing, Rhetoric, and Discourse at DePaul University. Their scholarship has appeared in *African American Review* and *American Literature*. Their current book manuscript, "Homeless Modernisms," unearths a literary archive of radical homeless activism in the 1920s, 1930s, and 1940s.

Virginia Thomas, PhD, is a scholar of visuality, aesthetics, and power. Her research, teaching, and public humanities work analyze the role of aesthetics in uprooting and decomposing white property relations. She is the founder of the Queer StoRIes Project, an oral history project for LGBTQ+ folx in Rhode Island with a focus on intergenerational skill and story sharing. Her work has been supported by the Institute for Citizens and Scholars, and she has published in *feminist review* and *Southern Cultures*. She is currently an assistant professor of women's and gender studies and art history at Providence College.

Stephen Vider is associate professor of history and gender and sexuality studies at Bryn Mawr College, with an affiliation in history of art. He is the author of *The Queerness of Home: Gender, Sexuality, and the Politics of Domesticity after World War II* (2021) and curator of the exhibition *AIDS at Home: Art and Everyday Activism* (2017). He was previously associate professor of history at Cornell University, where he was the founding director of the Public History Initiative. His next book project, *On Our Own: The Politics of Mental Healthcare after Deinstitutionalization*, examines the social and political aftermath of psychiatric deinstitutionalization in New York City and the state of New York since the 1950s.

Hentyle Yapp is associate professor of performance studies in the Department of Theatre and Dance at the University of California, San Diego. His research broadly engages the theoretical and methodological implications of queer, disability, feminist, and critical race studies for questions regarding the state and the transnational. He is the author of *Minor China: Method, Materialisms, and the Aesthetic* (2021) and a coeditor with C. Riley Snorton of *Saturation: Race, Art, and the Circulation of Value* (2020).

DOI 10.1215/10642684-11432700

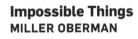

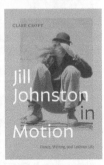